HILLTOP SCRIPTURAL MEDITATIONS FOR YEARS A, B WEEKEND SPIRITUAL NOURISHMENT

Rev. Benjamin A Vima

Trafford
PUBLISHING®   www.trafford.com
North America & international
toll-free: 1 888 232 4444 (USA & Canada)
fax: 812 355 4082

Contents

HILLTOP MEDITATIONS
For Year B Weekends

HILLTOP MEDITATIONS

For Year A Weekends

FIRST WEEKEND

First Advent Sunday

Waiting for Jesus not speculatively but realistically

> *...Therefore, stay awake! For you do not know on which day your Lord will come. Be sure of this: if the master of the house had known the hour of night when the thief was coming, he would have stayed awake and not let his house be broken into. So too, you also must be prepared, for at an hour you do not expect, the Son of Man will come.* (Matt. 24: 37-44)

This weekend, being the first one in the Year A, let us meditate on the active Presence of Jesus in our midst. Our entire Christian life in this world is built up on the biggest hope, as Isaiah once foretold, on Jesus' coming in our midst. While Jesus was alive physically he made all possible efforts to potentially establishing our dreamed-better world. Gospel writers as well as all the Apostles in their Letters, confirm their belief in the repeated promises of Jesus, before his death and even after, about his second coming. They heard him through his Spirit that *the Son of Man will come.*

In addition to his promise Jesus also cautioned us that his coming would be *at an hour we do not expect.* Knowing our human fragility and anxiety he encouraged us to stay always awake and wait with hope. In this precarious time of waiting he told us he will *not leave us orphans.* He too promised he would stay with us, even after his death, in disguise and in signs and symbols and sharing with us all resources of truth and fullness of life, peace and love, justice and unity. He has said: *"The kingdom of God is already in your midst."* As he was ready to be lifted up to heaven, he emphasized: *And behold, I am with you always, until the end of the age.*

Our Christian life is an active waiting for Christ's continuing coming. The stewards of Christ must always be ready for recognizing the Lord's coming by being faithful to the mission in life given them by Christ. Over the centuries, except here and there, we regret to find his foretelling has been realized but not completely and totally. We don't walk in the light of the Lord. Most of us are still slumbering, sleeping tight in our couches and also brooding over our past or groaning over what we lack in. As Paul depicts, we the humans still lead a life not in daylight but in dark night.

Every human person, young or old, dumb or smart, holds a view of his/her own about human life. There are two categories of people in this: People who go on behaving like small babies and people who live as reasonable adults. In fact everything of the world - our relationships, physical beauty, health, strength, mental and intellectual capacities, worldly possessions, name and fame, power, influence are none other than varieties of colorful balloons, very enchanting and attractive, but unfortunately, one day or the other they have to 'burst' and depart from us.

Even among these so-called reasonable adults there are three ways of approaching this stressful life: One group views it as *chronos,* which means in Greek, essentially life is unredeemed and cyclic. The second kind of people who use rationality more than anything else see life in *chaos.* In Greek it means unordered, confused, unfashioned, and essentially nothingness. And the third group's view is called *xairos*. They mean human life is redeemed by God in Christ Jesus and becomes a trustworthy ladder through which humans can climb up and ascend to their climatic destiny.

The third view is worth adhering to. It helps us to lead an optimistic life. Plus, we are enlightened by risen Jesus, through his Scriptures and the Tradition of his Church, we will be scheduling our daily life making it, not just waiting for him speculatively but actively and realistically performing certain spiritual and charitable deeds on his behalf ritually and socially he comes in various disguises-the needy, the sick, and the sacraments.

....

Second Advent Sunday

Repentance is conversion of attitude and action

In those days John the Baptist appeared, preaching in the desert of Judea saying, Repent, for the kingdom of heaven is at hand! It was of him that the prophet Isaiah had spoken when he said: A voice of one crying out in the desert, 'Prepare the way of the Lord, make straight his path'... Produce good fruit as evidence of your repentance...Even now the ax lies at the root of the trees. Therefore every tree that does not bear good fruit will be cut down and thrown into the fire. I am baptizing you with water, for repentance, but the one who is coming after me is mightier than I. I am not worthy to carry his sandals. He will baptize you with the Holy Spirit and fire. His winnowing fan is in his hand. He will clear his threshing floor and gather his wheat into his barn, but the chaff he will burn with unquenchable fire."
(Matt. 3: 1-12)

As we celebrate the coming of the new Messiah in this season of cold, freezing, snow and sleet, we take for meditation this weekend the preaching of John the baptizer, the forerunner of Jesus. John the Baptizer, the last Prophet of the Old Testament, being considered as the last hope for a desperate people at his time earnestly longing for the arrival of Messiah, started his ministry saying: *Repent, for the kingdom of heaven is at hand.*

Repentance is the translation of Greek word *metanoia*, meaning "after/behind one's <u>mind</u>"; *'to think differently after'*. Act of repenting means therefore a change of mind accompanied by regret and change of conduct, "change of mind and heart", or, "change of consciousness". It means simply a 'conversion' of attitude and action. John exhorts us to convert ourselves from the way we deal with our religiosity; to change from old twisted religion to new; from fake to genuine; and from reel to real.

He recommends a conversion from performing all religious duties not just as external rituals but as spiritual, interiorly on fire. He referred his own ritual action of Baptism in water, the relevance of which he didn't deny; but he wanted us to go beyond the mere ritual. He said: *"I am baptizing you with water, for repentance, but the one who is coming after me is mightier than I. He will baptize you with the Holy Spirit and fire."*

There is also another important dimension contained in the conversion process John proposed. He wants us to be prepared to meet the consequences of such conversion. Quoting Isaiah 'prepare the way of the Lord' he tells us to be prepared and to get ready for an awesome ground-breaking or radical view and conduct of our human life. We will be receiving a Messiah who is filled with and expecting us to be leading a life of justice, peace and love.

As the result of conversion, our human view regarding Messiah would be shattered; he is more humble than powerful; more merciful than judging; more peaceful than violent; more tolerant than intolerant. In simple term as John said of Jesus, *"This is the lamb of God who takes away the sins of the world".* This conversion is supposed to be total and wholistic. John was sent to us not simply ringing his tinkling and clattering jingle bell but rather he came with ax, a tool for cutting: *"Even now the ax lies at the root of the trees. Therefore every tree that does not bear good fruit will be cut down and thrown into the fire."* In the light of Christ we should interpret John's preaching not as a threatening but a positive tips for managing our life. Let us remember Jesus, who called himself as a vine tree, related us to him as the branches. (Jn. 15: 1-6) As John reminded, Jesus emphasized the Father will throw out into the fire if it does not bear good fruits in proper season; even if we are branches that bear good fruits Father would prune us so that we can bear more and better fruits.

The conversion Jesus the Messiah expects from us is not only a change in the moral behavior, but also it is an intellectual change; it implies a new way of thinking of God and of his religion. This is what John the Baptizer advised to his people as an immediate preparation for receiving the new Messiah. And Jesus continues the same demand from his followers as the primary requirement to see the modern life through the spectrum of fiery Spirit which never quenches until we change our mentality, our attitudes, our ways, so that Jesus can really live among us to make this world a place of unity and integrity, of justice and peace.

....

THIRD WEEKEND

Third Advent Sunday

Never-ending Joy through rare-blend life

The wilderness and the parched land will exult; the Arabah will rejoice and bloom; like the crocus it shall bloom abundantly, and rejoice with joyful song. The glory of Lebanon will be given to it, the splendor of Carmel and Sharon; they will see the glory of the LORD, the splendor of our God...Here is your God, he comes with vindication; with divine recompense he comes to save you. Then the eyes of the blind shall see, and the ears of the deaf be opened; Then the lame shall leap like a stag, and the mute tongue sing for joy... And the ransomed of the LORD shall return, and enter Zion singing, crowned with everlasting joy; they meet with joy and gladness, sorrow and mourning flee away. (Is. 35: 1-10)

Prophets of OT, while they foretold about the coming of a redeeming Messiah, prophesied also the inevitable results of his coming. One among them is a 'joy-filled life'. It is this prophetic message we meditate this weekend. Isaiah first underlines that at Jesus' coming the entire nature would be rejoicing; and then goes on stating how the needy, the sick, the handicapped, and the ransomed would be filled with joy. In this connection, we remember Jesus acknowledging that all the prophecies of Isaiah had been fulfilled in his coming (Lk. 4: 16-21). And Jesus too confirmed through John the Baptizer's disciples how his joy-oriented glad-tidings would be preached and acted out in the Way of religion he initiated. He said: *Go and tell John what you hear and see: the blind regain their sight, the lame walk, lepers are cleansed, the deaf hear, the dead are raised, and the poor have the good news proclaimed to them.* (Matt. 11: 4-5)

From the beginning of Jesus' Messianic mission he was firm that his followers would be filled with joy and that joy would be complete, if they not only talk his talk but also walk his walk of enduring love and compassion. Accordingly he blended both our hope-filled dreaming of and waiting patiently for rejoicing at his second coming as James writes, t*he coming of the Lord is at hand; and he is standing before the gates* (Jam. 5: 7-9), and our daily chores of love-based performance to make others more rejoicing as in 'persona Christi'.

For such rare-blended life, John the Baptizer is one among many rolemodels and messengers who is pointed out to us by Jesus during this Advent season. John was praised by Jesus for his remarkable life of this rare blend: that he was firm and unshaken-*not a reed that is swayed by the wind* in his enduring waiting for the Messiah; that he lived a simple and humble life-*not dressed royally in fine clothing*; that he was more than a prophet and teacher; that he repaired and renewed and turned the hearts of people to be fully complied with God's justice and compassion-When people asked him what they should do in day today life, he insisted they should lead a just and compassionate life (Lk. 3: 10-14)

All disciples of Jesus who profess our faith and love in our Master are asked by him to keenly observe the evidence of his words and deeds and to make a free and right decision in our discipleship. He expects us never to be tired of proclaiming his Gospel of mercy and compassion day in and day out; it should not be merely by words but much more so in activities. In his physical absence we must act as Jesus by making others joyful. The poor were Jesus' great concern. While we make the poor and the needy joyful, our joy is doubled; while they see Jesus the Messiah in our good works, we will be confirmed in hope, patience and faith.

It is this genuine joy Jesus wants us to enjoy. It is a joy of sharing and sacrificing for the uplifting of the poor, the sick and the needy. We try our best to move and work within the enlightened territory of God; however we should never think there will be no problems and hurdles. They are part and parcel of our discipleship. At those moments, as one leader said, *we better have our own vision, and we better have our own will and our own passion and determination; holding always in mind that now the life requires work and sacrifice and sometimes it's painful, but there is a lot of joy and there is a lot of hope and possibility."* This is the secret of Advent joy.

....

FOURTH WEEKEND

Fourth Sunday of Advent

An Unfathomable and Mysterious but Experiential Story

Now this is how the birth of Jesus Christ came about. When his mother Mary was betrothed to Joseph, but before they lived together, she was found with child through the Holy Spirit. Joseph her husband, since he was a righteous man, yet unwilling to expose her to shame, decided to divorce her quietly. Such was his intention when, behold, the angel of the Lord appeared to him in a dream and said, 'Joseph, son of David, do not be afraid to take Mary your wife into your home. For it is through the Holy Spirit that this child has been conceived in her. She will bear a son and you are to name him Jesus, because he will save his people from their sins.' All this took place to fulfill what the Lord had said through the prophet: 'Behold, the virgin shall be with child and bear a son, and they shall name him Emmanuel,' which means "God is with us." When Joseph awoke, he did as the angel of the Lord had commanded him and took his wife into his home. He had no relations with her until she bore a son, and he named him Jesus. (Matt. 1: 18-25)

We are now almost on the eve of the birth of Jesus. As we end the Advent season of waiting for Jesus' arrival, we are invited by the Spirit to go into the deeper meaning of Christmas celebration. We find Matthew narrating this event not as something happened in history or just a fairytale like those of Santa but rather, as an event of mystery. While proving that Jesus, son of Mary and Joseph is the fulfillment of the promises of God as the prophets foretold in OT, Matthew describes the threefold mystery contained in Jesus' birth.

The first mystery is that Mary, the Mother of Jesus, was ever virgin. If we deeply analyze the history and culture of Jewish people, such statement about a Jewish lady is unhistorical and unrealistic. The second mystery is that Jesus was born not by flesh but by the Holy Spirit. This too is an unethical, unrealistic and unnatural claim. The third is higher than everything and that is this Jesus is 'Emmanuel.' God with us. This fact sounds like any other pagan fairytales or Hindu puranas which talk about God coming to the world in many forms whenever humans need him.

Matthew and so all other NT Writers knew well how we the followers of Jesus, especially those born and grown after the Age of Enlightenment, would be facing tremendous problems both within us and outside of us by believing in this triple mystery of Jesus' birth. This is why Matthew connects the birth story to a popular prophecy uttered by Isaiah who was the greatest of all OT Prophets: *The Lord himself will give you a sign; the young woman, pregnant and about to bear a son* (Is. 7: 14), and the Evangelist adds to this prophecy: *which means God is with us.* This is the truth God invites us today to hold on as we celebrate Christmas this year. Thus anything we do and perform regarding Jesus' birth should turn out to be meaningful, resourceful and uplifting. Only when we believe this triple mystery happened in Jesus' birth we can really celebrate this Christmas truly religiously and spiritually. Otherwise it is just another national holiday as many refer to.

Any mystery according to its nature and identity is something not to be taught and debated and understood but rather, it is to be lived and experienced. As in Aramaic and Hebrew languages sentences are read in reverse, so the findings and writings were scripted reverse. First the writers experienced the resurrection of Jesus, then his passion and death, followed by his life and sayings and then, then only they interpreted his birth where they discovered the triple mystery. Throughout the human history, all those believed in this awesome mystery they have been cured, they have been filled with joy and peace and they became real 'Santas' to their kids and friends sharing the heavenly gifts.

We celebrate Christmas, reliving the same experience of the Mary, Joseph and Shepherds. Along with many fathers and mothers who work hard every day, making many sacrifices; along with the young, the sick and the poor, we celebrate, because it is the celebration of our encounter with God in Jesus. If we are convinced of this mysterious but realistic fact, we will certainly be able to transmit the joy of this friendship everywhere.

....

FOURTH WEEKEND-SPECIAL

Christmas
God-favored humans of Goodwill

For the grace of God has appeared, saving all and training us to reject godless ways and worldly desires and to live temperately, justly, and devoutly in this age, as we await the blessed hope, the appearance of the glory of the great God and of our savior Jesus Christ, who gave himself for us to deliver us from all lawlessness and to cleanse for himself a people as his own, eager to do what is good. (Titus 2: 11-14)

We are so happy and privileged to celebrate the birthday of our Master Jesus. A recent research study "culturometrics," (a fancy term to describe quantitative data analysis applied to individuals in society) demonstrates that among the top 100 historical celebrities Jesus is number one. Very frankly this is not the only reason why we are proud to be called Jesus' followers. There is something more about which let us meditate in this weekend. The celebration of Christmas announces a twofold important Good News to the world: *Glory to God in the highest; Peace and joy to those on whom God's favor rests-the people of goodwill.* God as a benevolent Father because of his uncontrollable love for us performs an unthinkable curious, remarkable but weird act for the sake of his adopted children and the entire human race. That is what we hear from the Letter to Titus.

I think our Father in heaven out of his recklessness of immense love not only he emptied his only begotten Son, made him take the form of a tiny little boy, vulnerable, weak and fragile like all the humans who are born like bundles of flesh and bones; in a way the Father ordered his Son to live like a slave of love, suicide himself handing himself over to his enemies freely to be murdered.

At the same time he also did a marvelous deed to his Son. Like the Italian dad did to his son, God made his Son resurrected and become King of glory and honor and take all the works of his Father in his hand. This is why we all fully agree with Prophet Isaiah to honor this Baby with words like: *he is Wonder-Counselor, God-Hero, Father-Forever, and Prince of Peace.* (Is. 9: 5-6). Thus he was immortalized like a diamond. The Baby was sent for our redemption, liberation, and attainment of fuller life overflowing with peace, joy and love. He therefore deserves fully glory and honor from us. God whom we worship is worthy of glory and honor.

By appropriating God's gratuitous favor through Baby Jesus, we, who begin to live a life, obedient and committed to God's Will-that is goodwill are filled with true joy and genuine peace. Scriptures abound in spelling out this endresults. *The people who walked in darkness have seen a great light; upon those who dwelt in the land of gloom a light has shone. You have brought them abundant joy and great rejoicing.* (Is. 9: 1-2)

Historically we observe these proven characteristics and qualities noticed in every person who has been committed to God's goodwill throughout the centuries. The friends of Baby Jesus have been always lovers of peace.

As they stand and walk erect with goodwill long to see true peace settled in the hearts and minds of the whole humanity. It is true today more than ever before, in front of the crib they may cry aloud as the Psalmist mourns in Psalm 120, *Long enough have I been dwelling with those who hate peace! I am for peace, but when I speak, they are for fighting.* However we can observe an internal peace settled inside of their minds and hearts. They are always smiling sunshine to people around them.

These humans of goodwill seem to be lovers of genuine love. They never flinch from what Paul exhorts about love. *Owe nothing to anyone, except to love one another; for the one who loves another has fulfilled the law.* (Rom. 13: 8-10) Their love always seeks the good of others; forgives everything others do out of malice and weakness; and never sells and buys other people for the sake of their personal profit. Out of such genuine love they never fear for plunging into even darkness and furnace of faith in order to bring others to Jesus. They have developed a personality that can both adopt and adapt as well: I took these two words from a wise saying: *"Adopt your own views and adapt with others' views too."* This is hundred percent true policy of any humans of goodwill. Adopting means approving, embracing and surely firmly implementing their values, being enlightened from the wisdom of their God; but at the same, they too amicably adjusting and even bending to the views and holdings of others according to the signs and situations of time and place. Let us try to be the friends of Baby Jesus.

....

FIFTH WEEKEND

Feast of Holy Family
Give Respect and Get Respect

For the Lord sets a father in honor over his children and confirms a mother's authority over her sons. Those who honor their father atone for sins; they store up riches who respect their mother. Those who honor their father will have joy in their own children, and when they pray they are heard. Those who respect their father will live a long life; those who obey the Lord honor their mother. Those who fear the Lord honor their father, and serve their parents as masters. (Sir. 3: 2-7)

We, in Christianity, are fortunate enough being brought up from early childhood with many golden rules and resourceful sayings and proverbs which staying permanently in our hearts direct us to walk in right path. Not as old religions which proclaimed some hateful sayings such as 'tit for tat, an eye for an eye and a tooth for a tooth, our Teacher Jesus gave us many precious love-based sayings. One among them is: "Do to others whatever you would have them do to you." (Matt. 7: 12) In simple words we can say this: "Give respect and get respect." During this weekend let us meditate how to apply this simple advice in all our relationships-in families and communities, to make them more joyful, peaceful and fruitful.

The word 'respect' means: appreciating, revering, esteeming, admiring other persons; and thinking a lot of another (not wickedly or badly but their goodwill and deeds); having a high opinion of them; showing consideration for them; having a high regard for them; and paying attention to them. This kind of respect we should give to others in the families: *Honor your father and mother* is the fourth commandment of God-very surprisingly it is placed just after the three commandments that are to be followed in our relationship with God; and this is the first commandment among all the other commandments that are to be followed in our relationships with our neighbors.

The passage from the Book of Sirach, which we have taken this weekend for our meditation, explains little more about this commandment of God. Repeatedly the Author emphasizes the excellence of respect in building up a family. Paul in his Letter (Col. 3: 12-21) affirms the duty of children to offer respect to their parents saying: *Children, obey your parents in everything, for this is pleasing to the Lord.* At the same time he also gives us a practical way of giving respect to each other in the family-husband and wife, parents and children and siblings to each other: *Put on heartfelt compassion, kindness, humility, gentleness, and patience, bearing with one another and forgiving one another, if one has a grievance against another.*

We witness this sort of respectful behavior in the Holy Family between Jesus, Mary and Joseph: Joseph who had a dream at midnight and admonished by the angel of God to flee to Egypt got up immediately, woke Mary and child Jesus who were in deep sleep, rose and took the child and his mother by night and departed for Egypt. Surely Joseph, being a person of justice, would have explained about his dream to Mary; so respecting each other they managed to adjust to the critical situations they were in and became refugees as so many families in today's world are homeless and hunting for asylum. Most of the time, we the members of the family lose our respect for each other only at the time of some crisis-problems of job, sickness, weaknesses of individuals and so on. Here in the Holy Family we notice all the three kept respect for each other, honored each other and thus preserved their peace and contentment.

Nonetheless we should understand our human nature always is prone to judge others; to put down others; to seek self-gratification; to compare and contrast with others. These are all human techniques for survival of the fittest. Certainly members of Holy Family were not exempted from this natural temptations. As a matter of fact they knew this kind of mutual respect is not possible for any human person; they too were well aware of the fact that any kind of self-oriented relationship never bring forth any peace or joy; rather only fight, war, separation and hatred. This is why all three in Holy family lived and moved on the basis of God's word and will. They were primarily respecting God as their Supreme Sovereign and Master. Undeniably our family or community that respects God as our all-in-all, we can witness there healthy and respectful relationships between husband and wife, and between children and parents. In this Holy family of Nazareth is indeed a remarkable rolemodel.

....

FIFTH WEEKEND SPECIAL

New Year's Day
*Start everything with Providential
Calculation and not with any other*

*But when the fullness of time had come,
God sent his Son, born of a woman, born
under the law, to ransom those under the
law, so that we might receive adoption.
As proof that you are children, God sent
the spirit of his Son into our hearts, crying
out, "Abba, Father!" So you are no longer
a slave but a child, and if a child then also
an heir, through God.* (Gal. 4: 4-7)

We are humans gifted with rationality and intelligence. Unlike animals or birds we are anxious about how, why, and how-long we survive and live our personal lives. According to my horoscope I am told that *"apart from some small health problems related to teeth and bones, the coming year will be full of good news. There will be a lot of new things happening and changing the face of my life in the New Year 2014. Most of the times, I will be seen roaming around the world, either for fun or work purpose."* It also advises me that *"precaution is better than cure will be the formula for success for me in New Year 2014, as there are chances for me getting tangled in some serious troubles if I won't take precautions on time."* This is our today's aching. And this is why we want to meditate now on some the Word of God that energizes us as we feel little slow and tilted.

From the day of humanity's origin humans attempted to calculate their living period in this world and how to avoid the curses of life and how to enjoy its blessings in their living period. Many apply a 'natural calculation' which is based on the stars in which we are conceived and born. Horoscope, Astrology, numerology, and Palm-Reading are some of the sciences generated out of such anxious calculation; some others an 'artificial calculation' through which in ancient period humans calculated and measured their living time by the sun moving; even by the shadow its light created on the ground. Gradually with the help of astronomy and mathematics each nation, each race created their own calculation called calendar that contains years, seasons, months, days, hours and seconds and now even by the calculation of light years (and megabytes and gigabytes) and so on.

There is also a third calculation in the circle of religious and spiritual humans, which is called 'providential calculation'. According to this, we are told that at one time the Supreme Spiritual being created the entire universe; every being on earth begins its life from Him and ends in Him; though He lives in timeless time, He recognizes and appreciates every kind of calculation of time we have introduced and are following. Only He knows fully well our beginning and our end. Though there is cyclic system He has created for other beings and materials, He has denied it in the lives of humans. There is only one birth and one death. Humans' lives are journeying in one way-traffic. Above all, He worries about our limitation of worrying too much about our life-time.

It is this 'providential calculation' most of us apply to our life as it progresses from birth to death. From Scriptures we are confirmed that everything existing in this universe moving and having its being only according to God's calculation. Our only time, hour, day and year is in his timeless time. He performs marvelous deeds in His own time and place. When we listen to Paul's way of calculating his and the entire human race's life we are encouraged to go forward from one year to another, and from one day to another with the relentless hope there is always a bright tomorrow reserved for us thanks to the providence of our 'Abba, Father'.

We too are convinced that *all things work for good for those who love God, who are called according to his purpose.* (Rom. 8: 28) All blessings are showered upon whom He favors. We continuously hear Him saying to us mainly through our elders and friends: 'I bless you.' (Ref. Num. 6: 22-27) Most importantly, such a calculation lets us believe that we are not alone in our life-journey; God is with us *Emmanuel* till our breath leaves.

The only thing we have to do, to realize the endresults of our 'providential calculation' during our limited life, is that as Mary, Mother of Jesus, *kept all these things, reflecting on them in her heart,* we must sleep daily on these promising words of God which are implemented here today by seeing through and calculating with our rationality all that had happened in the past and still happening today.

....

SIXTH WEEKEND

Epiphany of the Lord

Playing continuously the 'search and find' game

When Jesus was born in Bethlehem of Judea, in the days of King Herod, behold, magi from the east arrived in Jerusalem, saying, "Where is the newborn king of the Jews? We saw his star at its rising and have come to do him homage." When King Herod heard this, he was greatly troubled, and all Jerusalem with him... After their audience with the king they set out. And behold, the star that they had seen at its rising preceded them, until it came and stopped over the place where the child was. They were overjoyed at seeing the star, and on entering the house they saw the child with Mary his mother. They prostrated themselves and did him homage. Then they opened their treasures and offered him gifts of gold, frankincense, and myrrh... (Matt. 2: 1-12)

All disciples of Jesus are born as God's creation and reborn in Baptism and must show their worth as Jesus dreamed: they must be convinced their status as the children of God calling God 'Abba Father;' they too are established as the light of the world; and the salt of the earth; and as his delegates they must manifest his divinity, his glory, his power, and his priesthood. Along with, we should also acknowledge we are mere humans with limited physicality that can be rotten. Thus, every Christian-self is built in three dimensions: Powerful, Godly, and Breakable Vessel, made of clay and dust. Accepting this triple dimension of our true self as a whole and manifest it in daily life, by playing with it or plying with it, is very hard for ordinary humans. On this feast day of Epiphany the Spirit asks us to seriously reflect over such marvelous privilege bestowed to us. Sadly, we always try to show one or the other and hide the other two. Thus we fail Jesus and ourselves. The Spirit informs us that we can overcome such failures through the light appeared in human history. As Prophet Isaiah proclaims today such light is closer to our door: *"Rise up in splendor, Jerusalem! Your light has come, the glory of the Lord shines upon you...* (Is. 60: 1-6)

However, this 'enlightening manifestation of God' takes place in a slow but steady process. Every revelation God makes in history of mankind as his values, his teachings, events and so on, are occasions and channels to see his true Self. We the humans possess very little brain and that too often does not cooperate with us. God therefore slowly but gently reveals himself his truths to us. We are reminded by Paul that *"It* (God's revelation) *was not made known to people in other generations as it has now been revealed to his holy apostles and prophets by the Spirit."*

In Matthew's Epiphany story we read the sincere and enduring efforts of such searching God's light and how finally they were endowed with God's joy and peace. All the persons who are involved in this Magi event were searching for God's manifestation: While Mary and Joseph and shepherds have already sought and found God's Epiphany, still they were seeking him more: Mary kept everything in her heart and pondered over it; Joseph was always thinking about God and even in his sleep he had encounters of God. The Magi in particular were searching God very intensively. With the help of available media they started studying the stars and all possible Scriptures accessible to them. Their quest for meeting God born man might have been blended with curiosity and spirituality. But once they saw the star which guided them on their journey of searching, they were so glad. At one time it disappeared from them. They immediately went for human help. There is nothing wrong about it. They made some wrong choices as we do. The heavenly star again appeared and gave them proper directions. They finally reached their destiny. They found whom they were searching for. Herod too was searching and finding God's manifestation but he became wicked and cruel and turned out to be source of evil to others.

This is how, whenever we go on searching for the manifestation of God, we, as the characters in the story, would be first granted light to find our own true self. It may be either good or bad; if we try to be honest to ourselves and either improve upon the goodness and greatness or correct our wickedness and malicious character, then he will reveal himself, his true identity as heavenly light coming upon us. It may be surprising; to every one's bewilderment, God may reveal himself to us in ordinary way as he did through the customary gifts of Magi: Through the gift of gold Jesus' royal line; the incense his divinity; and the myrrh his humanity. Namely they observed all that they longed to see was found in the Baby Jesus.

....

SEVENTH WEEKEND

Feast of Baptism of the Lord

Plunging into the current of Jesus' salvation

Then Jesus came from Galilee to John at the Jordan to be baptized by him. John tried to prevent him, saying, "I need to be baptized by you, and yet you are coming to me?" Jesus said to him in reply, "Allow it now, for thus it is fitting for us to fulfill all righteousness." Then he allowed him. After Jesus was baptized, he came up from the water and behold, the heavens were opened for him, and he saw the Spirit of God descending like a dove and coming upon him. And a voice came from the heavens, saying, "This is my beloved Son, with whom I am well pleased." (Matt. 3: 13-17)

On Wednesday, 8 January, 2014 at the General Audience in St Peter's Square Pope Francis gave his catechesis on the Sacrament of Baptism. During his conversation with people assembled there he asked them 'how many of you know your Baptismal Date? Please raise your hands.' He was not at all surprised to notice majority didn't raise their hands. Then he added: It is important to know the day on which we were immersed in that current of Jesus' salvation.

What is this 'current of Jesus' salvation'? Jesus came to us to offer salvation from evil to Good; from darkness to light; from lies to the truth. It is an act of liberation from injustice to justice; from unrighteousness to righteousness. In the Gospel passage we meditate this weekend we hear that when Jesus came willingly to John the Baptist to be baptized at River Jordan he told John the real reason why he wanted it: *Allow it now, for thus it is fitting for us to fulfill all righteousness.* To be righteous means to be just both in front of God and people around us; to be truthful and honest to God and others.

As God predicted through prophet Isaiah 'Jesus knew that he came to this world to bring forth justice to the nations.' (Ref. Is. 42: 1-7) I want you to know the historical background of the Day of Jesus' Baptism: Slavery was prevalent in Judea and all over the world throughout the first century. The Roman Empire largely relied upon slavery in that period, where perhaps 40 percent of Judean population were slaves. Going against the justice of God, various world religions, especially the Stoics of Jesus' time, always encouraged this unjust slavery with their justifying philosophy that advocated "the acceptance of what kind of man God ordered you to be and where as a man you are placed." All political leaders, including High Priests and other power-holders at Jesus' time not only encouraged the slavery but also kept hundreds of slaves for their personal and domestic uses.

From the above-noted social backdrop, we know the legitimate reason why in that era so many rebels rose up to break this unjust bondage. No wonder Jesus was considered as one among them. In fullness of time the messiah came to rescue these people in the form of Jesus of Nazareth but with difference. As prophesied in OT, Jesus, from his early youth days, was very clear about his identity and mission; he recognized that he was the servant sent as

God's chosen one, with whom God was pleased; and upon whom the Creator had put his spirit. Jesus too felt within him an urge to fulfill the mission of bringing forth justice to the nations, but with non-violence and compassionate deeds. He willingly accepted an unprecedented evangelical life of justice, righteousness, truth and fidelity that would bring to his followers peace, goodness, healing, plus the active presence of Divinity. It is to this life Jesus was immersing into on the day of his Baptism. It is in this awesome stream of God's righteousness of justice and truth Jesus immersed into. He used the Baptismal ritual John as the starting point of his public ministry of salvation.

To mark the act of plunging oneself into the fulfillment of God's righteousness of salvation like the Master in our lifetime, his Disciples decided to observe the same ritual of Baptism as an initiation into the Christian life being committed to the Discipleship of Jesus. Through the sacrament of Baptism Christians pledge not just a faithful allegiance to Jesus' Church but more. Inside every baptized person heart begins beating at Baptism: *I will be one with God and always be a servant to please Him as his beloved child; I will be one with the humanity both in their joys and sorrows; I will be not simply generous but just and offer what is due to others who are also children of my God; I may encounter bleeding or persecution and other evils for the sake of righteousness and justice. Come what may! I will dive, I will swim, even going against the current.*

....

EIGHTH WEEKEND

Second Sunday in ordinary time

Christian Glory consists in being a Lamb of God

> *The next day he saw Jesus coming toward him and said, "Behold, the Lamb of God, who takes away the sin of the world... John testified further, saying, "I saw the Spirit come down like a dove from the sky and remain upon him. I did not know him, but the one who sent me to baptize with water told me, 'On whomever you see the Spirit come down and remain, he is the one who will baptize with the Holy Spirit.' Now I have seen and testified that he is the Son of God."* (Jn. 1: 29-34)

'What name do you give to your child?' It is a question that is asked from parents when they bring their child to be baptized. Name of a person is very important to himself/herself and not necessarily to their parents. For every human being his/her name is so precious because it identifies that person in a multi-billion population. It also in many cultures signifies the nominee's personality and quality. In Jewish culture this was hundred percent true. Every human name in the Bible is an emblem or symbol of what one is predicted to be or one is capable of accomplishing. For example, Christ was named 'Jesus' which was told by angels both to Mary and Joseph before his birth. In Hebrew name 'Joshua' meaning "Yahweh helps" was interpreted as "Yahweh saves."

In this weekend let us meditate on our own name received in Baptism. Our parents would have given funny names; we ourselves would have modified them according to our personal needs. But the only name that tops most is '*Christian*.' That is why the act of being baptized has been culturally regarded as 'christening'.

Our Master Christ was given a beautiful name 'Jesus', a heavenly name and a powerful name bestowed by his heavenly Father. On the basis of such identity and seeing Jesus' powerful deeds and accomplishments Jesus' followers gave him many names such as Messiah, Emmanuel, Lord, teacher, master, shepherd, light of nations, and so on. While Jesus accepted all these names and acknowledged them as true, he preferred to be named with certain names that depicted the other side of his personality. First he desired the term 'servant of God.' He was fully convinced that his Father sent him to this world as Joshua of Nazareth to be the Almighty's servant. As Isaiah predicted (Is 49: 3-6), Jesus heard from his heavenly Dad not only 'you are my beloved Son' but also 'You are my servant'; he was fully aware of the fact that God formed him as his servant from the womb. Jesus' one and only duty in this world was to be his Father's messenger and as God's voice, he announced God's love and mercy, justice and righteousness in the vast assembly; he took the role of a champion in raising up the Israelites and the Gentiles as well. Being aware of Jesus' indescribable obedience, humility, simplicity and innocence, John the Baptist named him 'the Lamb of God'. That was not only a nice compliment from John but much more a genuine and very descriptive apt name Jesus deserved and preferred.

We are prone to covet the honorable names as leader, guardian, protector, priest, prophet, king and queen, and so on. We are eligible to be called so, since we have been sanctified in Baptism and started our life of righteousness and justice with Jesus Christ. We are proud to be identified proclaiming, *we are indeed a chosen race, a royal priesthood, a holy nation, a people set apart to proclaim your mighty works.* (Ref. 1 Pet. 2: 9) But is that all we are to be?

Like Jesus Christ our 'Christian' name includes *'servants of God, apostles of God, messengers of God and surely lambs of God.'* Let us remember here what Jesus did and told in front of his disciples the day before he died at the Last Supper. *...I have given you a model to follow, so that as I have done for you, you should also do...* (Jn. 13: 12-17) Honoring the remarkable name 'Christian' we, who *call upon the Name of Jesus*, must lead a life worthy of that name. As Paul, we too are called to be apostles Christ. (Ref. 1 Cor. 1: 1-3) This means we become totally the servants of God in all our secular, earthly, spiritual and religious undertakings. At this critical moment when religious conflicts are spawned globally mainly by hostilities ignited by the arrogant supremacy attitudes of certain religious persons, we need to take a pledge before God that we would be faithfully following Jesus as innocent and meek and peaceful lambs.

....

NINTH WEEKEND

Third Sunday in ordinary time
Bend and repent for being renewed

When he heard that John had been arrested, he withdrew to Galilee. He left Nazareth and went to live in Capernaum by the sea, in the region of Zebulun and Naphtali, that what had been said through Isaiah the prophet might be fulfilled: "Land of Zebulun and land of Naphtali, the way to the sea, beyond the Jordan, Galilee of the Gentiles, the people who sit in darkness have seen a great light, on those dwelling in a land overshadowed by death light has arisen." From that time on, Jesus began to preach and say, "Repent, for the kingdom of heaven is at hand." (Matt. 4: 12-17)

From the day of its inception our Christian life revolves in and around the Kingdom of God which Jesus wants us to be immersed into deeply. In order to assist us in this effort, the Gospel passage, we take for this weekend meditation, offers us the first homily of Jesus, very short but filled with meanings. *Repent, for the kingdom of heaven is at hand.*

"To repent" means not simply brooding over but most importantly rethinking, revisiting, reviewing, and reevaluating' our life. It is because, as Jesus emphasized, the presence of God is within us; God's House in this world is built in more in every person's soul than anywhere.

Jesus therefore proclaimed *the kingdom of heaven or God is at hand, in our midst, among us, within us.* Therefore if we desire any change in our lives, Jesus asks us first to go inside of us and review our own attitudes, our won customs, our own holdings, our own value systems which we had coveted from our birth, our formation, and from our society. We become free to become original of God.

There are millions of people who live in sinful darkness of their lives. This situation of groping in darkness can be encountered by most of us while we are being tossed by doubts, worries, sicknesses, mental tortures, down-syndromes, unforgiving stressful life, discontentment in everything we handle and inability to discern, to manage ourselves, and to make right choices and so on. Such a dark road takes a surprise turn when we become fully spiritually and morally blind. Consequently we not only become useless to our family or society but also turn out to be social criminals harming others in everything we are engaged in.

This adherence to darkness can make us even the good things very badly. For example, many darkened souls, unfortunately mishandling the marvelous gift of faith, use it as source of their being stone-hearted, intolerant, very individualistic, becoming totalitarians, cruel leaders, and being ready even to destroy others on the basis of their faith-judgment that they are the only right persons while others are too bad to live. It is from this dark dimension or situation of human life today God wants us to be liberated. Undoubtedly the journey of this salvific liberation from darkness to light is a hard one. To be in darkness is easier, more comfortable and pleasurable. However, when we continue to live in darkness, we are outside the kingdom of God and in exile, pining for home.

Scriptures proclaim that this darkness can be easily overcome. As prophets preached, there is the way and source that leads us to the bright light (Is. 9: 1). Gospel Writers contend that this prophecy was referring to, none other than Jesus of Nazareth. Jesus, who is alive today in our midst, is waiting with his open arms to accept us though we feel or ashamed of our stupidity.

At the same time he expects us to fulfill certain prerequisites and conditions such as: To express our earnestness toward his promised life living in his bright house with the heartbeats of *The Lord is my light and my salvation. One thing I ask of the LORD; this I seek: To dwell in the house of the LORD all the days of my life* (Ps. 27); to unhesitantly reach out to Jesus, the spiritual doctor, with no fear whatsoever regarding our past sinful life; because he promised only sick person needs a doctor; and also to confess to him humbly the dark dimensions of our personal life with the intense longing to renew and reform our walk of life.

....

TENTH WEEKEND

Fourth Sunday in ordinary time

The Beatified Kingdom starts already here on earth

"...Blessed are the poor in spirit, for theirs is the kingdom of heaven. Blessed are they who mourn, for they will be comforted. Blessed are the meek, for they will inherit the land. Blessed are they who hunger and thirst for righteousness, for they will be satisfied. Blessed are the merciful, for they will be shown mercy. Blessed are the clean of heart, for they will see God. Blessed are the peacemakers, for they will be called children of God. Blessed are they who are persecuted for the sake of righteousness, for theirs is the kingdom of heaven. Blessed are you when they insult you and persecute you and utter every kind of evil against you falsely because of me. Rejoice and be glad, for your reward will be great in heaven. (Matt. 5: 1-12)

The Gospel passage we take this weekend for our meditation is the detailed followup of Jesus' first homily on 'the Kingdom of heaven'; it spells out who are eligible to be inducted into this 'kingdom'. In the past and still even now many of us hold a misunderstanding or misinterpretation about the term 'the kingdom of God' as Jesus used. Some say that Jesus congratulated the weaklings for their disabled status; for their neediness, homelessness. Many consider the kingdom of God referring to the heaven we are supposed to go after our death. Some others explain it as the political and social territory of our religion, the Christianity.

Unfortunately all those descriptions and definitions were not what the Lord intended to tell us. In the textual context the word 'kingdom' he used denotes our human life. Every one of us as we grow older begin establish or build our own life with self-respect, freedom and responsibility. Therefore each one of us forms our own life as our kingdom with its boundaries, walls, rules and formulas and codes; it includes first our individuality with its body and soul, then our family, and so on.

However as human experience shows almost all the time the kingdom we build as our own turns to be full of sadness, discontentment, and peacelessness, many times very destructive. Let us look at the human history where we observe the nonstop family-feuds, infights in communities, wars with destructive ammunitions, and even the problems existing perennially in the kingdom of our individual body and spirit. As the Scriptures indicate the whole human race in their own kingdoms live and move in darkness and gloom.

This is why God sent his Son as the Lamb, as the Light, as the Way for the humans to restructure once again their own kingdoms as realms of joyful and peaceful living. Jesus' entire life's ministry concentrated on this matter and taught us how to keep our kingdom, our realm of life as God's. He firmly convinced us that we the humans are the children of God and created as God's image and likeness and therefore we possess the capacity to rebuild our kingdom into God's kingdom.

The 'kingdom' which Jesus pointed out is a realm and it is a life full of justice, full of love, full of contentment, full of joy and full of peace. He wanted his disciples to live such a Godly life and make earthly life into a kingdom of God. In that kingdom there is always blessing; always fraternity, always balanced mindsetup and always level-ground walking. He longed that in all steps of life, his disciples should be joyful. In order to understand the 'beatified' tips Jesus offered in the Gospel, as Paul advises, we have to look at Jesus himself, *who became for us wisdom from God, as well as righteousness, sanctification, and redemption.* (1Cor. 1: 30) Paul also, expounding this truth, exhorts us, *Let the same mind be in you that was in Christ Jesus...* (Phi. 2: 5-8)

As Jesus preached about the 'beatified' steps for the kingdom, he was so much concerned about our present life rather than what comes after this life. Undeniably he emphasized that there is heaven beyond this earthly life but only as its extension or continuity. In order to enter fully the heavenly kingdom we should start it here before we die. Jesus expects us to be fully dependent on God as he was. The Gospel slogans of Beatitudes of Christ therefore challenge us to accept the kingdom of God and live accordingly and try to make our lives as truly the kingdoms of God.

....

ELEVENTH WEEKEND

Fifth Sunday in ordinary time

We are enlightening Light but always seasoned by Salt

> *You are the salt of the earth. But if salt loses its taste, with what can it be seasoned? It is no longer good for anything but to be thrown out and trampled underfoot. You are the light of the world... your light must shine before others, that they may see your good deeds and glorify your heavenly Father.* (Matt. 5: 13-16)

In the Gospel passage taken for this weekend meditation Jesus tells his followers: *You are the salt of the earth. You are the light of the world.* The metaphor 'light' is frequently used in Scriptures describing the identity and action of God and his Son: *God is light and in him there is no darkness* (1Jn. 1: 5). Jesus proclaims himself *the true light of the world come to light every man* (John 1: 5; 8:12). Very surprisingly, Jesus adds that all his followers are also the light. When he identified himself as the light of the world coming from heaven, his enemies were scandalized that he equalized himself with God; worse still, when he publicly admitted that his followers were also the light like himself we can imagine how much their hearts would have been pulsating.

At the same time we should know he never missed the chance to add some more fact about this role of light he transmitted to his followers: First of all, he differentiated our role of light from his own. While he proclaimed in John 8: 12 that *he is the light of the world,* we hear him say in John, *"While I am in the world, I am the light of the world."* (John 9: 5) In other words, as long as he was physically present in the world, he has been the light of the world, but when he is no longer physically present, his followers are to assume the role of being the light of the world. This role, as Jesus has been pointing out, is not something naturally inherited by their birth; rather, it was purely a gratuitous gift from God.

Besides, Jesus emphasized that this 'light' entrusted to his disciples has to be nurtured and preserved safely burning within them. To underscore this truthful fact he added another dimension of Christian identity and he said: *You are the salt of the earth.* From early days of humanity salt was used both for social and religious purposes: In ancient Near East, there was a covenant of salt, a synonym for an inviolable covenant; as Jesus himself stated it is the source of human love and peace. (Mk. 9: 50). In our daily life, we know salt has been the ultimate seasoning that gives taste to food. Plus, it has the power to keep food safe and intact.

In saying that we are the salt of the earth, Jesus indicates that all human nature corrupted by sin has become tasteless, but through our ministry of testimony, the grace of the Holy Spirit will regenerate and preserve the world, if only we melt like salt in the spiritual fire and living waters of God, like Jesus. By his death as a sacrificial lamb and libation being poured out, the humanity was reconciled to God. He gave to human life a fullness of meaning and taste along with safe direction.

Jesus considers the light shared by God within us is to be like salt. *If salt loses its taste what is the use of it?*

So light first must shine within the hearts and minds of the followers and then it will shine outside and will do its accomplishment. He too gave a doable strategy for preserving and increasing the inner light burning and the inner spirit of salt tasteful. To abide in such light Jesus said: ...*He who loves his brother abides in the light*... (1 Jn. 2: 8-11)

This is why whenever we hear OT Prophets proclaimed that people of God can be light shining in darkness, they never missed adding the source of such role of lighting others, namely love deeds. (Is. 58: 9-10) Joining hands with our Master, let us declare and try to live upto the concrete way of being light and salt in this world as God's proxies through our orderly effective and concrete charity that bends toward the needy, poor and the suffering. Consequently we can give flavour to the life of the world and we build a culture of life and a civilization of love.

....

TWELTH WEEKEND

Wisely Revisiting but Faithfully Adhering to God's Laws

> *Do not think that I have come to abolish the law or the prophets. I have come not to abolish but to fulfill. Amen, I say to you, until heaven and earth pass away, not the smallest letter or the smallest part of a letter will pass from the law, until all things have taken place. Therefore, whoever breaks one of the least of these commandments and teaches others to do so will be called least in the kingdom of heaven. But whoever obeys and teaches these commandments will be called greatest in the kingdom of heaven. I tell you, unless your righteousness surpasses that of the scribes and Pharisees, you will not enter into the kingdom of heaven.* (Matt. 5: 17-37)

Our meditation this weekend is about God's commandments which are proposed and recommended to humanity by our Master Jesus. Judeo-Christian Traditions uphold the source and dignity of these Commandments by quoting repeatedly God saying: *"See, I have today set before you, life and good, death and evil...* (Deut. 30: 15-18) In other words, the Commandments of God are to be honored simply a resourceful guide for our survival and success in this world. These are supposed to be strategies for our life-management. Very sadly the humans, especially we who have been born and bred in this Age, being swayed by this sophisticated individualism, hate laws and regulations; we are proud to disobey and violate them. Worse than the adults, young people of today are very hostile to laws and rules as they consider these laws 'limiting their freedom'. They dream how much happier life would be without so many do's and don'ts!

This wrong attitude against God's Commandments is originated not by mere outward 'modern isms' but much more so from within, namely out of ignorance of the richest benevolence of those Commandments. Actually God's laws are optional instructional manual for our life. There is an ancient adage: "Keep the rule and the rule will keep you." As this ever-guiding principle for victorious life, God wanted his humans take to heart all his Commandments. Persons who are sincere to strive for joy-filled and peaceful life in this world have been fully aware of this option God has entrusted to them. We can hear this truth repeated many times in the Scriptures.

Jesus never denied the necessity and resourcefulness of God's Laws in human lives. From the Gospel passage we read for our meditation we observe Jesus was well aware of the facts that those Laws are God's special gift to his people; they express his love for the people since observing them they would walk in his ways and come to share his life and happiness; they in turn show their gratitude for his love by obeying the laws and by sharing his love with one another. Hence he was totally conformed to those Laws and was zealous in institutionalizing and more enhancing them in the hearts of his followers. *Do not think that I have come to abolish the law or the prophets. I have come not to abolish but to fulfill.*

He was very sad to observe God's chosen people abusing his Laws as they paid more attention to the letter and not to the spirit of the Law. He was disturbed by the abusive efforts of religious leaders and teachers of his time being engaged in hair-splitting interpretations of the law. This created a bad perception among the people about relationship with God which was no more based on love but on the legalistic observance of so many man-made laws. Therefore he revisited those commandments and renewed them in their core spirit. He too capsuled them in a simple package so that his disciples-educated and uneducated, may be kept these Laws in their inner memory and be reminded always. *Love God with all your heart....and love your neighbors as yourself.* He too asserted: *The whole law and the prophets depend on these two commandments.* (Matt. 22: 40)

In this postmodern Age, every one of babyboomers and millennials tries to revisit and reinterpret those Laws according to our situations and needs. Personally I think there is no problem in it. God's plan of action is not dead, it is alive and growing. Like Jesus we too can reread and revisit those Laws. Nonetheless our only problem lies in our engagement with the Laws. On this matter, we should follow exactly what our Lord has entrusted to us as criterion for making choices. It is nothing but the package he gave to us. He named it: "The Gospel of Charity." The word Charity Jesus used mysteriously includes all virtues, especially justice, freedom and purity.

....

THIRTEENTH WEEKEND

Seventh Sunday in ordinary time
Our Enemies are Neighbors in Need

"You have heard that it was said, 'An eye for an eye and a tooth for a tooth.' But I say to you, offer no resistance to one who is evil. When someone strikes you on your right cheek, turn the other one to him as well... You have heard that it was said, 'You shall love your neighbor and hate your enemy.' But I say to you, love your enemies, and pray for those who persecute you, that you may be children of your heavenly Father...So be perfect, just as your heavenly Father is perfect. (Matt. 5: 38-48)

To many of us, Jesus' words, taken for this weekend meditation, may seem confusing or challenging or very hard sayings to digest. Certainly love for enemies seems madness to common reason and in the public square of post-modern society. On seeing so much evil in the world, especially when that evil affects us deeply, our reaction is always anger and perhaps revenge. But Jesus tells us not let evil force us to fight it with its own weapons of evil. He commands us to fight it with the weapons of God himself: mercy, forgiveness, even love of the evildoer and prayer for the ones who have hurt us. Nonetheless we see in history the true followers of Christ firmly believed and continue till this day to recognize that Jesus' command of loving enemies is very realistic. Why?

God's Archenemy, the Devil, who started his rivalry-engagement against God from the creation of the world, is sowing the evil continuously in the hearts of humans. The endresult is we can find millions of tombs and monuments full of skeletons buried by wars of hatred, retaliation and revenge. Even today we hear and see such cruel and horrible violent and bloody conflicts globally being enacted in the name religious affiliation or political isms.

In this unending spiritual battle the followers of Christ discovered victory can be attained only by the strategy Jesus handled in his own life: Forgiving and loving and praying for those victimized by the cruel Devil. He demonstrated it to us while he was hanging on the Cross. *However we should never think such a meek and forgiving style of life as surrender to the evil-situations with sour-grape attitude or by an attitude of pacifism. Rather there is something more to this. First we should know the* 'enemies' are the neediest People

According to Jesus' Gospel of Charity our neighborly charity should be need-based and not by one's own liking and disliking. Unfortunately because of our self-centered perception we make our own calculation to practice the command of charity. According to it, we judge divide our neighbors as those who like and love us; those whom we like and love; those whom we don't like yet love; and those, who hate us, do all kinds of evil against us. Among them we are prone to show love the first three groups of neighbors whereas we dislike and sometimes hate others. These are the ones whom we judge as sinful, alien, unworthy to live with us. In other words, we, with our selfish shortsightedness, name certain neighbors as enemies. But in themselves they are not.

As any other humans the so-called enemies also have their needs. Especially they are in need of a merciful and compassionate touch from God through us. Indeed they are truly our neighbors. Jesus suggests to us today to come out of our self-centered shortsightedness and to love the wrongly-named enemies as our neighbors. Jesus had an incredible dream about his followers, namely they should *be perfect as the heavenly Father is perfect.* All that he lived, experienced and preached centered on this motif. He defined this goal of perfection as going beyond themselves and not living as average humans; their religious life surpassing that of the Scribes and Pharisees; loving neighbors, especially our enemies.

'Loving our enemies' is indeed a miraculous act, very hard to perform. Yet it is possible if each one of us closely stand by the Cross remembering the words of Paul: *All belong to you, and you to Christ, and Christ to God.* (1 Cor 3: 22-23)

....

FOURTEENTH WEEKEND

Eighth Sunday in ordinary time
Restful Settlement in God we Trust

No one can serve two masters. He will either hate one and love the other, or be devoted to one and despise the other. You cannot serve God and mammon. Therefore I tell you, do not worry about your life, what you will eat or drink, or about your body, what you will wear. Is not life more than food and the body more than clothing? Look at the birds in the sky; they do not sow or reap, they gather nothing into barns, yet your heavenly Father feeds them... So do not worry and say, 'What are we to eat?' or 'What are we to drink?' or 'What are we to wear?' All these things the pagans seek. Your heavenly Father knows that you need them all. But seek first the kingdom of God and his righteousness, and all these things will be given you besides... (Matt. 6: 24-34)

All of us are overwhelmed with so many worries that intensify our stress: We are worrying when jobs are scarce and homes with overdue mortgages are being repossessed in record numbers. Yes, there are a lot difficult situations swirling around us nowadays. Yes, there are many things we require to make it thru each day: food, clothing, shelter, and so on. One author very truly compares worry to a "god, invisible but omnipotent.'

Jesus was fully aware of these injurious results of worries in his disciples. As a human being, he himself had gone thru such intensive worries and stress. If we look back his life as narrated in the Gospels from his early days he was snowed under stress. So he knew well what humanity's fate is. He had great concern for us. He didn't want to leave them in that stressful situations and also never allowed them to use their own devices to solve it. He desired that his disciples learn from him the ways to cope with worries and stress as he applied in his own life. He found a deep rest even in the midst of such deplorable lifesituation.

In the Gospel passage we meditate today Jesus reminds us emphatically worrying about life, we cannot add a single moment to our life-span. It is sheer useless to worry about tomorrow because *tomorrow will take care of itself. Sufficient for a day is its own evil.* Worry is futile. We cannot, by worrying, add anything to our lives and improve our situation. It is said that 'today is the tomorrow we worried about yesterday'. Like Paul we should never worry about ourselves and our limitations and sinfulness because our judgment about us won't be as correct as the Lord's. Nor should we be worried about the complaints, remarks and other gossips from others; again it is because they are not the true judge on us; it is only God. (1 Cor. 4: 1-5)

After offering some wise and reasonable facts of human life, Jesus asks us to trust in God because we are God's precious children. He loves and cares for us. As Isaiah points out (Is. 49: 15-16) God is to us more than a parent: *Even should a mother forget, I will never forget you.* This means we are worth very much in God's eyes and he loves us deeply. We are forever *engraved in the palm of his hands.* Therefore Jesus counsels us to stay put in God's trust. It means to settle oneself single-hearted. *You cannot serve two masters.* Those masters are: God who has established his kingdom already in us; and the Satan who, trying his best to destabilize God's kingdom, longs to establish his own. In continuation of this advice, Jesus adds we should keep God as our priority. *First seek the kingdom of God and everything will be added unto.*

We have to trust in God, who provides for our every need, no matter how small and insignificant we are. God has a wonderful plan for our lives, and part of that plan includes taking care of us. Even in difficult times, when it seems that God doesn't care, we can put our trust in the Lord and focus our attention on his Kingdom. This is because of our faith in Jesus' words: *Your heavenly Father knows that you need them all.*

God in Jesus confirms to us constantly that when we settle in him with trust, we become very restful, safe, secure and peaceful. We hear the outcry of the Psalmist about his conviction on this fact. (Ref. Ps. 62) The restlessness we feel many times is generated by our imbalanced way of approaching our life issues, especially our human relationships. This critical situation flies away when we move and live in him keeping him as a rock.

....

FIFTTEENTH WEEKEND

First Sunday of Lent

Temptation is inevitable but always conquerable

> *Then Jesus was led by the Spirit into the desert to be tempted by the devil. He fasted for forty days and forty nights, and afterwards he was hungry. The tempter approached and said to him...At this, Jesus said to him, "Get away, Satan! It is written: 'The Lord, your God, shall you worship and him alone shall you serve.'" Then the devil left him and, behold, angels came and ministered to him.* (Matt. 4: 1-11)

As we start the Lenten season of forty days, like Jesus went through before starting his public ministry, Church invites us to meditate on a very crucial and inevitable factor in our Christian life, namely the temptations which the Master himself encountered.

Temptation is simply a lure, enticement, inducement or coaxing from within or without of ourselves. The temptations we reflect this weekend are the compulsions happening in the spiritual dimension of our life. They are the events occurring in the battlefield between good and evil, truth and lie, darkness and light, God and the Devil. This battle is not happening somewhere beyond the space or in other planets; rather it happens within each one of us.

Every spiritual temptation comes to us only when we are facing a situation or occasion to make choices for God. Satan enters in those situations and lures us either to reject or to deviate ourselves from our connections, our commitments and our observances toward loving God. The main cause of these failures is none other than the Devil, Archenemy of God. He is a roaring lion, roaming about to devour all God's children (1Pet. 5: 8-9); he is very smarty and performs his actions in a very subtle way; he never appears directly and shows his face of arrogance and cruelty to his clients. He comes in various disguises, like a serpent; and in the disguise of a lovemate (Gen. 3: 1-7).

This shrewd but fallen angel waits for the weak moments of humans to devour them. We are rare-blending of both physical and spiritual dimensions. However, in our hunger and thirst for fulfilling basic needs physically and emotionally we become weak. During those moments Satan enters into our life to gobble us. Many of us at those moments forgetting the other side of us-the children of God, like Adam and Eve, succumb to Satan's temptation. In the Gospel passage we meditate today Jesus too as human was approached by Satan in his weak moments. But we know he didn't yield but drove him out of sight. Thus, Jesus is given to us as a rolemodel in handling these temptations successfully. Very faithfully he used the Word of God as ammunition in his battle against his Enemy.

Besides, the most striking factor we have to understand is that Satan picks up only those who are good-willed people as his priority victims. Before he was tempted by the devil Jesus was at the Jordan; baptized by John, anointed by the Holy Spirit and given recognition from his heavenly Father as *my beloved Son;* soon after, the Spirit takes him to perform a forty days retreat as immediate preparation for his ministry. During this holy period Satan enters to tempt Jesus as usual taking hold of his regular strategy of feeding through human weaknesses. He tempts Jesus to misuse his self-awareness, in other words, his own goodness.

Christian Life indeed is a risky business. It is a wild road jampacked with temptations. As Pope Francis is quoted saying, *Temptation is our daily bread. So much so, that if one of us says that 'I have never been tempted' the right response would be, either you're a cherub with wings, or you're a little stupid.* Satan continues to go after people, like Jesus, who are spiritually well-groomed, well educated, well trained, well positioned, and well aware of their identity. A disciple can never be more than the Master but can follow his footprints. Let us therefore try like our Master to handle with care our self-identity, our well-established individuality especially in our life's weak moments.

Second Sunday of Lent

*Hilltop encounter always pulls us down
to the valley of needs and tears*

*After six days Jesus took Peter, James,
and John his brother, and led them up a
high mountain by themselves. And he was
transfigured before them; his face shone
like the sun and his clothes became white
as light. And behold, Moses and Elijah
appeared to them, conversing with him.
Then Peter said to Jesus in reply, "Lord, it
is good that we are here. If you wish, I will
make three tents here, one for you, one for
Moses, and one for Elijah." While he was
still speaking, behold, a bright cloud cast
a shadow over them, then from the cloud
came a voice that said, "This is my beloved
Son, with whom I am well pleased; listen
to him"... As they were coming down from
the mountain, Jesus charged them, "Do
not tell the vision to anyone until the Son
of Man has been raised from the dead."*
(Matt. 17:1-9)

We lead in this world a life filled with temptations that
hinder us to be faithful and trustworthy disciples, and even
sometimes drifting us away from our Master. Plus, it is like
a journey of Abram to a 'land of destiny' unknown to us
but known only to God. (Gen. 12: 1-4); it seems as living

an exilic and deserted life hopelessly hoping for better future. As committed disciples of Jesus many of us feel often that we are surrounded by the lawless and unruly, the godless and sinful, the unholy and profane, murderers, the unchaste, sodomites, kidnapers, liars, perjurers, and so on. (2 Tim. 1: 9-10)

We are led by the Spirit this weekend to reflect on how to conduct ourselves with our 'utmost for the highest result.' Observing Jesus in the Gospel passage from Matthew, we discover some effective and productive tips to snatch the win. We know from all the Gospel writers that Jesus never missed a single moment without communing with God. His heartbeats were ceaselessly infusing within him not only blood but also inebriating his spirit elevated. However he chose special hours and special environment to be immersed in prayer. One of those hours is narrated in the Gospel passage of today.

He chose a 'hilltop' environment, in order to be secluded from the mob; as he had preached, 'going to his inner sanctuary of spirit, closing all the doors of outside world, he prayed to his Father in secret.' Such kind of commune with God was his primary tool to be nourished, strengthened and renewed during his personal exilic journey. He too endorsed the one-heart-and-one-mind group prayer by taking disciples this time to pray with him.

Another tip Jesus offers to us is not to be self-centred during prayer. We can see the difference between Jesus and Peter in performing hilltop prayer. While Peter was preoccupied with not losing that 'split-second' spiritual ecstasy, Jesus, despite his full awareness of his glorious transfiguration, seemed more attentive to conversing with his spiritual mentors and getting their advices and directions. More importantly Jesus, being strengthened in his will to accomplish his Father's Will, rushes back to the down valley where his vision and mission will be realized; he never gave even a single minute to discuss with his disciples what happened to him at the hilltop; rather he warned them not to mention about it to other people.

Those tips of Jesus for managing our life in this world, in the light of the Word, are based on the covenantal relationship with the Supreme Being. From the beginning of human life, as the Bible underlines, God proposes to humans his covenantal love and demands from them the same. Persons like Abram consented to God and amazingly wherever his consent took him, even to lead an interim nomad and exilic life, leaving his land, relatives, and his father's house, he persevered in his faith and fidelity to his Creator. The same way Jesus reciprocated his faith and love to his Father by emptying himself, becoming very fragile human, and undergoing ignominious death on the cross.

That is the way we, his disciples must cope with this treacherous earthly life. The hardships we undergo during this deserted life must be borne with the convictions that in this life we were called by God to be holy and that everything that happens in this life-journey is designed already by the grace of God. As we are meditating now at the hilltop, Jesus touches us and wakes us up telling: *Get up; don't stay only on the hilltop; but get out, and go down with me; walk with your friends and relatives. Go forth; continue to evangelize and make the poor and the needy joyful.*

Third Sunday of Lent

Be the River of Living Waters from the Divine Spring

Jesus came to a town of Samaria called Sychar, near the plot of land that Jacob had given to his son Joseph. Jacob's well was there. Jesus, tired from his journey, sat down there at the well. It was about noon. A woman of Samaria came to draw water. Jesus said to her, "Give me a drink"...The woman said to him, "Sir, you do not even have a bucket and the well is deep; where then can you get this living water?... Jesus answered and said to her, "Everyone who drinks this water will be thirsty again; but whoever drinks the water I shall give will never thirst; the water I shall give will become in him a spring of water welling up to eternal life"...Many of the Samaritans of that town began to believe in him because of the word of the woman who testified, "He told me everything I have done." When the Samaritans came to him, they invited him to stay with them; and he stayed there two days. Many more began to believe in him because of his word, and they said to the woman, "We no longer believe because of your word; for we have heard for ourselves, and we know that this is truly the savior of the world." (Jn. 4: 5-42)

In this holy season, the Spirit provides for our this weekend meditation a relevant Gospel story that offers guidance for how to quench our unending thirst during this deserted earthly life. In the Gospel story we see Jesus and his disciples feeling thirsty as they were walking through the desert from Galilee to Judea under Palestinian scotching sun. Jesus requests a Samaritan woman to give water to him and his crew. As the Spirit of God moved Jesus, using the natural and physical need of thirst for water, to discuss about what the real spiritual thirst of humans and how it should be quenched.

God the Creator has been never tired of claiming himself as the 'rock of our salvation'. We read in the Book of Deuteronomy (Chapter 32) he speaks through Moses how he had been their rock who could bring out their life resources breaking through any kind of rocks found in this earth. In fact he demonstrated his claim, as we hear in OT, by a miraculous deed. While people were stranded in the desert on their way to Promised Land, in their thirst for water, they grumbled and groaned. God indeed listened to their cry and he arranged cool water flow from the hot rock. (Ex. 17: 3-7) And therefore all his messengers like David exhorted their people to *acclaim the Rock of our salvation.* (Ps. 95) Undoubtedly God to us who are marching on in the deserted life is the rock on whom we can rely and the source of life-giving water.

Even the physical rocks that seem to be giving troubles to us in walking the walk of our Master can turn out to be the source of energy, nourishment as the Living waters. Abiding in his Father, he spelt out his own identity of being that divine rock from whom we can receive spiritual waters that can quench our thirsts. W*hoever drinks the water I shall give will never thirst...* (Jn. 4: 14)

Humans of this Age are affected by too many thirsts: Thirst for power, dignity, freedom, pleasure, fulfillment, prosperity and on and on. According to Jesus, whatever we do by our natural, artificial, earthly ways in order to quench our thirsts, will not confine or control all those thirsts. The one and only permanent solution for this plight is drinking the Living waters that come from the heart, words and sacraments of Jesus. To drink this living water means: Welcoming Jesus into our life; accepting his lifestyle of love; boasting in hope of the glory of God; boasting even of our afflictions, knowing that affliction produces endurance, and endurance, proven character, and proven character, hope. (Ref. Rom. 5: 1-8)

We observe in the Gospel story the Samaritan woman tasted this living water and she was so intoxicated by this water that she went around proclaiming its greatness. Other Samaritans believed the witness of the woman, but remained steadfast in their belief because they themselves had tasted the living water. Similarly, let us not limit ourselves to the hearing of the greatness of Jesus, but experience his greatness in our personal lives, so as to remain steadfast in his love.

EIGHTEENTH WEEKEND

Fourth Sunday of Lent

Anointed Soul's Sudden Awakening

As he passed by he saw a man blind from birth. His disciples asked him, "Rabbi, who sinned, this man or his parents, that he was born blind?" Jesus answered, "Neither he nor his parents sinned; it is so that the works of God might be made visible through him. We have to do the works of the one who sent me while it is day. Night is coming when no one can work. While I am in the world, I am the light of the world." When he had said this, he spat on the ground and made clay with the saliva, and smeared the clay on his eyes, and said to him, "Go wash in the Pool of Siloam" (which means Sent). So he went and washed, and came back able to see...So they said to the blind man again, "What do you have to say about him, since he opened your eyes?" He said, "He is a prophet"...Jesus said to him, "You have seen him and the one speaking with you is he." He said, "I do believe, Lord," and he worshiped him. (Jn. 9: 1-41)

Helen Keller, who became blind in her early childhood and remained blind till her death, writes about this experience she says: *"I came up out of Egypt and stood before Sinai and a power divine touched my spirit and gave it life."* Later in her life she went on to experience the beauties and mysteries of life with such clarity that she was able to share what she called her "soul's sudden awakening" with others.

The Gospel story we meditate today is about one such blind person who was cured of his blindness by Jesus' anointing. It is a metaphoric explanation of the Spirit about every human's spiritual journey from blindness to sight; from unbelief to faith, from darkness to light. It is all about the daily encounter of us who have been enlightened by Christ in sacramental anointing. All who get this spiritual anointing begin to see very differently their own self and all that are outside of them.

First, we fully see that Jesus is our savior who helped us in this liberation process of coming out from blindness, darkness to light-filled life. Jesus' anointing of the blind man in the Gospel brought light and renewed hope into the man's darkened life. Liberated from his blindness, the man began to see and to believe in Jesus. His seeing and his believing challenge us to leave behind our personal darkness and to live in the light of Christ. The same way we begin to see, that the one who offered us such healing anointing, namely Jesus the Messiah is our Light. We begin to be fully aware of our life gets its fullness in him, through him and with him.

Secondly we see everything and every person around us as God sees. We hear the Spirit telling at every point of judging others, as it was in the life of Prophet Samuel: *Do not judge from his appearance or from his lofty stature, because I have rejected him. Not as man sees does God see, because, man sees the appearance, but the Lord looks into the heart.* (1 Sam. 16: 1-13)

Moreover, after the Lord's anointing our inner eyes are opened to see the fact that we are not alone in our journey of life which is like a desert, like climbing up the high mountain, like floating over or swimming against the current of natural waters. This is because our mind and spirit are in full agreement with the truth that there is God in and around our life like a Good Shepherd and sheep. Therefore we start feeling safe and secure, not living in timidity and fear. (Ps. 23)

We too begin to know our true identity. We are weak, clay, dust but at the same time we possess a dignity and a freedom that had previously eluded us. As Paul writes, we were once darkness, but now we are light in the Lord. (Eph. 5: 8) At the same time we have the daring attitude as Jesus' disciples to call God our Abba, Father; we love to wear the faith-glasses and see through our glorious identity of being anointed by Jesus as God's adopted children, plus Jesus' own possession.

With this enlightenment, we are endowed with the power of the Spirit; we start with no inhibition or fear proclaiming that Jesus is the Lord and Messiah, as the cured blind man gratefully accepted and cooperated with the anointing Jesus offered him. He not only went and washed, as he was directed, but he also became a witness to God's anointed, Jesus. Since Christ has already won the ultimate victory, we are assured a share in his strength with which wherever we live, we initiate causing darkness to recoil; all our words and works contribute to the liberation and advancement of the whole human race.

NINETEENTH WEEKEND

Fifth Sunday of Lent

Death has no final say over our life

...Jesus loved Martha and her sister and Lazarus...When Jesus arrived, he found that Lazarus...Martha said to Jesus, "Lord, if you had been here, my brother would not have died. But even now I know that whatever you ask of God, God will give you"...Jesus told her, "I am the resurrection and the life; whoever believes in me, even if he dies, will live, and everyone who lives and believes in me will never die"...So Jesus, perturbed again, came to the tomb...Jesus said, "Take away the stone"...So they took away the stone. He cried out in a loud voice, "Lazarus, come out!" The dead man came out... (Jn. 11: 1-45)

The Gospel passage taken for our meditation is John's narration of a miraculous event of Jesus raising Lazarus from his death. The core message God's Spirit proposes to us through this story is: we should never give up hope even in the most hopeless of situations in which we find ourselves as individuals, as a community or as a nation. It is never too late for God to revive and revitalize a person, a community or a nation.

Scriptures state it is possible to hold such hope if we have strong faith in Jesus as the Living Word that came from God who demonstrated Himself as merciful and compassionate Father, plus made promises of revival and renewal of life. He is the Son of a God who shouts out that he does not desire any human to die. And he is the one who uninterruptedly promises us: *I will open your graves and have you rise from them; I will put my spirit in you that you may live, and I will settle you upon your land.* (Ez. 37: 12-14) In the Gospel Jesus reclaimed his Godly identity of Life-giving ability. Jesus expected Martha to believe in him not only that he has power in giving eternal resurrection on the last day, but also to revive and revitalize the darkened lives of humans who believe in him. *I am the resurrection and the life; whoever believes in me, even if he dies, will live, and everyone who lives and believes in me will never die.*

We should be convinced that Jesus continues to perform such miracles of revival in our lives. The wonder of wonders is that we, the baptized disciples of Jesus, have already risen from ungodliness, darkness, filthy wickedness because of the living presence of the risen Jesus within us. Paul expounds this marvelous deed of God repeatedly in all his Letters. While he underlines that all of us were dead in our transgressions and sins in which we once lived following the age of this world (Ref. Eph. 2: 1-3), he too insists that *God, who is rich in mercy, because of the great love he had for us, even when we were dead in our transgressions, brought us to life with Christ, raised us up with him, and seated us with him in the heavens in Christ Jesus.* (Eph. 2: 4-6)

Unfortunately, as Paul bemoans (Rom. 6: 2-8), forgetting the glorious status we were bestowed with, most of the baptized children of God today are still living in the tomb of hopelessness and decay in the bondage of sinful habits and attitudes. Thus we walk around more dead than alive. However, we should never be discouraged and frustrated or get angry against ourselves. The Lord constantly inspires us to keep on trusting and loving him and letting our friendship with him be evergreen.

According to Jesus, any deviation or wrong choice we make which makes us dead spiritually is not totally to be considered as death; rather, Jesus wants us not to be squirming on our spiritual downfalls, instead to believe that it is an occasion, as he told his disciples about the death of Lazarus, for more glorifying God's immense love and patient compassion for us. *This illness is not to end in death, but is for the glory of God, that the Son of God may be glorified through it.* He highlights that any evil things happening in our lives are very temporary; all the sufferings we undergo are not the end of all; they are all simply stepping stones to the ultimate fullness of eternal life.

If we suffer or die enduring in our friendship with Jesus, we can hear his commanding but compassionate voice: *Lazarus, come out.* Immediately Lazarus wades his way out of the tomb; and the Lord urges other disciples to help him untied. God calls us today to come out of the tombs of our hardness of heart, out of the graves of our fears and selfishness, of everything that keeps us imprisoned. Let us always be available to lend our hearts and minds to God in Jesus who is our Life and Resurrection.

Palm Sunday/Holy Week

The Paradigmshift lived and proposed by Radical Jesus

> *...The disciples went and did as Jesus had ordered them. They brought the ass and the colt and laid their cloaks over them, and he sat upon them. The very large crowd spread their cloaks on the road, while others cut branches from the trees and strewed them on the road. The crowds preceding him and those following kept crying out and saying: "Hosanna to the Son of David; blessed is he who comes in the name of the Lord; hosanna in the highest." And when he entered Jerusalem the whole city was shaken and asked, "Who is this?" And the crowds replied, "This is Jesus the prophet, from Nazareth in Galilee."* (Matt 21: 1-11)

Practically all radicals, being redden down in life but always ended it up in glory. This is historical and perennial truth which is not just narrated in classics and novels, but can be traced out through the centuries in real lives of chivalrous men and women who have been the causes of ushering historical 'paradigmshifts' in human civilizations. We can say boldly Jesus of Nazareth was number one of that kind who has become an eternal icon for spiritual and religious radical ever lived. It is about his unique radicalism we meditate this weekend as we enter into holy week.

The word "radical", coming from the Latin *radix* meaning 'root', has been historically used (quite distinct from the modern usage to denote political extremes of right or left) to designate individuals, parties, and movements that wish to alter drastically any existing cultural, social and religious practice, institution, or system. In this historical sense, Jesus of Nazareth seems to be a typical radical. We discover this fact in Matthew's Gospel narration we meditate today.

From the day of his youth, Jesus was so anxious to fulfill his Father's Will of bringing radical changes in all his children. In Luke we read Jesus saying to his parents, *I must be in my Father's house* (Lk. 2: 49). This saying, according to Biblical scholars, can also be translated, "I must be about my Father's work." Referring it as the fire of purifying and refining the twisted and distorted holdings of humans, he is quoted saying (Lk. 12: 49-50): *I have come to set the earth on fire, and how I wish it were already blazing*! In his program of bringing about radical changes in human society he chalked out through his life and sayings the list of those changes:

First, Jesus' radicalism proposed that humans should choose God and his covenantal love as their life's priority. He preached: *Seek first the kingdom [of God] and his righteousness, and all these things will be given you besides.* (Matt. 6: 33) Righteousness he recommended is nothing but a change of heart and conduct, a turning of one's life from rebellion to obedience towards God; to submit to the plan of God for the salvation of the human race. Undoubtedly he first lived upto it and that is why he could willingly accept the people's hosanna greetings which included the reality of his identity: '*He comes in the name of the Lord*'. Nothing more nor less.

The second radical change Jesus endorsed was that we should lead a life not self-centered but self-sharing. He wanted us to become matured persons who love to share, rather than to accumulate the good things of life. In his own life he upheld this radical life. Though he was in the form of God, as Paul beautifully writes, *"he did not regard equality with God something to be grasped. Rather, he emptied himself, taking the form of a slave, coming in human likeness; and found human in appearance, he humbled himself, becoming obedient to death, even death on a cross."* (Phi. 6-8)

It would have been a shock for many to see Jesus being greeted with a triumphal entry amidst pump and pageantry of a whole city. Clearly, people who welcomed him had their own idea of the Messiah. This was not the first time that the people recognized Christ as the king they expected. It had already happened after the miraculous multiplication of the loaves, when the crowd wanted to carry him in triumph, he fled away from their enthusiasm. But today Jesus surprises us with his silent acceptance of it, even retorted his enemies who wanted him to stop such nonsense-outburst of people: *I tell you, if they keep silent, the stones will cry out!* (Lk. 19: 39-40) The reason behind this is very clear when we fully understand his radical view of his own life. On this day he was entering Jerusalem where his entire vision and mission would be finally completed by freely taking up the cross, suffering and dying on it. According to his value system, that was his life's goal and final triumph to fulfill his Father's Will and bringing salvation to his fellowmen.

At the same time Jesus kept in his mind his third challenging paradigmshift in human life. He envisioned that there should be a radical change in us from arrogant power-play to merciful and compassionate serviceability;

from proud mindsetup to humble melting heart-setup. Let us closely look at the entry procession. While Jesus was hailed by the crowd as the king, he preferred to ride on a donkey. It may sound funny and humorous; but there is a deep implication to it. Matthew was correct in his writing about an OT prophecy being fulfilled in this event: *Behold: your king is coming to you, a just savior is he, Humble, and riding on a donkey...(Zech. 9: 9)* The animal chosen indicates that it was not a triumphal entry, but that of a king meek and humble of heart.

However the humanity, being beguiled by power-display and triumphalism, almost unaware of this expression of humility and not recognizing in it a messianic radical paradigmshift, went on glorifying Jesus. They forgot the difference Jesus was making in his entry from secular leaders' procession which was militaristic, triumphal entry with war horse, chariot, and weapons. He pointed out his radical change to be ushered in his followers: To be faithful service, even when it's a burden; be ready for humble service; not caring who gets the glory, resisting a "hero" image; not getting enthralled or overwhelmed by the crowds, their noisy praises; and being obedient to the will of the One who holds the reins.

It is very hard to do such radical changes within ourselves, and even just to hear them seems madness. However thousands of saints tried to imitate Jesus in his radical and controversial ways. Come, let us follow their footsteps.

TWENTY FIRST WEEKEND

Easter Sunday

We are an Easter people

Are you unaware that we who were baptized into Christ Jesus were baptized into his death? We were indeed buried with him through baptism into death, so that, just as Christ was raised from the dead by the glory of the Father, we too might live in newness of life. For if we have grown into union with him through a death like his, we shall also be united with him in the resurrection. We know that our old self was crucified with him, so that our sinful body might be done away with, that we might no longer be in slavery to sin...Consequently, you too must think of yourselves as [being] dead to sin and living for God in Christ Jesus. (Rom. 6: 3-11)

Our indomitable Christian creed is: *"I believe in the resurrection of the body and life everlasting."* However, according to the Scriptures, such heavenly resurrection will not come to us as a sudden, magical touch of any heavenly angel. Apostle Paul and other NT Writers and Church Fathers teach firmly it is a life-long journey of continuous deaths and resurrections. There are many deaths we are prone to undergo: Paul profusely speaks in all his Letters about two of those deaths: *Death in sin and death to sin.*

Scriptural Tradition testifies that we the humans, born of Adam and Eve, originally enslaved by the snare of Evil and Christianity names it as 'original sin'. Bible refers this human state as 'spiritual death'. When God warned about this death to be resulted by human disobedience he said: ...*in the day that you eat of it (forbidden fruit) you shall surely die.* (Gen. 3:6) The phrase 'you shall surely die' is interpreted as a continuous state of death that began with spiritual death. As God foretold, all of us experience the ripple effects of the original spiritual death: countless spiritual and physical deaths. Paul makes this clear writing that sin and death entered the world and spread to all humans through Adam's sin. (Rom. 5: 12)

Humans daily face many deaths, such as, the nonstop deaths of acute suffering and pain by chronic and terminal diseases; the daily dying of marginalized people out of hunger, thirst, emotional imbalance, unjust rejection and discrimination and exploitation; deaths of going to the downhill by material and physical deprivation. Plus knowingly or unknowingly every human hurts each other by their sinful and silly words and actions. Thus they bring deaths to each other. Due to the original and mutual co-ushering of deaths among humans, none of us is capable of bringing any solution of uplifting each other, in Biblical term, regenerating or resurrecting one another from those inevitable deaths. Jesus repeatedly claims that we cannot come to him without God's enabling (Jn. 6: 44).

As a matter of fact, we are so blessed to see and hear from Jesus and his disciples that we, who are naturally born dead in sin, are bestowed with a power to rise from those deaths by the amazing grace of God through Jesus' death and resurrection. Christian Tradition insists human salvation depends on both the death and resurrection of Jesus.

Yes, by Jesus' death we are saved; by his blood we are saved; by his breathing out last his Spirit is ready to possess us. However Jesus' redemptive work is not over. By his resurrection his Spirit has entered into humanity and started his saving work subtly and effectively. First and foremost his resurrected Spirit makes us die to original sin and daily sins and secondly he raises up from the dark pits of ignorance, indifference, faithlessness, and hopelessness and above all from selfishness. God is never tired of promising to us: *"I will give you a new heart and place a new spirit within you...I will put my spirit within you...you shall be my people, and I will be your God."* (Ez. 36: 26-28)

This is what Paul highlights on this day of Easter. We are buried with Jesus and simultaneously we are risen with him and start walking in newness of life. *Whoever believes in the Son has eternal life* (Jn. 3: 36). All Christians, believing in Jesus' promises of resurrection and through his continuous compassionate actions, receive resurrection of forgiveness, mercy, enlightenment, healing, power and heavenly support. By that belief those who hurt others rise up from their death of losing joy and friendship by getting forgiveness from those whom they have hurt by sincere apologies; those, who die and go to their blues or dark moments of isolation and depression, rise from this death by truly forgiving those who hurt them and get life of joy. Such moments, which I boldly name, are the "earthly resurrections." Thanks to the risen Jesus, *We are indeed an Easter people."*

TWENTY SECOND WEEKEND

Second Sunday of Easter

Easter Church proclaims 'the Lord is truly risen'

> *On the evening of that first day of the week, when the doors were locked, where the disciples were, for fear of the Jews, Jesus came and stood in their midst and said to them, "Peace be with you." When he had said this, he showed them his hands and his side. The disciples rejoiced when they saw the Lord. Jesus said to them again, "Peace be with you. As the Father has sent me, so I send you." And when he had said this, he breathed on them and said to them, "Receive the Holy Spirit. Whose sins you forgive are forgiven them, and whose sins you retain are retained...* (Jn. 20: 19-31)

Humans are social animals. No man is an island. Each one of us needs to belong to a community for our survival, growth and safety. As human beings we belong to a global community of human race. As Christians we belong to the Community we call 'the Church' which was originated from the Easter Encounter. This weekend the Spirit invites us to reflect on the identities and qualities proper to any community which deserves to be called an 'Easter Church' as the risen Lord exposed to the world at its dawn.

First of all the 'Easter Church' was a faith-filled and consequently Spirit-filled community. From the Gospel passage we come to know that together with Thomas everyone in that community was bonded with the risen Lord and with one another as well by the basic and central point of Christian faith that professes in season and out of season that Jesus is '*my Lord and my God.*' At the dawn of Christianity the disciples of Jesus began preaching about the risen Jesus as their Savior. At the start it was very difficult for them as they were surrounded by enemies of their Way. Some people even doubted about the identity of Jesus as Thomas did. However the spirit of Jesus inspired them by his merciful touch and made them understand the truth about his unique identity: He alone is Lord and God and none other. Due to such Jesus-centered situation, all his believers were filled with his Spirit. He breathed on them and said to them, *Receive the Holy Spirit.*

Easter Church was also a community united and peaceful. As we hear in Acts (Acts 2: 42-47), church members were together as one family in listening to the teachings of their elders; in sharing together in love and justice all their property and possessions; in celebrating the Breaking of Bread, the Eucharist; and in praying together continuously and regularly. The repeated greeting words from the mouth of the Risen Lord were, *Peace be with you.* Those powerful wishes brought permanent peace to the community. It was a Peace Loving Community.

Decisively Easter Church was a joyful community. When the risen Lord appeared to the disciples, they were overjoyed. This joy, throughout centuries, has been an important sign of the community of the risen Lord. The risen Lord gives complete joy to his disciples. The community that experiences such joy is ready to do any sacrifice. Peter the Apostle testifies to it writing in his Letter: *In this you rejoice, although now for a little while you may have to suffer through various trials... even though you do not see him now yet believe in him, you rejoice with an indescribable and glorious joy.* (1 Pet. 1: 6-8)

As an outcome, Easter Church was a missionary Community. The risen Jesus, after empowering the disciples with his Spirit, entrusted to them a grand commission. John writes about this succinctly: *As the Father has sent me, so I send you. Whose sins you forgive are forgiven them, and whose sins you retain are retained.* However the three other Gospel writers elaborate it according to their vision. They writer that Jesus sent the disciples to all over the world to proclaim the Good News of forgiveness and of healing, through their teaching and administering the Sacraments, especially the sacrament of Baptism. (Ref. Matt. 28; Mk. 16; Lk. 24)

Besides the universal Church, there are indeed numerous local Easter communities made of so many disciples whose faithfulness inspires the world. They are the ones who trust the Spirit's presence, even in the midst of adversity. They are the ones who raise their children to do the same. They are the ones who accept their own illnesses as opportunities to reveal God's love to others. They are the ones who quietly feed the hungry and share their own resources with faithful abandon, and shape the next generation so they will do the same. And they are the ones who gather their families in the face of approaching death and remind them that *the Lord is truly risen.*

TWENTY THIRD WEEKEND

Third Sunday after Easter

Earthly Encounter with the risen Lord

Then Peter stood up with the Eleven, raised his voice, and proclaimed to them, "You who are Jews, indeed all of you staying in Jerusalem. Let this be known to you, and listen to my words...My brothers, one can confidently say to you about the patriarch David that he died and was buried, and his tomb is in our midst to this day. But since he was a prophet and knew that God had sworn an oath to him that he would set one of his descendants upon his throne, he foresaw and spoke of the resurrection of the Messiah, that neither was he abandoned to the netherworld nor did his flesh see corruption. God raised this Jesus; of this we are all witnesses. (Acts 2: 14-32)

The risen Jesus is alive today in our midst as he had promised before he left this world; and the NT Books and the Church Tradition uphold that he can be encountered by any disciple of Jesus. It is to this unfathomable truth Peter preached 'witnessing'. The Spirit invites us today to meditate on this mysterious but historical matter. These remarkable incidents of encountering the resurrected Lord began from the day he rose from the dead. According to my calculation, risen Jesus' appearances reported in NT are 12 at different times, to various disciples ranging from one, like Mary Magdalene, Peter, Paul, and Jesus' brother, to five hundred, as Paul points out (1 Cor. 15: 6).

There is no doubt as cradle and converted Catholics we firmly believe that risen Lord is still alive in our midst, knocking at the doors of our hearts, our families, our communities, and surely our personal and private lives. However, after hearing and reading all these testimonies found in Scriptures and Tradition, one question always arises in the modern minds: "Is this possible even today?" Can we experience such apparitions of the risen Lord as the disciples had in early days of the Church? Many may contend we don't. Due to this failure and disappointment some among us are dejected and discouraged and even stopped our pursuit of these marvelous encounters...may be with some sour-grape attitude! But the Lord invites us today not to stop our pursuit for the Lord's encounters, to rethink of our approach toward this faith-fact.

If we, with the Spirit dig into all those appearances of risen Jesus we can find some particular life situations in which the disciples met him. The encounters occurred either when they were in search of the Master (Jn. 20: 11-18); or planning to perform the usual rituals to be done for Jesus (Mk. 16: 1); or conversing about the Master's life and death (Lk. 24: 14); or living behind closed doors out of frustration and fear (Jn. 20: 19); or by special arrangement of the Master to entrust his Gospel works to his disciples (Matt. 28: 16-20; Acts 9: 3-6). Particularly in the Gospel of Luke we read a narration (24: 13-35), about two disciples encountering the risen Savior, which seems to be very closely related to our daily lifesituations. Like them we are travelers in life; we too continuously converse, analyze and meditate on the Master's personality and deeds; at the end of our all spiritual and religious attempts we fail and intensely frustrated. In such grim situation we notice one of the wonderful heartwarming encounters of the risen Lord happening in the lives of those disciples. They testify clearly at what time they exactly became fully aware of the risen Lord's presence. They said at the *breaking of bread*, which was a customary ritual performed by disciples of early Church.

Unquestionably Jesus' disciples possess the ability to encounter the risen Lord in prayer, in visions and dreams, in moments of sufferings. There are so many Christians in history witnessing to this truth. However, that is not a regular occurrence for every ordinary human disciple of Jesus. There is one more very tangible, very visible and very plausible and very regular encountering of the risen Lord in each one's life. He is found, touched, heard, read first and foremost in Scriptures and surely in the intimate connection we have with the Church. At the end of his earthly life he left behind his unique path of human life as a self-actualization. This self-actualization of Jesus is found in the written Scriptures and lived Tradition, namely the Church. *"Very surprisingly the heavenly Word became flesh and later more miraculously his flesh and Spirit became the Words of scriptures and Traditions of the Church."* Therefore willingly and longingly when I reach out to Scriptures and more faithfully when I involve myself in the Traditions of the Church I do encounter Christ, the risen Lord. He is walking with us! He is talking to us! *Are not our hearts burning within us while we read and hear scriptural words? While we are in the Church as Eucharistic Christians? While we are caring the sick and the elderly as Good Samaritans?*

TWENTY FOURTH WEEKEND

Fourth Sunday after Easter

Jesus is the only 'safety Gate' to us

So Jesus said again, 'Amen, amen, I say to you, I am the gate for the sheep. All who came before me are thieves and robbers, but the sheep did not listen to them. I am the gate. Whoever enters through me will be saved, and will come in and go out and find pasture. A thief comes only to steal and slaughter and destroy; I came so that they might have life and have it more abundantly.' (Jn. 10: 7-10)

A group of tourists traveling in the Middle East were introduced to an actual shepherd. He talked with them at length about his work. He showed them the fold into which the sheep were led at night. It consisted of four walls, with a gap that was wide open. One tourist observed, "But there is no door to close and shut out the wild animals. How are they protected from danger?" The shepherd replied, "I am the door." Then he explained, "When the light has gone and all the sheep are inside, I lie in that open space. No sheep can go out without crossing my body, and no predator can enter without stepping on me."

A good shepherd is supposed to be the gate of his sheepfold. In the Gospel passage we take for this weekend meditation Jesus states that he is the gate, through which those of us who choose to enter, will be saved. How? First he is so good a Shepherd he doesn't hesitate to fight against the evil intruders like wolves trying to enter into the sheepfold and planning to devour his sheep. He promised he would do anything for his sheep's safety and security, even at the cost of his life. He said, 'I came so that they may have life' and even he fulfilled it by dying on the cross. We observe him continuously present, not inactive or indifferent or sleeping tight, but ever-vigilant at the door of his sheepfold. *I am with you always, until the end of the age.* (Matt. 28: 20)

This amazing 'gate' is not only the right entrance for entering into the divinely designed sheepfold but also the proper exit to go out for green pasture and the living waters of God. *No one comes to the Father except through me.* (Jn. 14: 6) Nonetheless there are millions of sheep among us who feel unsafe, insecure and deprived of proper nourishment of spiritual food and water. The main reason for such deplorable condition is nothing but being unaware of the worth of this 'Gate', not listening to his voice that repeatedly cries out: *Come to me all who labor and are burdened; I will give you rest* (Matt. 11: 28); and not caring his demand that the sheep inside must open their inner home for his relationship: *I stand at the door and knock. If anyone hears my voice and opens the door, then I will enter his house and dine with him, and he with me.* (Rev. 3: 20)

As a Shepherd does to his sheep, Jesus the risen Lord is to us supports us as our Leader, Guide and Provider. It is this faith in Jesus that opens our minds and hearts to him to drink deeply from the inexhaustible riches of life and forgiveness. *"Out of the fullness of his grace he has blessed us all, giving one blessing after another"* (Jn. 1: 16). "Come to me..." Jesus invites us today 'Come to me, I will satisfy and feed you...I will quench all your thirst...I will fill all your emptiness and powerlessness... I will heal and strengthen you in your sickness and sorrow... I will teach you and enlighten you in your ignorance and darkness...and I will give life eternal when you die.

Jesus also expects us to be fully aware of the difference existing between us, his sheep and those who are outside of his fold. We hear constant exhortation from the Apostles: *Save yourselves from this corrupt generation.* (Acts 2: 40) Jesus was the one who insisted this awareness of difference existing between his disciples and others. We are in the light, they are in darkness; we are chosen but they are not; we are sheep but they are only goats; we follow the good Shepherd, they are led by the thieves and robbers; we follow the Spirit, they follow the flesh.

Very sadly some of us are still hesitating to honor and choose our present state in Jesus' fold. We are like the contestants in the game show 'Let's make a Deal', who are invited to choose among three doors. Prizes hidden behind the doors could be as valuable as a new car or a great vacation, or as worthless as a pile of straw. After choosing a door, the contestant would be tempted with another offer in exchange for the first choice. In the end, because of their indecisiveness or desire for more, some contestants left with little or nothing at all. Jesus offers us a choice, he assures: *I am the only door that can offer more abundant life. Check 'yes' or 'no'.*

Fifth Sunday after Easter

Faithless Heart is always a Restless Heart

Jesus said to his disciples: "Do not let your hearts be troubled. You have faith in God; have faith also in me. In my Father's house there are many dwelling places. If there were not, would I have told you that I am going to prepare a place for you? And if I go and prepare a place for you, I will come back again and take you to myself, so that where I am you also may be...I am the way and the truth and the life. No one comes to the Father except through me... Believe me that I am in the Father and the Father is in me... Amen, amen, I say to you, whoever believes in me will do the works that I do, and will do greater ones than these, because I am going to the Father." (Jn. 14: 1-12)

Jesus' unique strategy: There are many modern prophets in media and in secular as well as religious circle who conduct many crisis management workshops, write so many books about it. Contrary to those secular world philosophers' empty promises and solutions, Jesus' words are full of truth and revelation from God the source of consolation and power. Jesus our Master offered us a Gospel of life management, which includes crisis management too. This is what the Spirit invites us today to meditate on.

Not only did Jesus speak about it but he lived it also. As a Good Samaritan and Good Shepherd Jesus throughout his life went all the way out of his self to console and strengthen by deeds the people affected and hurt by human life's crises. He led a serviceable and sacrificial life for others' liberation from crises. During those hectic days of his public salvific ministry he, as every one of us, underwent so many crises such as deprivation, rejection, separation and so on. Unimaginably he was able to withstand all of them and reached his final destiny of resurrection.

We hear Jesus telling his disciples: *Let not your hearts be troubled.* The Lord said these consoling words to his disciples who were so much anxious, dejected and discouraged at the separation of Jesus from their physical life; they were very much troubled about their present and future; they were worried about the rejection Jesus and they experienced from their enemies. He didn't stop there simply with his advising words but, with his eternal wisdom and human experience, he offered them a principle that would make them free of troubling. In the light of Scriptures, we discover that principle is a 'twofold faith': Faith in him and faith in ourselves.

He said: *You have faith in God; have faith also in me.* By these words Jesus confirms that his disciples' faith in his Godly identity, which is powerful and efficacious, will bring peace and needed strength to bear the pains and sufferings. In addition to their belief of his divine identity, he suggests they should concretize that faith in following him as *the Way, the Truth and the Life.* That is the way to make their faith most effective and fruitful. His requesting his disciples to follow his *Way* of love... forgiving, patiently forbearing, and merciful; being consecrated to his wholistic *Truth*, being honest and sincere in all their undertakings. He also preferred that they should lead a *Life* of service and sacrifice; helping and supporting the needy even at the stake of sacrificing one's life as he did.

The second dimension of faith Jesus proposed was that we, however clay and dust we may be, are born again by his Blood and in his Spirit. We were once no people and now we are adopted as children of God and disciples of God's Son. Apostles were empowered with such faith and hope and preached about it day in and day out. They state: *You are a chosen race, a royal priesthood, a holy nation, a people of his own; like living stones, let yourselves be built into a spiritual house...* (1Pet. 2: 9) We must read attentively this statement of Peter. While he honors Jesus as the 'Living Stone' prophesied by the Prophet, T*hus says the Lord GOD: See, I am laying a stone in Zion, a stone that has been tested, a precious cornerstone as a sure foundation* (Is. 28: 16), he too surprisingly qualifies us as the 'living stones' of the edifice Jesus has established.

Upholding firmly this two-dimensional faith, we are assured by Jesus that we would be esteemed very precious in the sight of God. We would accept the bitter sweet life in this world joyfully as Jesus' disciples have been living happily even in their crises. Plus, we would be accomplishing great things, even greater than our Master's, as Jesus promised: *Amen, amen, I say to you, whoever believes in me will do the works that I do, and will do greater ones than these.*

TWENTY SIXTH WEEKEND

Sixth Sunday after Easter

The Secret of the Survival of the Fittest Christians

> *If you love me, you will keep my commandments. And I will ask the Father, and he will give you another Advocate to be with you always, the Spirit of truth... I will not leave you orphans; I will come to you...Whoever has my commandments and observes them is the one who loves me. And whoever loves me will be loved by my Father, and I will love him and reveal myself to him.* (Jn. 14: 15-21)

They say a person needs just three things to be happy in this world: *"Someone to love, something to do and something to hope for."* When we reflect upon the situation of the early disciples, we can readily observe that they found all three of those things in Jesus. The Spirit calls us this weekend to meditate on this 'survival kit entrusted to Jesus' disciples. Scriptures inform us that the disciples of Jesus *had someone to love and to be loved*: Jesus' love for them, which was found its fullest expression on the cross, engendered in them a love for him and for God that they expressed in their love for others. In the Gospel we hear Jesus talking with his disciples expressing his love and concern for them: *I will not leave you orphans; I will come to you.* He guarantees that their love for him will connect them to his Father: *"Whoever loves me will be loved by my Father, and I will love him and reveal myself to him."*

Besides these words, Jesus also confirmed that *as the Father loves me, so I also love you. Remain in my love.* (Jn. 15: 9)

Secondly the disciples *had something to do*: Having learned in Jesus' School of Love, they were inspired to do something precious; they served the needs of others, and even when they were made to suffer for doing good, they persevered. They never forgot the first and the last lesson they underwent on the new commandment: *Love one another as I have loved you.* It was this love-command that urged them to perform so many acts of love, service and sacrifice. This is why, as history testifies, *they went from town to town; they proclaimed the Gospel of Jesus; they baptized them in Jesus' name; they prayed over the people to receive the Holy Spirit; they performed signs and wonders such as: Casting out unclean spirits from many possessed people; many paralyzed or crippled people were cured; and because of all these, they created an atmosphere of joy in wherever they stepped in.* (Ref. Acts 8: 5-17)

They too had *something to hope for*: Their steady perseverance was fueled by their hope, a hope that probably made others wonder at their spiritual stamina. Explaining the sufferings early Christians undergoing, the Apostles exhorted all disciples to bear them patiently like Jesus and for the sake of getting crowned by him for such patient endurance and be ready to explain the reason for such hope. (1 Pet. 3: 15-18) In this light the disciples who know that God will ultimately bless and protect them, have been enduring any human suffering and, in many cases, make it an occasion for proclaiming the Gospel. They were inspired by the Holy Spirit that this painful sense of loss was an essential aspect of their mission. It was a sharing in the passion of Christ. Their suffering became an expression of their love for God and for the fellowmen. Although their suffering could have made them downhearted they radiated joy. They had an unsinkable hope, and it was evident to all who met them.

Jesus expects us today to buy from him this 'survival kit' free of charge: Jesus is to be the One to love; his love-command is something to do; and his Promised Land is something to hope for. On the other hand, for most of us that 'someone to love' is some human or humans; 'something to do' is worldly enterprise; and 'something to hope' for seems the earthly accomplishment. However we, the committed disciples of Jesus, being enlightened by the Spirit, well know the reality that not any human or worldly enterprise can satisfy us all the time and fully. Therefore we need Christ alive as the ultimate resource for our survival.

We are called to be in the world but not of the world. We can neither withdraw in arrogant aloofness from the world nor fully victimized by the worldly pleasures and accomplishment. We have to be light where there is darkness, salt where there is apathy, and leaven that elevates the quality of life. Surely these are the challenges of Jesus' disciples. But Jesus affirms today that we are never alone or without resources for whatever we are called upon to be or to do. Always we should be mindful that Jesus is the reason for our joy, our love, our faith and our hope. This is the secret contained in the 'survival kit' the Master offers for the *survival of the fittest Christians*!

Feast of Ascension

The Unquestionable Glory of the Risen Lord

...When he had said this, as they were looking on, he was lifted up, and a cloud took him from their sight. While they were looking intently at the sky as he was going, suddenly two men dressed in white garments stood beside them. They said, "Men of Galilee, why are you standing there looking at the sky? This Jesus who has been taken up from you into heaven will return in the same way as you have seen him going into heaven." Then they returned to Jerusalem from the mount called Olivet, which is near Jerusalem, a Sabbath day's journey away. (Acts: 1: 1-11)

At the end of our forty days of reading and meditating about our exciting relationship with the risen Lord Jesus Christ, Church welcomes us today joining with Mary, and the Apostles and some other first disciples at the Mount of Olivet to meditate on our intentional relationship with the risen Lord especially when we notice our life at its edge. As Luke ascertains, Jesus did and taught until the day he was taken up, after giving instructions through the Holy Spirit to the apostles whom he had chosen. But they couldn't grasp fully all his teachings and sayings about his identity. That is why when he met them after his resurrection he scolded them: *Oh, how foolish you are! How slow of heart to believe all that the prophets spoke!* (Lk. 24: 25)

Even after Jesus presented himself alive to them by many proofs after his death, appearing to them during forty days and speaking about the kingdom of God, they still showed their ignorance and foolishness to get the glimpse of the risen Lord's identity and mission. However gradually and slowly they got enlightened in those Jesus' mysteries as the risen Lord encountered them, most importantly at the time of his ascension. On Pentecost day the whole enlightenment-process was complete. During this event of Jesus' ascension we notice the most central truth about Jesus and his mission through two symbolic factors Jesus chose for this event:

First Jesus selected a *location* for his ascension proving his mighty powerful identity of his Lordship. Luke indicates it as Mount of Olives. Such a mountain locale signifies the biblical reference to God the Almighty. According to all religions, especially Judaism, mountains are the symbols of mighty God's dwelling place. The second symbol Jesus used on this occasion to demonstrate that He is God and Savior was a *gesture*. Luke picturizes it in his Gospel (Ref. 24: 50-52), saying: Jesus raised his hands, and blessed them. Lifting up the hands, suggests a priestly blessing. The reaction of the disciples was to worship him. Only here do we learn that the disciples had responded appropriately paying homage to Jesus, whose true identity and status they at last recognized. Their worship of Jesus signified that they had, at last, recognized Jesus for who he was.

This ascension-factor was the starting point for the disciples' strong faith in Jesus as their Lord and Savior. Their whole mind and heart were filled with only one faith element: Jesus Christ is the Lord and Savior. We know well how then all the disciples of Jesus receiving power from on High began speaking about this creed; in every sermon and worship they proclaimed this unique belief and asked others do so in order to be saved. The core of Paul's teachings and preaching was this truth about Jesus Christ. ...*In accord with the exercise of God's great might he worked in Christ, raising him from the dead and seating him at his right hand in the heavens, far above every principality, authority, power, and dominion, and every name that is named not only in this age but also in the one to come...* (Eph. 1: 17-23) 'Human salvation is possible only by the proclamation of the faith that Jesus Christ is Lord and Savior'. This has been the one and only message all disciples preached.

This belief in Jesus and in our mission of life continues intact in the spirit of today's Church. To this there is no exception in status or whatever role each one of us takes in daily life. All of us, as members of the Church, while we are waiting to join our Head who has already entered into heaven hold very important role. Pope Francis, in his talk to the leaders and representatives of all Catholic religious congregations-priests, brothers and nuns, said: *I wish to leave you three suggestions for your religious life: The centrality of Christ and his Gospel, authority as a service of love, and 'feeling' in and with the Mother Church.* This clarion call is certainly that of the Master Jesus to all his disciples, living in the postmodern Age.

TWENTY EIGHTH WEEKEND

Feast of Pentecost

Holy Spirit is the Breath of Fresh Air

On the evening of that first day of the week, when the doors were locked, where the disciples were, for fear of the Jews, Jesus came and stood in their midst and said to them, "Peace be with you." When he had said this, he showed them his hands and his side. The disciples rejoiced when they saw the Lord. Jesus said to them again, "Peace be with you. As the Father has sent me, so I send you." And when he had said this, he breathed on them and said to them, "Receive the Holy Spirit. Whose sins you forgive are forgiven them, and whose sins you retain are retained." (Jn. 20: 19-23)

On this day of Pentecost let us meditate on the Dynamic Presence of God's Spirit that comes through the risen Jesus. The struggle of understanding and communicating about the Holy Spirit who is invisible but proactive inside Jesus' Church, is perennial. However NT writers have tried their best to do this job, especially in writing about the 'Pentecostal Event'. In spite of the differences, basically all of them agree on the fundamental truths hidden in the event and modes of the Holy Spirit's manifestation such as, that there is a strict unity between Jesus and the Spirit; and that with the descent of the Spirit, a new era in the history of God's dealing with humanity has begun.

John says that Jesus breathed on the disciples and said "receive the Holy Spirit." The Spirit is esteemed as breath, which is one of the four constitutive elements of the universe. The breath is the extraordinary force which brings forth energy. Therefore, the Spirit is the creative force in God, in man and in the universe. Everything that is good and true comes from the Spirit. In the event of Pentecost Jesus acted, as his Father Creator did at creation of humans, in breathing his recreating breath into the selected humans who were open to such redemptive renewal. That Breath seemed to the disciples at times like a tempest shaking houses, and uproot trees but not destructive; and other times like a gentle, refreshing breeze. The Spirit has been always a Breath of Fresh air of love for the hearts and minds of the disciples; refreshed their faith and their understanding of Gospel values.

Such a historical event has become a nonstop occurrence for two millennia. In performing this remarkable act of breathing His Fresh Air, Jesus wants us to uphold one important point about our today's church life. Anything that happens in the church or in our individual life as change because of the Holy Spirit is not a total change as topsy-turvy. On Pentecost day Spirit brought forth a new system of religion. But it was not altogether brand new. Spirit made disciples to maintain the symbols of the old era; they revered the sacred symbols of the past, all the while ruthlessly revising them. That is what we mean by the Spirit's actions in us as 'breath of fresh air'.

We know how there are millions of humans walk around in this world and surprisingly in the churches with their bad-smelling mouth. The air they inhale as well as exhale is very much contaminated. Therefore other people notice how badly they speak and behave. Pope Francis in one of his morning masses identified three specific groups of Christians who live among us with bad-spiritual smell: Some are *uniformists* who, being confused of Jesus' teaching on unity or equality, prefer everybody and everything in the Church must be rigidly uniformed. The second group of Christians, whom Pope calls *alternativists*, are those who always have their own ideas about things and who do not want to conform their minds to the mind of the universal Church. Clinging on to their certain 'pickups of Jesus' values' they have one foot out of the Church. And many others, whom Pope names *exploitationists,* are those whose only concern is to seek the personal benefits and consequently end up doing business in the Church.

These bad-smelling Christians, we well know, do possess many wonderful natural and spiritual gifts from the Creator God; but they use them for their own self-gratification and self-glorification. Through Paul the Lord tells all of us (1 Cor. 12: 3-13) that we should use them in the church for others and the Church out of love. Our human mind, on its own, is inadequate to understand Jesus and God. Jesus' disciples only understood fully, when he breathed this Spirit into them after his resurrection and the assembled church when it received the Spirit at Pentecost. Certainly it is not easy to do so because, the worldly temptations are many. This is why we should make recourse to the Holy Spirit to be renewed in His Breath of Fresh Spiritual Air.

Feast of Holy Trinity

The mindblowing Triune Love is Our God

God so loved the world that he gave his only Son, so that everyone who believes in him might not perish but might have eternal life. For God did not send his Son into the world to condemn the world, but that the world might be saved through him. Whoever believes in him will not be condemned, but whoever does not believe has already been condemned, because he has not believed in the name of the only Son of God. (Jn. 3: 16-18)

God can be called in various beautiful names according to the Ages, Cultures and Experiences of human beings around the globe. However the most striking and the closest one to our hearts and minds is the name that NT authors have used in their writings. And that is *God is Love*. Every other explanation about Him is centered on and swirling around this Name 'Love'. Our Christian uninterrupted faith is that God is 'love' not only in relation to us or to the created universe but also He is so in himself, in his intimacy, essentially, infinitely, eternally. And Augustine rightly insists: *If we see love, we see the Trinity.*

Love in God is His origin, basis, process and His total Life. Love is His Personality. 'Love' means a spirit of relating; a sense of togetherness; a reality of bending and binding with the other. Therefore God, the Love, is not solitude but communion, the ocean of his being vibrates with an infinite movement of love, reciprocity, exchange, encounter, family and celebration. This is the background of our identifying God as the 'Triune God' about whom this weekend let us meditate and pray.

From Scriptures and Traditions we discover the *Creative Love* of God as Father who formed the universe out of chaos and nothingness. But the deeper truth is he created this world out of love for human beings. Moses, writing about one of his encounters with God at Mount Sinai, says: *The LORD passed before him and cried out, The LORD, the LORD, a merciful and gracious God, slow to anger and rich in kindness and fidelity.* (Ex. 34: 4-9)

We too are instructed by our faith resources about the *Redemptive Love* of the Son who reformed the world through his passion, death and Resurrection. This redemptive love was meant for all but especially for those who had strayed away from the divine Love. *God so loved the world that he gave his only Son, so that everyone who believes in him might not perish but might have eternal life.* God's Son Jesus therefore went in search of the least, the lost and the last in the society. His love broke the barriers of division and built the bridges of love among people, social groups, and religious compartments. His love embraced all the spheres of human life: tax collectors, lepers, sinners, prostitutes, the prodigals, the abandoned and the unwanted. He still continues to redeem people from all these bondages through his representatives.

From the Biblical and Church history we too learn that the unchangeable *Sanctifying Love* of the Spirit of God from the beginning of creation and continued through the centuries sanctifying the kings, the priests and the prophets, Apostles and disciples of Jesus who were chosen to lead the people of God. The same Spirit performs the same work of sanctifying love in our midst. Pope Emeritus Benedict XVI explains in one of his Encyclicals: "The Spirit, in fact, is that interior power which harmonizes the hearts of the believers with Christ's heart and moves them to love their brethren as Christ loved them" (*Deus Caritas Est*). The Spirit immerses us in the rhythm of divine life, which is a life of love, making us personally in relations between the Father and the Son. When the Spirit dwells in us, the Word, Son of God, who bestows the Spirit is in us too, and the Father is present in the Word.

When we hold strongly that God is the Triune Love, then we begin to understand God much more easily and appreciate what he has done for us. We discover that he keeps loving us as a forgiving, and merciful Father who cares and is tender as a mother, as the Son who became one of us and made us free at the cost of his life, and as a Spirit of love and unity and strength who keeps guiding and inspiring us. This is why, Paul never misses in his greetings to Christians an emphasis on the Trinitarian nature of God: *The grace of the Lord Jesus Christ and the love of God and the fellowship of the Holy Spirit be with all of you.* (2 Cor. 13: 13)

THIRTIETH WEEKEND

Feast of Corpus Christi
Let there be Bread

Jesus said to the Jewish crowds: "I am the living bread that came down from heaven; whoever eats this bread will live forever; and the bread that I will give is my flesh for the life of the world...Whoever eats my flesh and drinks my blood remains in me and I in him. Just as the living Father sent me and I have life because of the Father, so also the one who feeds on me will have life because of me... (Jn. 6: 51-58)

The Food and Agriculture Organization (FAO) is a specialized agency of the United Nations that leads international efforts to defeat hunger. Its Latin motto "*fiat panis*" translates into English as "let there be bread". Obviously the world organization has the noble intention of finding out ways and means of eliminating the problem of hunger in the world. The origin of such a globally-coordinated community-efforts comes from the grand Master Jesus Christ's Heart. In his Godly heart he foresaw the personal and social difficulties of the whole human race and he put forward to us a Way, weird but genuine, ritual but resourceful and personal but combined with communal dimension. That is called traditionally the Eucharist about which we will meditate today.

The Eucharistic Christians who participate regularly in the Church Communion Services firmly believe an astounding miracle occurring in those rituals: 'The ordinary bread and wine change into Body and Blood of Christ'. And they too hold that through this ritual action Jesus had established a very resourceful Way in this world to feed the hungry, to quench the thirsty, to shelter the homeless and to satisfy the needy.

Judaism is a faith largely based on its memories of the past deeds of their God, especially of his merciful and miraculous acts of feeding their forbears and quenching their thirsts while they were acutely afflicted in the desert-journey. This is why Moses, their respected Leader, repeatedly exhorted them and their posterity to preserve and cherish in their memory those gracious deeds of 'Manna'. (Ref. Deut. 8: 2-16) OT prophets and teachers endorsed the ritual remembrance of the 'merciful Manna-deeds' of God and advised people to be merciful in the same way God has been. They envisioned the 'ritual' turning out to be 'actual'.

At the backdrop of this Jewish religious holding and practicing, Jesus established his own creative ritual of the same kind but with difference. During this ritual we remember, listen, meditate, sing and praise, as the Israelites, what the Lord God has been to us as Creator, Provider and Caregiver. Especially we reminisce with gratitude and awe his redemptive deeds performed through his Son's broken Body and poured out Blood. Alongside, we eat Jesus' Body and drink his Blood we are intrinsically connected to his risen Spirit and become the Body and Life of the same Lord. As the saying goes: *You are what you eat.* As Jesus promised, we are nourished spiritually with all heavenly blessings and gifts and begin to feel the spirit of eternal life. The Eucharistic-food offers us the possibility 'to share in the divinity of Christ who humbled himself to share in our humanity.'

Jesus uses food, materially and symbolically, to build community that was pointed toward the Promised Land. To eat is to acknowledge our dependence both on food and on each other. Despite the cruel life's losses and limits, broken hearts of tears and defeat, and our mistakes and missteps, we can still depend on the sufficiency of love come down to save us. Through the Eucharistic participation we have amalgamated; and we have been transubstantiated. And part of the process is, as Paul portrays (1 Cor. 10: 16-17), eating from the one loaf makes us one body. We don't have to be self-sufficient anymore. Unlike the people who see themselves, first and foremost, as self-sufficient individuals, we who share this bread see ourselves, first and foremost, as a community caring for one another. It is precisely that connectedness that allows the human self to be as sufficient as possible.

Dorothy Day beautifully underlines this remarkable result of the Eucharist in her autobiography, 'The Long Loneliness': *The most significant thing is community, others say. We are not alone anymore...We cannot love God unless we love each other, and to love we must know each other. We know him in the breaking of bread, and we are not alone any more.* When we receive the Eucharistic bread we commune with God, and we experience fellowship with our brothers and sisters. We then start our own family and community projects or join in hands with other friends' programs to break the bread, to shed even our blood and sweat in labor to take care of the needy. Mohandas Gandhi once said, *If Christ ever comes to India, he'd better come as bread.* The entire world is still hungering for the miraculous 'Manna' from Jesus. Such miracle can possibly be done today by those disciples who make their 'Eucharistic ritual' into 'life-sharing ritual.'

Twelfth Sunday in ordinary time

Fear kills natural human; but Jesus'
disciple conquers the 'fear'

Therefore do not be afraid of them. Nothing is concealed that will not be revealed, nor secret that will not be known. What I say to you in the darkness, speak in the light; what you hear whispered, proclaim on the housetops. And do not be afraid of those who kill the body but cannot kill the soul; rather, be afraid of the one who can destroy both soul and body in Gehenna...Everyone who acknowledges me before others I will acknowledge before my heavenly Father. But whoever denies me before others, I will deny before my heavenly Father. (Matt. 10: 26-33)

Fear is one of the rarest gift from God that takes care of our survival. Fear helps us to be cautious of what we use and handle in daily life for better or for worse. But such wonderful feeling of fear should not become dangerous factor as 'Phobia', which in Greek means an irrational and intense fear of certain persons, situation or things. In common usage this term refers to 'social phobia' of negative attitudes or prejudices against certain persons or groups, such as: Christianophobia: fear or dislike of Christians or Christianity; Islamophobia: fear or dislike of Muslims or <u>Islamic culture;</u> and <u>Xenophobia</u>: Chauvinism, racial intolerance, racism and dislike of foreigners.

Biblical heroes like Jeremiah the prophet was not exempted from this fear-complex because of which they were panicked: *"I hear the whisperings of many: "Terror on every side! Denounce! Let us denounce him!" All those who were my friends are on the watch for any misstep of mine...* (Jer. 20: 10) Gospels portray at length how much Jesus' disciples were afraid of suffering, persecution and other life's challenges. Many times he advised them not to be afraid of anything and anybody in the world. He wanted them to fear only one and that is his Father who the consolidation of Truth, Love and Justice. His Spirit also through his disciples taught us that the total destruction of our life would be happening only by the violation and going against the fullness of truth, justice and love. Jesus always wants his disciples to be free of fear. On the contrary we know from the Gospels how timid and puny were his disciples, being intimidated by anything and everything until they received the power from Jesus' Spirit.

Invariably all humans have to go through three phases in our development: In the first phase we are situated in a horrible surrounding where so much slavery, selfishness, maneuvering, injustice, insensitiveness and coldness are pervading. At that period most of us are like dumb stony age barbarians who either are not fully aware of what is going on or for their survival, simply and coolly satisfied with them. When we reach to a second phase of life-development we become aware of all those outside atrocities strangling us; we start reacting against the existing system or situation. Out of this reactionary move the world has witnessed so many civil wars, community struggles, infights and so many isms and unions.

And the third phase of human development in which humans are supposed to act, in a proactionary mode, matured enough, well-balanced in their in and out communications, in their dialogues, in their dealings and relationships and above all in their leadership. Unfortunately since 'fear' holds its dominion over many of us, even though they have gone through the first two phases of development, continue still to live only a reactionary life. In our deal with these people we need to be very cautious in words, even a slip of tongue; we have to keep a distance from them; anything and everything that we speak, do and act would affect these people. They are adults, yes indeed, but only in physical but not in emotional or intellectual or spiritual levels. While they react against us out of fear they keep us in fear.

It is to these disciples Jesus tells: 'Do not fear. Trust in God, he is your Father who loves you so much. He has sent his Son Jesus to die for us and took away all your sins and transgressions.' Paul, though living in anxiety of sinful burdens and working out his salvation in trembling, never was he discouraged and overturned his trust in the mighty power and friendship of Jesus. He writes: *For if by that one person's transgression the many died, how much more did the grace of God and the gracious gift of the one person Jesus Christ overflow for the many.* (Rom. 5: 15) Master Jesus expects all of us to join with the Prophet to say to God everyday: *Yes Lord. We trust you; for to you I have entrusted my cause; you are with me, like a mighty champion; surely my persecutors will stumble, they will not triumph. In their failure they will be put to utter shame, to lasting, unforgettable confusion.* (Jer. (Ref. Jer. 20: 11-13)

THIRTY SECOND WEEKEND

Thirteenth Sunday in ordinary time

Be prepared for surprises from Jesus

One day Elisha came to Shunem, where there was a woman of influence, who pressed him to dine with her. Afterward, whenever he passed by, he would stop there to dine. So she said to her husband, "I know that he is a holy man of God. Since he visits us often, let us arrange a little room on the roof and furnish it for him with a bed, table, chair, and lamp, so that when he comes to us he can stay there." One day Elisha arrived and stayed in the room overnight. Then he said to his servant Gehazi, "Call this Shunammite woman." He did so, and when she stood before Elisha, he told Gehazi, "Say to her, 'You have troubled yourself greatly for us; what can we do for you? Can we say a good word for you to the king or to the commander of the army?'"... Gehazi answered, "She has no son, and her husband is old." Elisha said, "Call her." He did so, and when she stood at the door, Elisha promised, "This time next year you will be cradling a baby son"... and by the same time the following year she had given birth to a son, as Elisha had promised. (2 Kgs. 4: 8-17)

Through the OT story taken for our today's meditation, the Spirit teaches us that we, the disciples of Jesus, must always welcome God's messengers in our life and be open to their message. To welcome God's message through theses messengers brings so much blessing to us as it happened in the life of the Shunammite woman. It is a very ordinary story about a woman who offered her TLC hospitality to Elisha, whom she esteemed as 'Man of God'. Elisha, as most of the God's messengers would do, offered to repay her hospitality with power and security. But she did not want any help in return from the prophet. But Elisha desired by all means to do some good deed for her. With his spiritual intuition, he discovered a secret sadness filling her heart and soul. Something was missing from her life. Namely, the woman and her husband were childless. Elisha promised that, despite her barrenness, she would embrace a son. What we notice in this story is that when the woman welcomed the messenger of God into her home, she got much more than she bargained for. Along the way, she learned that welcoming God's message and living with it is rarely easy and seldom simple; but often surprising and sometimes risky. Nonetheless ultimately his word, that is welcomed and hosted lovingly, performs miraculous deeds in human lives which even the entire world cannot contain.

Unfortunately most of us do not offer a warm welcome to God's words because they are very difficult to observe and at times very risky. Take for example the demands of Jesus, the Great Messenger of God Gospel. His most demanding words are: *Whoever loves father or mother more than me is not worthy of me, and whoever loves son or daughter more than me is not worthy of me; and whoever does not take up his cross and follow after me is not worthy of me. Whoever finds his life will lose it, and whoever loses his life for my sake will find it.* (Matt. 10: 37-39) His faithful Disciple Paul echoes our Master's demands repeatedly in his Letters. In sincerity he testifies he lost everything, even his very self as dying before he died and thus fulfilling Master's hardest demand. He too advises us that as we were buried with Jesus in Baptism, we also should be dead to sins. Consequently *you too must think of yourselves as [being] dead to sin and living for God in Christ Jesus.* (Rom. 6: 3-11)

Besides God's Words, the instruments or agents through whom he makes us to hear those words are also very hard to be welcomed. They seem to us either cranky and strange and low to our standard or typically weak and fragile like any humans. The woman in the story accepted the prophet into her home though in that region any prophet of his kind was not well accepted by the public. We read about the same prophet Elisha who was jeered at by even little boys at Bethel, who stoned at him, shouting, "Go away, baldy; go away, baldy!" (2 Kgs. 2: 23); we too hear in NT how the public treated unjustly and viciously by jeering, stoning at Jesus, Paul and the Disciples. These messengers were rejected by most of the people either as strangers and weird in their proclaiming God's words.

The same is true today in this modern world. Due to such wrong notions about the vocation to proclaim the Gospel demands of Jesus, as a recent survey study shows, the society today does not esteem this vocation, of becoming God's messengers, as an honorable one. The world considers these ministers of God's word as useless and leading a strange life. The Spirit expects us to examine ourselves how we relate to God's words and his messengers. These messengers of God's word today are two kinds.

First group consists of those men and women who are chosen and ordained for this sole purpose. These are the priests, bishops, religious monks, sisters and so on. The second group of the messengers of God's word is comprised of those ordinary people whom we meet daily but overlook them because of their strangeness. Many don't consider our human life is itself a vocation to discipleship. All men and women are called to "follow after" Christ the Lord. Married or single, ordained or lay, every human person finds ultimate fulfillment in answering Jesus' call to "take up the cross" which brings life out of death and to "lose life" that it may be found in all its fullness. Among them there are many who by birth or by formation or by any accident carry their crosses temporarily or permanently. They may be in the form of the homeless, the poor, orphans, widows, the handicapped, the disabled, socially and physically spoiled ones by drugs and alcohol and so on. Jesus asks us today to be their hosts and welcome them into our hearts and homes. Hospitality to a fellow human being -- even giving a cup of cold water to someone who is thirsty -- is inseparable from receiving Christ and the one who sends him to us. In hospitality there is certain loss but it always turns out to be a gain at the end. (Matt. 8: 40-42) I found a remarkable plaque fixed on the wall in my friend's dining room where it was written: *"Every stranger is our guest of honor at our home because he is Christ in our midst."* Hosting strangers is simply hosting Jesus himself. Let us warmly welcome God's messengers with their divine words; I promise, 'be prepared for surprises!'

Fourteenth Sunday in ordinary time

My soul rests in God alone

At that time Jesus said in reply, I give praise to you, Father, Lord of heaven and earth, for although you have hidden these things from the wise and the learned you have revealed them to the childlike... Come to me, all you who labor and are burdened, and I will give you rest. Take my yoke upon you and learn from me, for I am meek and humble of heart; and you will find rest for yourselves. For my yoke is easy, and my burden light. (Matt. 11: 25-30)

Jesus, being so irritated by the hardheartedness of unrepentant people at Chorazin, Bethsaida and Capernaum, reproached them with curses (Ref. Matt. 11: 20-24). Soon after that, Matthew inserts the Lord's sayings which we have taken for our today's meditation. First of all, we should understand that Jesus doesn't invite us to take a nap when he says 'Come, I will give you rest.' Undoubtedly taking a short rest by nap, medically speaking, can result in less stress, more patience, better reflexes, increased learning, more efficiency and better health. Jesus' intention is not to offer such petite rest; rather, he points out to a spiritual pause and a place to rest and be refreshed so that we will be fortified in faith and energized in our service.

Jesus' invitation to pause and rest is deeply rooted in the spirituality of Israel. In Psalms we hear God summoning us repeatedly: *Be still and know that I am God* (Ps. 46: 11). *Be still before the LORD; wait for him* (Ps. 37: 7). And the Psalmist exhorts himself do the same: *My soul, be at rest in God alone* (Ps. 62: 6). The Hebrew imperative "Be still" found in Scriptures has also been variously translated as "Desist!"; "Give in!" and "Let be!" as in an authoritative order to a contentious person to "Shut up" or "Stop it"; rather than be overwhelmed by life's troubles, we are to let go and let God act. Therefore God's bidding is not simply to rest, as in "Take a load off" or "Put your feet up." To be still and take rest refers to more than all these: It is 'to go deeper always with Jesus into ourselves, as I personally label 'in-traveling' into our inner sanctuary where the kingdom of God has been already established.'

At that sacred space we get to know who God is; get to listen more clearly the true voice of God and teachings; get to discover and be amazed of the marvelous pearls of God in Jesus. We will be very close to Jesus and we will listen more clearly what he teaches us. Also, during those holy resting moments, as Jesus mentions in the Gospel passage, we will be the 'little ones' who will be able to know and understand most of his heavenly secrets. These heavenly mysteries are not merely some revelations about God's mysteries; they are very secondary. We will fully understand the most remarkable strategy for successful life in this world and deeply come to terms with it. That hidden heavenly secret is leading a life of meekness and humility. To be meek means, in its God-ward glance, perfect trust, willing obedience and lived faith; in its posture toward others, meekness means force of character and inner strength that invite admiration and a desire to emulate such virtue. These are the lessons we learn from the Lord when we pause, be still and come to rest in him.

As the endresults of our rest in and with Jesus, first our attitude will be changed into Jesus' likeness who is meek and humble of heart. We begin to live always in the Spirit, as Paul writes; we will be no more in the flesh; we will not be debtors or slaves to the flesh, to live according to the flesh; but by the Spirit we will put to death the deeds of the body and thereby we will live a qualitylife, an eternal godly life. (Ref. Rom. 8: 9-13) Secondly getting into the true restfulness of Jesus, we begin to feel all life's burdens easy and light. Jesus' promise of an easy or well-fitting yoke does not mean that his followers would be freed of all challenges of unfairness of life or burdens of human roles and duties; rather, he did not bring a Gospel of prosperity, or that of comfort. When the burden of love and service is laid upon us and shared by a loving yokemate such as Jesus, then, as an ancient rabbi once said, "My burden is become my song."

For many of us, such a pause for rest and renewal in Jesus seems impractical, a waste of time; some others consider it a mark of laziness. Nevertheless, these pauses are as necessary to our busy lives as breathing, for within those few moments of rest in the Lord, we grow and deepen and mature. St. Augustine's prayer was: "God! Our hearts are restless until they rest in thee." Most of us are restless because we have not fully accepted Jesus' invitation of rest in God. It is to those of us God prophetically said: *"This people's heart goes astray; they do not know my ways." Therefore I swore in my anger: "They shall never enter my rest."* (Ps. 95: 8-11) Let us pray today and every day that those of us who are restless may soon hear Jesus' invitation to go in-traveling and take rest in him.

Fifteenth Sunday in ordinary time

Spoiled Freedom can damage our spiritual Growth

> *On that day, Jesus went out of the house and sat down by the sea. Such large crowds gathered around him that he got into a boat and sat down, and the whole crowd stood along the shore. And he spoke to them at length in parables, saying: "A sower went out to sow; and as he sowed, some seed fell on the path, and birds came and ate it up. Some fell on rocky ground, where it had little soil. It sprang up at once because the soil was not deep, and when the sun rose it was scorched, and it withered for lack of roots. Some seed fell among thorns, and the thorns grew up and choked it. But some seed fell on rich soil, and produced fruit, a hundred or sixty or thirtyfold. Whoever has ears ought to hear"...* (Matt. 13: 1-23)

This weekend the Spirit of Jesus invites us to reflect over how we should lead a fruitful life in God's garden where God works as a dutiful and generous sower and gardener who takes care of our inner land the soul very attentively. In Psalm 65 we hear David proclaiming that 'God is a hard-working gardener who stays continuously connected to his land, cultivates it, drenching its furrows and breaking its clods and once he sows, he regularly waters it and consequently prepares its grain'.

God acts as a generous sower in nature. When we look at living beings, plants, and animals of all kinds, we see how much seed is generously sown. There is plenty of it, and yet few spring up and reproduce fruit. The same gardener; the same sower; the same natural ground or field; yet at the harvest time the world reaps different results and fruits. Yet the Lord of generosity himself keeps on sowing the seeds abundantly.

As a sower of human body and soul, the same God works with us more intensively for our spiritual growth. Our soul is nothing but God's product. The seed he sows in humans' creation is part of 'his image and likeness'. This is why he is so attentive to our spiritual development. Human soul is a treasure land where he wants to dwell as his sanctuary and help us grow in his holiness more and more and bear his godly fruits outside for his glory. For this august soul-management, according to Scriptures, God uses his powerful Word as ammunition and source of nourishment as well. Isaiah writes about the power of his Word: *Just as from the heavens the rain and snow come down and do not return there till they have watered the earth, my word that goes forth from my mouth shall not return to me void, but shall do my will, achieving the end for which I sent it.* (55: 10-11) From the days of creation we notice the endresults of God's mighty word with which he created the universe and everything in it by His Word. When the time of fulfillment arrived God uttered his final and complete Word who became flesh among us.

This miraculous Word-story continues in the form of Jesus' Spirit till this day, and will be so till the end of time, accomplishing what God has planned for humanity through his Son Jesus. God's Word always accomplishes in power and force the goodness and beauty, joy and peace, order and harmony among his humans of good will. As Paul writes, God's word also accomplishes retribution against the power of ungodliness and injustice of human beings who in their injustice hold back the truth (Rom. 8: 18).

Jesus also reminds us today how God's soul-management in humans' lives meets seemingly with failure. As we encounter in nature the fact of lavishing seeds sown every season on the land but very few sprout and bear fruits at the harvest, God sows his powerful words in every human heart with no hesitation but only out of sheer love for us. Unfortunately not all of us are receptive and fertile soil; some like the walkway, some others as rocky ground, and others are filled with thorny bushes; and only a few of them are like rich soil, even in these fertile grounds some are good, some better and some others best.

The main reason for this is, as Jesus identifies, the human weakness of pride, arrogance, self-righteousness, superficiality, faint-heartedness, worldly possessions, and anxiety. Most of us either misuse or abuse the greatest gift God has shared with us, the 'freedom'. The Gardener who sowed the seed within us pours out his Word over that seed which is nothing but an invitation, a call and a challenge. God continually calls us to a better and more fruitful life. But not all show due to their twisted freedom and independence, their willingness to long to listen and obey his word.

Wherever God's word is received properly it yields a miraculously bountiful return. It is within our capability to obstruct the divine sower's purpose and prevent or curtail its growth. Those, who close their minds against him, receive less. At the end of our meditation, let me quote a thoughtprovoking proverb: *Sometimes a way seems right, but the end of it leads to death!* (Pro. 14: 12)

THIRTY FIFTH WEEKEND

Sixteenth Sunday in ordinary time
Salvific Patience is need of the Day

Jesus proposed another parable to them. "The kingdom of heaven may be likened to a man who sowed good seed in his field. While everyone was asleep his enemy came and sowed weeds all through the wheat, and then went off. When the crop grew and bore fruit, the weeds appeared as well. The slaves of the householder came to him and said, 'Master, did you not sow good seed in your field? Where have the weeds come from?' He answered, 'An enemy has done this.' His slaves said to him, 'Do you want us to go and pull them up?' He replied, 'No, if you pull up the weeds you might uproot the wheat along with them. Let them grow together until harvest; then at harvest time I will say to the harvesters, "First collect the weeds and tie them in bundles for burning; but gather the wheat into my barn." (Matt. 13: 24-30)

For our weekend meditation today God in Jesus brings to our attention through the Scriptural words the eternal truth of his Triune Personality as a just and merciful Owner and Proprietor of our lives. The entire Bible is abounding with the details of this truth. In the Book of Wisdom for example we hear a song of praise to that God of mercy and justice, the God of power and leniency. God's power is made most manifest by being merciful. Mercy seems to be almighty power at its best and most revealing. Those familiar with God are called to trust the loving power of mercy so that they need not be fearful. The Psalmist too constantly sings and proclaims that the Lord is good and forgiving, merciful and gracious (Ps. 86: 5). Jesus preached the same truth as his eternal Gospel of mercy which he portrays splendidly by a tiny 'parable of the Weeds'.

The good seed of God's kingdom, according to Jesus, sown in us both by first and second birth is very well sprouting and growing by the bountiful providence of the Creator. However through some evil sources, both from inside and outside of us, bad weedy seed is being sown in and around us and it also sprouts and grows very well. Though this metaphor Jesus emphasizes that God is not the source of evil; rather he is good in himself in everything. God as our gardener planted only good seeds but some enemy, an opposite force to God has done the weeds. The Satan's kingdom of darkness (as he comes at night) loves confusion and doubt. This evil enemy has taken part ownership of the field, or at least has taken out a lease.

Imprudently and foolishly most of the times we love to move and have our being not in light but in darkness. There is a part of our earthliness which wants to be left alone. It desires not to be tilled and cultivated and of course, weeded. Yielding to Satan's vicious analysis about God's Command of avoiding the forbidden fruits (Ref. Gen. 3: 4-5) most of us feel the tension of holding ownership of ourselves and our life, and consequently we make our inner sacred field not only bad soil but also we permit either ourselves or outsiders to sow bad weeds in our hearts somewhere at some time.

Since such evil seeds and deeds are sown and spread lavishly in and around us when we are enlightened by the Spirit and led by him we begin to see the ugliness and sinfulness of human life and we start trembling before a God who is just in all his ways as we are told by our Master that there is going to be a harvest time during which the crop of wheat and the disordering-weeds will be collected: one for the burning and the other for union and life. Therefore we feel desperate and by all means we try to destroy the weeds as early as possible. However God tells us today to imitate him in his patience.

We, the patient disciples of Jesus, see the best in others and do not judge their motives or their actions; moreover we are instructed by the Scriptures that leniency, kindness, justice, mercy and clemency are shown by God to those whom he loves as very dear children. Despite our frequent failings and repeated sins, our patient God gives us what is perhaps the greatest gift of all, time as second chance, to repent of our sins.

The bad weeds, like the unbelieving, the weak, the heretics, the false teachers and the backsliders, continue to grow among us from the beginning of the church to this day. While we distinguish clearly between good and evil, we must aim at being tolerant and merciful as God is. The time for judgment is not yet come. In the meantime, withholding our condemnation against the evil doers, and continue our relationship of love with them, we should always pray for their conversion to the Lord. At times we may find it hard to do so but as Paul exhorts us, we can avail ourselves of the aid of the Spirit, who aids us in our weakness and intercedes for us with inexpressible groanings. (Ref. Rom. 8: 26-27)

We belong to a community of believers, who though are weak, have immense potential for growth and good works. We should then put our heart and soul together patiently in cooperating with God in his gardening of His Kingdom.

THIRTY SIXTH WEEKEND

Seventeenth Sunday in ordinary time
Are we real or fake still?

The kingdom of heaven is like a treasure buried in a field, which a person finds and hides again, and out of joy goes and sells all that he has and buys that field. Again, the kingdom of heaven is like a merchant searching for fine pearls. When he finds a pearl of great price, he goes and sells all that he has and buys it... (Matt. 13: 44-52)

People often dream of finding a treasure or winning the first prize in the state lottery and get big jackpot in the bingo games in casinos. According to Scriptures there is a treasure greater than that the humans dream of. Every disciple of Christ born and reborn possesses this treasure of fine pearls, such as God's Kingdom established, Jesus' Gospel values and the Holy Spirit's gifts of faith, wisdom, hope and love. Today the Spirit invites us to meditate on acquiring this awesome treasure.

Jesus has points out this treasure of God is buried already in the field of human soul as every one of us has been designed and created in God's image and likeness. It is like the mustard seed, smallest but full of potentials to be enlarged and richer. As the smarty man in the Gospel's parable we have to discover it as soon as possible. This is possible by reading, listening and experiencing the words and actions of God in various ways. The words of God are very powerful instruments in discovering those treasures as the Bible underlines: *The revelation of your words sheds light, giving understanding to the simple.* (Ps. 119)

Jesus also suggests to us that when we find God's treasure buried within us we should start to do some prudent and wise actions about it. First, we must safeguard them, protect them and secure them from God's enemies as the person in the Gospel parable hid the treasure which he found in his field. Here comes the need of religion. We must use as fervently and frequently as possible what our church offers us in the form of sacraments, devotions and other religious practices. We shouldn't follow what some of elders did in our lives in order to safeguard our faith. My dad was a staunch Catholic. He fully believed his Catholic faith and so wanted me to possess this as he did. He never allowed me even to read or look at the pagan temples and shrines. Whenever I walked with him through the streets where there were many Hindu temples and their idols he would ask me to close my eyes not to expose myself to any such abominable sights.

Our Master is famous for taking risk in life and so he wants us do the same in detaching ourselves from all worldly treasure for the sake of seizing the other-worldly treasure. As we grow older we begin collecting so many riches, positions, qualifications, properties and hoarding them as our earned treasures through talents, power, IQ and luck. Now we have on one side this treasure of worldly and material possessions and on the other God's treasure. As faithful disciples of Jesus we should judge wisely which treasure is more beneficial and richer. Certainly for such prudent decision-making we need the gift of wisdom from God. This is why as we read in OT, when God appeared to King Solomon and promised him 'whatever you ask I shall give you', the King pleaded to offer him only wisdom and not worldly treasures: *Lord! Give your servant, therefore, an understanding heart to judge your people and to distinguish right from wrong.* (Ref. 1 Kgs. 3: 5-12)

The last but not the least advice Jesus offered to us in this matter is that once we wisely prefer the heavenly treasure to temporary ones, we should dispose all that we have in the kind of material goods and cling on to God's treasures. Let us remind ourselves here what Jesus told the youth who wanted to inherit heavenly treasure: *There is still one thing left for you: sell all that you have and distribute it to the poor, and you will have a treasure in heaven. Then come, follow me.* (Lk. 18: 21-13) He too has cautioned us: *What profit is there for one to gain the whole world yet lose or forfeit himself?* (Lk. 9: 23-25)

In spite of all the ups and downs in life, life itself is worth living, because it is a precious gift of God. One can make one's life beautiful or miserable depending upon one's attitude towards life God has offered us. We should appreciate every bit, every moment of this life and make the best use of it with all its hidden treasure. We too must try to behave like Paul who treasured his faith in the love for Jesus and realized that all things work for good, for those who love God. (Ref. Rom. 8: 28-30) Jesus expects us to be real and no more fake disciples of him. This is how we, the disciples of Jesus, lead a fruitful life *like the head of a household who brings from his storeroom both the new and the old.*

The Transfiguration of the Lord

It's good to be at Hilltop but better to be at Hilldown

After six days Jesus took Peter, James, and John his brother, and led them up a high mountain by themselves. And he was transfigured before them; his face shone like the sun and his clothes became white as light. And behold, Moses and Elijah appeared to them, conversing with him. Then Peter said to Jesus in reply, "Lord, it is good that we are here. If you wish, I will make three tents here, one for you, one for Moses, and one for Elijah." While he was still speaking, behold, a bright cloud cast a shadow over them, then from the cloud came a voice that said, "This is my beloved Son, with whom I am well pleased; listen to him." When the disciples heard this, they fell prostrate and were very much afraid. But Jesus came and touched them, saying, "Rise, and do not be afraid." And when the disciples raised their eyes, they saw no one else but Jesus alone. (Matt. 17: 1-9)

Human life is a desert-life where, we, like Jesus, are tormented by Satan's temptations; nonetheless, Scriptures and Christian Tradition proclaim that we can overcome these temptations and win the victory through our split-second but very intense and intimate encounters God offers us in daily life. The Scriptural passage we have taken for our Transfiguration-Feast Day meditation demonstrates what and how of these intimate encounters with God possible and actual.

We read in the Gospel when Jesus took his disciples to mountaintop and stayed with them in prayer, the disciples encountered one of those ecstatic experience of seeing the transfigured Lord. Indeed, they had been captivated by his visionary ideals and by his missionary miraculous deeds of mercy and compassion. Sometimes they thought he was the Messiah, other times a Prophet, a Healer and grand Teacher. But they never noticed the other glorious dimension of their Master who is a 'beloved Son of God' and a great person closely connected to their Jewish traditional Prophets and Teachers like Moses and Elijah. In this hilltop encounter they witnessed it. They observed their Master standing like 'the son of man' as the Prophet Daniel saw in his vision. (Ref. Dan. 7: 9-14)

Many mystics and saints call this moment of ecstasy *'a split second.'* Though this may seem like a second, during this encounter with transfigured Jesus the disciples were really overwhelmed with wonder and awe. So much so, Peter wanted to stay on permanently in the experience. Forgetting his own self and needs he said: *Lord, it is good that we are here...*Indeed it was a pleasurable trip to heavenly bliss. In the Bible we hear both heroes and heroines of OT and NT encountering such ecstatic moments in their prayertimes. Paul had conversion of heart by getting a 'split-second' encounter (that blinded him and threw him down to the ground) with the risen Lord. Later days, as the Apostle portrays in his Letters, he had been granted so many such 'split-seconds' and was taken many times to the 'third heaven'. In all of these human encounters with God-in-Jesus humans were bestowed inner strength and power and clear understanding of who they were and what kind of Leader they follow.

The main motif for God to grant these mystic experiences to the humans is nothing but to deliver to them a personal call or invitation or an order from his Throne purely out of his bountiful mercy. For instance, Abraham, Moses, Prophets, judges, Kings and Queens of OT were called to do even the most difficult errands among people on God's behalf. As for the disciples who encountered the transfigured Lord they were bestowed a unique vision and declaration from God to listen to the glorious Christ and witness his wholistic identity –both human and divine, to humanity, as a reliable prophetic message. (Ref. to 2 Pet. 1: 16-19)

While the disciples were in awe the ordinary Jesus of Nazareth came upto them and asked them to climb down the hill in order to face the challenges ahead in their lives. Though they didn't relish his order, but remembering what the heavenly Father had told them, they immediately obeyed Jesus and joined with him walking toward Jerusalem. In our life, most of us do everything we can to avoid hardships, suffering and crosses. However, we should know the road to glory will never be trodden, unless we accept and endure them in love and commitment, as Jesus himself did and wants. The event of Transfiguration motivates and challenges us to be disciples to Jesus. Undoubtedly we may get many 'split-second' ecstasies in our hilltop meditations; we can receive the gift of mystic joy and cry out, *"Lord, it is good that we are here!"*

Concomitantly these hilltop 'split-seconds' surely empower us to be agents of change and renewal, who would be invited by Jesus to go down the hill and mingle with the needy, the poor, the sick and the dying. Therefore, when the poor and needy look to us for help, we might also be moved to say, *"Lord, it is good that we are here."*

Nineteenth Sunday in ordinary time
Only Faith in Jesus is our Lifesaver

Then he made the disciples get into the boat and precede him to the other side... Meanwhile the boat, already a few miles offshore, was being tossed about by the waves, for the wind was against it. During the fourth watch of the night, he came toward them, walking on the sea. When the disciples saw him walking on the sea they were terrified. "It is a ghost," they said, and they cried out in fear. At once Jesus spoke to them, "Take courage, it is I; do not be afraid." Peter said to him in reply, "Lord, if it is you, command me to come to you on the water." He said, "Come." Peter got out of the boat and began to walk on the water toward Jesus. But when he saw how strong the wind was he became frightened; and, beginning to sink, he cried out, "Lord, save me!" Immediately Jesus stretched out his hand and caught him, and said to him, "O you of little faith, why did you doubt?" After they got into the boat, the wind died down. Those who were in the boat did him homage, saying, "Truly, you are the Son of God." (Matt. 14: 22-33)

All our religious practices are not end in themselves; rather, they are performed to realize the biggest goal in life, namely to encounter God in his glory and power, not just during this meditation time as the disciples had at hilltop, but in everyday chores, especially in life's critical situations. This is what the Spirit teaches through the Gospel event of Jesus calming the storm, chosen for meditation.

We notice in this event the disciples hitting upon a natural disorder as wind and waves tossing their boat about. Their fear of capsizing is aggravated by wrongly thinking Jesus, who comes to join them, as a ghost approaching them. In that dangerous situation, though they show their weak faith, Jesus insists that they should have courage and asking them, *do not be afraid.* Even though Jesus has demonstrated at some other time his power of calming the roaring sea (Matt. 8: 23-27), in this event he doesn't do anything about it but compels his disciples to hold on to their faith in his continuous mighty presence. Even when Peter is daring enough to ask Jesus to prove his worth, Jesus asks him to walk by his own faith on the water. Since Peter does not possess strong faith at that moment, he fails walking on the water but using this event as a grace-filling occasion Jesus strengthens his faith. Jesus tells through this event that the mighty encounter from heaven is always open to every human but it requires a strong and sincere faith in him.

We discover this truth from many of our forebears. For example, read about Prophet Elijah's encounter with God, especially during one of his worst lifesituations. (Ref. 1 Kgs. 19: 9-13) Elijah earning the wrath of Jezebel, wife of Ahab, because he spoke on behalf of his true God. As a result, the prophet had to flee into the desert. There, he was in despair and frustration. He sat under a broom tree and prayed for God to take his life. While he felt lonely and helpless, he would have expected God to encounter him. The compassionate Lord indeed had his inner mourning; first he sent an angel providing the prophet food for his journey. But Elijah wanted more, namely an intimate experience of God's divine presence. God certainly tried to satisfy the heart's desire of his messenger but in His own unique way. Like most of the humans, the Prophet expected God's powerful presence in wild natural forces like strong heavy wind or earthquake or in burning fire. But God had his own way as high way. He made the Prophet experience the divine presence in a tiny whispering sound of breeze. This is to say to us that God will meet us surely in our trials and tribulations but at his own time and in his own way. Our only faith-filled job is to vigilantly wait for God's interaction.

God has been behaving the same way in human history. Especially in the light of the Bible we know so many great things God has done in the midst of his people Israel. (Ref. Rom. 9: 1-5) Very sadly, as his Son Jesus, God lamented many times over his adopted children's stubbornness and unfaithfulness. We are told by Jesus the reason for the absence of such miraculous deeds of God not happening is the lack of faith among us. God continues to do great things for us, his people, through the Church and continues to manifest his name to us. Today, more than ever before, as we are in this postmodern Age, thwarted and tossed in every aspect of life, God does want us to encounter Him. We are in the midst of a roiling sea. Can he still be found in the perils of our time? Yes, He is there, but it is hard to recognize him because the true faith is not found among us. If we really encounter the Lord in faith, friendship and deep love, then the Lord makes everything become quiet, even when the stormy wind keeps blowing, for the Lord makes his presence felt.

Twentieth Sunday in ordinary time

Merciful and Just Faith guarantees our Salvation

Now I am speaking to you Gentiles. Inasmuch then as I am the apostle to the Gentiles, I glory in my ministry in order to make my race jealous and thus save some of them. For if their rejection is the reconciliation of the world, what will their acceptance be but life from the dead? For the gifts and the call of God are irrevocable....Just as you once disobeyed God but have now received mercy because of their disobedience, so they have now disobeyed in order that, by virtue of the mercy shown to you, they too may [now] receive mercy. For God delivered all to disobedience, that he might have mercy upon all. (Rom. 11: 13-32)

Many times I ask myself, "Am I saved?" In other words, "Do I belong to the elite group of God in Jesus? Will I go to heaven?" I have valid reasons to doubt about my salvation. First of all, nobody, even God has directly told me that I had been saved nor has anybody from heavenly Government supplied me with an ID card. Only the church, where I belong to or registered in, embraces me and offers me all licenses to participate in any activity in earthly kingdom of God. Nonetheless, I do not think any church can monopolize nor can guarantee for my salvation.

The right to enter into God's heavenly Kingdom totally depends on the gratuitous mercy of God. This is what Paul underlines in all his Letters, especially in the passage we picked out for today's meditation. According to him, all humans, both Jews and Gentiles, are equally the same in their disobedience to God and in being forgiven and saved by God's bountiful mercy.

From the beginning of God's interactions with humans, we notice God never dividing humans and not showing any partiality in his approval or condemnation, and blessing or cursing. He esteems every human is his child. **Those who seem foreign to us are not foreign to God;** those who are marginalized are never marginalized by the King of kings; and those who seem to be a minority are not a minority to the Creator; because he loves them without condition.

Through Prophet Isaiah God clearly spelt out his truthful relationship with the humans. Highlighting his greatest attribute of being eternally just, and commanding his chosen ones to be the same, God states: *Observe what is right, do what is just, for my salvation is about to come, my justice, about to be revealed. And foreigners who join themselves to the LORD...to become his servants...and hold fast to my covenant. Them I will bring to my holy mountain and make them joyful in my house of prayer... For my house shall be called a house of prayer for all peoples.* (Is. 56: 1, 6-7) The Spirit also moved the Psalmist singing the universality of faith: O God, let all the nations praise you! (Ps. 67)

When we look upto Jesus to get more on this matter, we observe his attitude is the same as that of his Father toward how to esteem our 'faith-enrollment'. One day when Jesus was approached by a stranger to get his help or miracle, he behaved both as human and divine. The person who asked his help was literally a stranger, as a woman who at that time should not be out of her home, and if so, she would be considered either as a prostitute or as a strange figure in the society; she was also a Canaanite woman, a non-Jew who was esteemed by the Jewish Community as pagan, gentile and an alien who was to be scorned as dog. Jesus took that occasion to teach us something his father had proposed already, to look those who seem strangers or foreigners to us through the 'specs of faith'. He admired at her faith and said, "O Woman, great is your faith! Let it be done for you as you wish."

Those who are not like us, those on the margins, outcasts, or foreigners, must be approached with the faith we uphold on the mercy and justice of God, whose compassion and love transcends geography, or nationality, or creed, or our own feeble human limitations. We, as his beloved children, should not create any check box and living in that cubicle as inclusive and exclusive persons. Surprisingly God continually thinks outside of those boxes and his grace and mercy will not be contained in them. He is even waiting even for our renewal of mercy-filled and justice-oriented faith-life. All he requires from us, in return, is to persistently stand by just and compassionate faith.

The possible way of getting miracles is to have this genuine faith: Holding on to a faith not in what we profess but in whom we profess. For salvation and for miraculous intervention of God, it does not matter where we belong to, but it matters to whom we belong. We should honor and respect any faith in God found in different colors-in different dimensions, in different phases, and in different terminologies. By such faith in the compassionate and just faith our salvation is guaranteed.

FORTIETH WEEKEND

Twenty First Sunday in ordinary time
*Evil never prevails against anything
built on the rock of faith*

*When Jesus went into the region of
Caesarea Philippi he asked his disciples,
"Who do people say that the Son of Man
is?" They replied, "Some say John the
Baptist, others Elijah, still others Jeremiah
or one of the prophets." He said to them,
"But who do you say that I am?" Simon
Peter said in reply, "You are the Messiah,
the Son of the living God." Jesus said to
him in reply, "Blessed are you, Simon
son of Jonah. For flesh and blood has not
revealed this to you, but my heavenly
Father. And so I say to you, you are Peter,
and upon this rock I will build my church,
and the gates of the netherworld shall not
prevail against it. I will give you the keys
to the kingdom of heaven. Whatever you
bind on earth shall be bound in heaven;
and whatever you loose on earth shall be
loosed in heaven." (Matt. 16: 13-19)*

Our religious or spiritual relationship with the Divine
and because of which, all that we perform and practice
seem to be full of challenges, surprises, and awards and
frustrations. The Spirit today calls us to sit down in silence
and meditate how God has been dealing with humans in

history and how we should respond to them reciprocally as disciples of Jesus. God always behaves with us the sole Master and Proprietor of human life-management. He is the prime CEO but plays a low key and invisible in all his undertakings. Paul, admiring the depth of the riches and wisdom and knowledge of God, writes: *How inscrutable are his judgments and how unsearchable his ways! For who has known the mind of the Lord or who has been his counselor?* (Rom. 11: 33-36)

In the Gospel event taken for today's meditation we find God secretly inspiring Peter to go first to answer Jesus' question: *Who do you say that I am?* This we know by the words of Jesus: *"Blessed are you, Simon son of Jonah. For flesh and blood has not revealed this to you, but my heavenly Father."* Then comes the investiture of power on Peter as the rock on which God's Church is to be built and the entire responsibility of godly binding and loosing was entrusted to Peter. From the Gospels we know how delinquent and feeble Peter had been. Soon after this remarkable investiture event we read how Peter was rebuked by Jesus saying: *Get behind me, Satan! You are an obstacle to me.* (Matt. 16: 23)

Such unsearchable deeds of God are numerous as we read in the Scriptures, one of which I admire the most is the dealings of God with the man Sabena. Shebna, a household treasurer in the court of King Hezekiah, was a wicked, deceitful, and proud man who had conspired with Assyria in an attack on Jerusalem. Seeing Shebna's malpractices, God proclaimed judgment on him through Isaiah. Consequently Shebna was brought down from his prestigious position, while the same Lord raised Eliakim, a faithful and trustworthy servant of the Lord, from a lower position to become a great officer in the court. (Ref. (Is. 22: 19-23)

This is the way how God deals with his humans demonstrating that he is in total control of everything. He, the Supreme, is in control of all promotions and demotions of us. He creates, as he likes; he destines his creatures as he plans. Mary, Mother of Jesus rightly sang when she realized such unfathomable dealings of the Creator in human history: *He who is mighty has done great things for me, and holy is his name. He has shown strength with his arm, he has scattered the proud in the imagination of their hearts, he has put down the mighty from their thrones, and exalted those of low degree; he has filled the hungry with good things, and the rich he has sent empty away.* (Lk. 1: 49-53)

While all these invisible secretive managerial or providential activities going on in the realm of God among human beings, though we cannot fathom his wisdom in this regard, we can notice a single behavioral trend in all his deeds. Invariably he is so enticed and attracted by a strong faith, *chutzpah* that he offers wonderful power to those who possess it, if absent he throws them out. Even if they are pagans, not belonging to the elite groups of the society or weak and sinful and timid God seeing their *chutzpah* receives them, elects them and makes them solid rocks by his grace. Jesus does the same to Peter who is so weak and fragile, sinful as much as to deny him, and yet finding Peter's *chutzpah* from his public testimony about him: *You are the Messiah, the Son of the living God,* he elects him as the first pope of his church and strengthens him by grace as unshaken rock which then will never be prevailed by Satan.

Definitely by proclaiming that Jesus is the Messiah and witnessing to it by our personal and humble obedience to God's will, we will become genuine and true rocks on which God will build up his towers of glory and blessings and minister to his people who shelter in his House.

FORTY FIRST WEEKEND

Twenty Second Sunday in ordinary time

Cross means the Crisscrossing of God's seducing & humans' surrendering

You seduced me, LORD, and I let myself be seduced; you were too strong for me, and you prevailed. All day long I am an object of laughter; every one mocks me. Whenever I speak, I must cry out, violence and outrage I proclaim; the word of the LORD has brought me reproach and derision all day long. I say I will not mention him, I will no longer speak in his name. But then it is as if fire is burning in my heart, imprisoned in my bones; I grow weary holding back, I cannot! (Jer. 20: 7-9)

Prophets like Jeremiah, Isaiah, Ezekiel, proclaimed to their people the one and only message from God who told: 'Return to Yahweh.' Before they began sharing this God's message with people, they personally listened from the same God who compelled them to obey his message and then preached about it. In the OT Scriptural passage, selected for our today's meditation, we hear from Jeremiah that he truly returned to his God but seemingly and surprisingly the Person, whom he returned to, didn't offer him a lot of hope and consolation. Being duped by God, as the Prophet confesses, he was compelled to preach about the 'reform' at the time of the destruction of Jerusalem and subsequent exile; very sadly obedience to God's call brought him great misery and abuse. Showing his negative reaction, he tried to evade from performing this onerous duty, but, as he indicates, it became like fire burning in his heart, imprisoned in by bones; he grew weary holding it in, he couldn't endure it.

His relationship with God seemed destroying his youthful life. Not only did it force him to remain unmarried, it created situations in which his fellow Jews regarded him as a traitor to them and their country. In truth more than any other Prophets, Jeremiah suffered the worst and this is why Biblical Scholars name him as "*A man of constant sorrow.*" Delivering God's word brought to the Prophet tremendous pain and woe; worst still, not delivering it brought him even greater pain and woe. This is why he felt as if he was trapped by God. However Jeremiah survived many ordeals to compose the majestic verses of both lamentation and consolation that encompass Israel's exile and restoration. His fidelity through trial to triumph made him one of the great voices in the Bible.

This sort of being seduced and overpowered by Almighty God is not an experience only of Jeremiah or any other OT Prophets. Anyone who was and is fully committed to God the Supreme has been undergoing such ordeals in their spiritual and social lives. As David, they constantly have been crying aloud: *My soul is thirsting for you, O Lord my God!* (Ps. 63)

Jesus, our Master, was the embodiment of that costly and bleeding encounter with God in his life. God created within him certain voracious hunger and unquenchable thirst for fulfilling God's will. Throughout his life he was fully aware of what God wanted him to accomplish even though sometimes he could spell out his inability to carry on. We can remember what he experienced while he was in prayer at the Garden of Gethsemane: *"Father, if you are willing, take this cup away from me; still, not my will but yours be done." He was in such agony and he prayed so fervently that his sweat became like drops of blood falling on the ground.* (Lk. 22: 42-44) During the time of his crucifixion he had the same agonizing moment: *My God! My God! Why have you forsaken me?*

Jesus esteemed the possessive and compulsive deal of God with him is the most burdensome cross in his life. But knowing the benefits thereof, he carried it willingly and freely because that is the only way for attaining the 'ultimate destiny'. Hence he advised his disciples to follow him strenuously in taking up our crosses. Before he underwent his final agony of that 'cross', he advised them not to be afraid of this 'cross' of life and resurrection, even it demands from them denial of one's self, relatives, and even very life. (Matt. 16: 21-27) True discipleship happens only after we hear and accept this challenge. Jesus' statement helps us understand that carrying one's cross originally didn't refer to patiently enduring some dramatic moment of suffering. It described an ongoing, generous, open and honest relationship with God, a daily quest to discover what God wishes of us during this specific day. Such a quest involves a real death to self and real sacrifice.

Paul explains to us his understanding of 'carrying this cross' in his revelatory style. He repeats frequently that we need to die with the Master to sin so that we would rise resurrected to eternal life. This death is not once but lifelong. He describes that we should 'not to conform ourselves to this age; rather, we should offer our bodies as a living sacrifice, holy and pleasing to God, our spiritual worship.' (Rom. 12: 1-2)

Twenty Third Sunday in ordinary time
Do the best you can, God will do the rest!

If your brother sins against you, go and tell him his fault between you and him alone. If he listens to you, you have won over your brother. If he does not listen, take one or two others along with you, so that 'every fact may be established on the testimony of two or three witnesses.' If he refuses to listen to them, tell the church. If he refuses to listen even to the church, then treat him as you would a Gentile or a tax collector. Amen, I say to you, whatever you bind on earth shall be bound in heaven, and whatever you loose on earth shall be loosed in heaven. Again, amen, I say to you, if two of you agree on earth about anything for which they are to pray, it shall be granted to them by my heavenly Father. For where two or three are gathered together in my name, there am I in the midst of them. (Matt. 18: 15-20)

All evil deeds, done by humans, are rooted on what the Bible calls as 'wickedness.' Many of those sins may be committed either unknowingly and ignorantly or deliberately and intentionally. Due to this wickedness, conflicts and maladies, such as wars, infights, peacelessness, insecurity, dissension and rebellion and even schisms have become part of human life. Most of us are aware of the historical fact that the God of our Scriptures and Traditions from the day of creation has been doing the task of purifying the sinful and wicked hearts of humans and trying to bring them back to him. For accomplishing this redemptive job he sends out clarion call to all his Son's disciples to join in his combat. The Gospel passage today expounds to us more on this call and offers some tips for performing the noble task of correcting our fellow-humans.

The problem with us is, we ignore or don't care about his invitation. This is because to be involved in God's redeeming works is so hard, bitter and painful. Undoubtedly, to convert our brothers and sisters to listen to God and return to him is the most cringe-making job. Even Jesus, who was the Greatest Miracle Worker in history, despite his immense power, failed in this. In his life he did numerous miracles in which water obeyed and made itself into wine; broken limbs, bones of humans obeyed him and cured; nature resource like wind obeyed him and became still; much more so, when he ordered the dead bodies 'rise up' they all obeyed. But when he approached humans to open their hearts for him and still continues knocking at their doors, they retort him: "Stop; we have our time; in our own time we will respond to you because God has provided us with freedom and intelligence."

It is to this sort of job God wants us to join him, as he reached out to his Prophets and to his other chosen ones and expressed his longing to become partners in redeeming affairs. As he did to Ezekiel, he commands all Jesus' disciples: *You, son of man—I have appointed you as a sentinel for the house of Israel; when you hear a word from my mouth, you must warn them for me.* (Ez. 33: 7)

To accomplish this cooperative redemptive work fruitfully and with light burden, God offers us today some guidelines: First, we should start and fulfill this duty only in Jesus' name-through him, with him and in him. Since the task is too onerous to be performed by our human strength, Jesus recommends to include him in our team of work as its center and source. Therefore he promised: *For where two or three are gathered together in my name, there am I in the midst of them.*

Secondly all our efforts of correcting others must be based on the spirit of love and mercy only. Pope Francis deliberates this guideline of love and mercy in his apostolic exhortation *The Joy of Love*: *No one can be condemned forever, because that is not the logic of the Gospel!* He too adds: *We put so many conditions on mercy that we empty it of its concrete meaning and real significance...It is true, for example, that mercy does not exclude justice and truth, but first and foremost we have to say that mercy is the fullness of justice and the most radiant manifestation of God's truth.* (Chapter 8) God indeed exhorts us through Paul *Owe nothing to anyone, except to love one another.* (Rom. 13: 8) This implies, we should take the first step toward the 'wicked' as a loving icebreaker and not as a tough law-binder.

Thirdly, Jesus wants us to proceed in this task very slowly, gradually, little by little with patience and tolerance and do what we can all the possible tactics. First do individually one-to-one; if we fail, do it as a group of one mind and one heart. In other words, we should try to be together as one team of God. Today God repeats his invitation to us to cooperate in his redemptive plan. He says aloud in our inner sanctuary: *Go and tell all your neighbors that the Kingdom of God is at hand; and ask them to repent and join Jesus' Club. I have appointed you through the Cross of my Son Jesus as the watchmen, watchwomen, and custodians of all my children. Please do the best you can; I will do the rest."*

Twenty Fourth Sunday in ordinary time
We die by others' wrongdoing but
always rise by our forgiving

> *Then Peter approaching asked him, "Lord,*
> *if my brother sins against me, how often*
> *must I forgive him? As many as seven*
> *times?" Jesus answered, "I say to you,*
> *not seven times but seventy-seven times.*
> *That is why the kingdom of heaven may*
> *be likened to a king who decided to settle*
> *accounts with his servants...So will my*
> *heavenly Father do to you, unless each of*
> *you forgives his brother from his heart."*
> (Matt. 18: 21-35)

In the Gospel reading we choose for today's meditation we hear one of Jesus' hardest sayings: 'So will my heavenly Father do to you, unless each of you forgives your brother from your heart'. We have to pay serious attention to his words: 'From your heart.' This means, as many preachers interpret, to forgive others out of one's will; to forgive out of sheer love. It also denotes a forgiveness, which is total and not partial; not just once or twice or even seven times but 'seventy-seven times', namely with no count.

Human will, as we know, doesn't perform its task of loving without the cooperation of human rationality for its final success. God's Word therefore offers us some valid reasons why we should forgive others from our heart. First of all, as Jesus underlines in the Parable of the Unforgiving

Servant, the amazing eternal factor that God who loves us and forgives us as soon as we beg his mercy and pardon, expects us to be so in our dealings with others.

Secondly the duty of forgiving others emerges from the obedience to God's love-commandment. *Remember the commandments and do not be angry with your neighbor* (Sir. 28: 7) Thirdly from Jesus we know that there is one and only condition God demands from us for being forgiven by him and that is to forgive other people's sins and mistakes. *Forgive us our trespasses as we forgive those who trespass against us.* He surely based this crucial demand on the teachings of OT sages: *Forgive your neighbor's injustice; then when you pray, your own sins will be forgiven.* And in addition, *Could anyone refuse mercy to another like himself, can he seek pardon for his own sins?* (Sir. 28: 2 & 4)

The fourth reason for forgiving others lies on our human frailties. One of life's challenges is our physical and spiritual illness. So we regularly pray to God for healing of all our sickness and infirmities. God has promised he will surely grant such miraculous healings. But most of us do not get it from God. Why? The Teacher Sirach, tells us the reason: *Could anyone nourish anger against another and expect healing from the LORD?* (Sir. 28: 3) Hence, in order to get healings from the Lord we need to forgive others.

One more reason for forgiving others is that 'still we are going to die'. A day will come we will die and become food for the earth. Let us remember our death and what will happen afterwards. Before we die let us set right everything before God and others. We hear in OT: *Remember your last days and set enmity aside; remember death and decay, and cease from sin!* (Sir. 28: 6) Therefore Jesus does not want us to carry a heavy burden of hatred and vengeance in our soul. With that burden it is very hard for the soul to fly toward heaven.

All the above-listed arguments are for any human being who adheres to God. There is a most compelling reason for Jesus' disciples who believe and follow the exalted Jesus for forgiving others. Our forgiveness of others comes out of our intimate connections with God the Most High. First of all both God and we have made covenant with each other in Jesus and therefore we have to live up to that promise. As OT points out, we have to *remember the Most High's covenant, and overlook faults.* (Sir. 28: 7) In addition, we Christians are baptized in Christ Jesus. Therefore we live, move and have our being through him, with him and in him. All that we do and say should occur in that environment. As Paul says, *none of us lives for oneself, and no one dies for oneself. For if we live, we live for the Lord, and if we die, we die for the Lord; so then, whether we live or die, we are the Lord's.* (Rom. 14: 7-8)

In other words such deeper love and union with Christ makes us lose our very self, including its prestige, respect and glory. Most of the time we are hurt terribly by others only because they hurt our self-prestige, good name or good life. Certainly every hurt others inflict on us is tiny little death before we face the grand death. But as Christians our entire life containing those deaths belongs to Christ. Surprisingly when we totally forgive the wrongdoers Jesus resurrects us to new life, may be also that of the opposite party! Our glory, our prestige and our good name come only by our union with Christ. So others' sins or evil deeds against us do not in any way affect us, even it does, by the Christian forgiveness we will be raised to new life in Christ.

FORTY FOURTH WEEKEND

Twenty Fifth Sunday in ordinary time
*In God's Vineyard all are equal but
with difference in Attitude*

*Seek the LORD while he may be found, call
upon him while he is near. Let the wicked
forsake their way, and sinners their
thoughts; Let them turn to the LORD to
find mercy... For my thoughts are not your
thoughts, nor are your ways my ways. For
as the heavens are higher than the earth,
so are my ways higher than your ways,
my thoughts higher than your thoughts.*
(Is. 55: 6-9)

We know there are so many exhortations and
admonitions written in the Bible don't share with our
opinions nor do they correspond to the ideas and feelings of
us who take pride living in very civilized and very illumined
Postmodern Age. One such Scriptural passage is what we
have chosen for our today's meditation, especially the
repeated oracle of God as stated by Isaiah: *My thoughts are
not your thoughts, nor are your ways my ways.*

This sort of God's proclamation should have been
humiliating even all the prophets, preachers and teachers.
But when we consider this Scriptural message seriously,
relating them to other Biblical verses, we run into
what seems to be an almost inescapable truth about the
dimension of our human condition. Through our spiritual
eyes we can discover some experiential truths about our

human life and also some practical guidelines to swallow those inevitable bitter capsule of truths.

The eternal truth that God has been proclaiming from the day of creation is our humanness is very fallible and limited though he had created us 'in God's image and likeness. We want to contain him in our wallet so that we can use his presence as a credit or debit card in buying or coveting anything we want at any time and at any place. But God would not behave that way. We prefer God to be blind to all our faults and sins and never should he chide us. But God never hesitate reprimanding us saying: You Scoundrels! Forsake first your wicked ways and turn to me for mercy. We wish God be angry against all the sinners and criminals and evil-doers around us; but surprisingly he loves to be good to all, generous in forgiving and compassionate toward his creations.

Many of us feel human death is a big loss. God indicates, life is Christ and death is gain (Ref. Phi. 1: 21). Some of us, especially the elderly, mourn and groan daily to get away soon from this world; we want to die before we die. But God points out through Paul though it is far better to leave this valley of tears and sufferings to be with Christ in heavenly mansions, God lets us remain in flesh for some more time for the benefit of our neighbors. (Phi. 1: 23-24) The Creator wants our sickbed or deathbed as the reverberating pulpit of proclaiming God's Sovereignty and Christ's holiness we carry within us in patience, endurance, and continuous communion with heavenly hosts.

We hear from Jesus about one of the most startling and unexpected managerial dealings of our God in his interactions with humans. We totally agree with Jesus when he proclaims in his parable 'Workers in the Vineyard' (Matt. 20: 1-16) that God is the proprietor of this whole universe, which is, according to the Bible, his sole vineyard. He hires men and women in the environment of the Church to cooperate with His works of gardening at any time of humans and at any Age of the world. So far, we can agree on this statement of Jesus. Yet, what we cannot digest is at the end of his parable Jesus echoing the Gardener's declaration: *'My friend, Take what is yours and go. What if I wish to give this last one the same as you? Or am I not free to do as I wish with my own money? Are you envious because I am generous?'*

By this, Jesus seems to underline the plight of so many of us who have been toiling tirelessly in God's Vineyard, the Church, from our birth; we cannot expect from our Creator more than what he considers just and right to be handed down to us at the end of days of work in his Vineyard. Our human spirit expects that God would reward us more in comparing with other people during this life and in the otherworld. But since *our thoughts are not God's thoughts*, all of us with no discrimination or variation will be remunerated by our Gardener equally as any other workers, including the latecomers. Nonetheless the Spirit enlightens us with an amazing truth: In the eyes of God what we do is less important than what our attitude is toward him. What matters to him is our sincerity of purpose to live a life according to the promptings of his Spirit, nothing more nor less; other things like our accomplishments or our performances are very secondary. He will remunerate us only according to our good-willed and truth-filled relationship with him. If we fulfill our daily labor with this unquestionable truth, then as the Psalmist sings (Ps. 145: 17-18), the LORD will be near to us always and surely fill us with satisfactory rewards.

Twenty Sixth Sunday in ordinary time

Saying total yes is the right choice in life

What is your opinion? A man had two sons. He came to the first and said, 'Son, go out and work in the vineyard today.' He said in reply, 'I will not,' but afterwards he changed his mind and went. The man came to the other son and gave the same order. He said in reply, 'Yes, sir,' but did not go. Which of the two did his father's will?" They answered, "The first." Jesus said to them, "Amen, I say to you, tax collectors and prostitutes are entering the kingdom of God before you. When John came to you in the way of righteousness, you did not believe him; but tax collectors and prostitutes did. Yet even when you saw that, you did not later change your minds and believe him. (Matt. 21: 28-32)

Every one of us respects our individuality. To say yes or no to others is our individual right and prerogative. We choose to say either 'yes or no' absolutely or change them anytime we want. The Spirit of God offers us today a small parable of Jesus and in its light we are asked to meditate on the right use of our individual right for fullness of life. In our personal lives, whatever be our status, we have repeatedly behaved as the sons in the parable. Either, as the elder son we may initially say yes and later not to do its followup or as the younger one we may say no first but then after reflecting we may act positive.

For example, many couples, starting from the dating day till their wedding ceremony, dreamed, wished and pledged to commit themselves to one another for life; they celebrated that love and their life together with the exchanging of vows and the declaration, "yes, I do!" In order for their love to grow and their marital commitment to deepen, every day of their lives they together would have affirmed and reaffirmed by an endless litany of "I dos". However in truth how many of them are keeping upto their 'dos'? In some cases some might even decide to say "I don't" or "I won't" or "I can't!"

And so it happens among with priests too like me. I as priest, from the starting of my priestly training upto the day of ordination, had repeatedly said 'yes, I do' to almost all that had been presented to me by the Church I would be serving, as vows, commands, rules and regulations. But honestly so many times I didn't comply with what I had promised either personally or thru my authorities! It is all due to our human right and freedom to change one's mind and heart as we wish.

Basically almost all of us, as Christians, have said to the Lord at our Baptism 'I do' and repeatedly renewed the same answer throughout the year. The tragic fact is we fail in our relationship with God by not adhering to the 'yes' and consequently we fail also other humans in our social relationship. Knowing the seriousness of human prerogative of uttering 'yes or no', our Creator God has been continuously reminding every human being to say always 'yes' to him-to his commands and his directions. If we don't listen to him, then we have to reap its consequences.

When disasters occur, wreaking havoc, like hurricane, bomb-blast, tornado, cyclone, earthquake, and claiming lives, usually humans look for someone to blame. OT Israelites too were blaming God and others for their misfortunes. But through Prophets God exhorted them, rather than looking for a scapegoat upon whom to heap their guilt, or even finding fault with God foolishly, they should look only to themselves and to their own responsibility for conversion. He urged them to say "yes" to him by turning away from their own wickedness; in that way, they would preserve their lives and would find the hope they needed to await their deliverance. (Ref. Ez. 18: 25-28) Jesus continued the same ministry of coaxing all humans, especially his followers, to say a total yes to God.

Through the Parable of the Two Sons, he reminded his disciples how Israelites behaved like the first son, saying yes first but then didn't follow suit; and how the sinners and pagans, though they said no but then warmly said yes to God. Besides, he pointed out himself in this regard as a pattern to all his disciples. As Paul wrote, his whole attitude was simply saying yes to God and that too total and absolute. However this absolute 'yes' to God seemed to take the toll of the very life of Jesus. For his every yes to God Jesus had lost more and more of himself. First he agreed to surrender his equality with God, then his freedom 'taking the form of a slave', then his dignity as 'he humbled himself', then his independence, 'becoming obedient', then his very life, 'even death on a cross'. (Phi. 2: 1-11) Surely saying yes to God may appear like a very risky business in our earthly life. But we should never lose sight of the endresult of this marvelous yes. We know Jesus, for his total yes to God was exalted as the Lord of glory, by whose saving efforts sinners are saved. Therefore following Jesus let us be bold enough to respond yes to God's will totally and consistently.

FORTY SIXTH WEEKEND

Twenty Seventh Sunday in ordinary time
When rejected, don't react but proact

> *...Jesus said to them, "Did you never read in the scriptures: 'The stone that the builders rejected has become the cornerstone; by the Lord has this been done, and it is wonderful in our eyes'?... I say to you, the kingdom of God will be taken away from you and given to a people that will produce its fruit.* (Matt. 21: 33-43)

We take for today's meditation Jesus' Parable of the Tenants'. What struck me, as I was meditating in my prayertimes, was the Biblical quotation with which Jesus was concluding his parable, and in particular the term 'the rejected stone'. Undoubtedly any stone, being a material thing, whether kissed or rejected, doesn't feel anything. But its reference to humans, like Jesus and his disciples, clearly indicates the feelings they experience: either feeling joy when good things occur or encountering painful trauma if they are rejected or scorned. The Spirit bestows us today very practical guidelines for tackling those painful feelings.

We are fully aware of the perennial truth that every privilege we enjoy comes with a price tag. 'No pain, no gain'. Some people who are granted the favor of being positioned as cooperators in God's deeds, misuse it trying to take advantage of others, of the society, and even of God. We see this in Jesus' parable of the rebellious farm managers; while enjoying the benefits they withhold to themselves from the landowner. Because of their unjust dealings, when their Landowner took some stern efforts to correct them, they felt uneasy, irritated and began to react against the Landowner and tried all crooked and malicious ways to reestablish their 'stone'-status. Instead, if they had proacted, namely having repented for their misdeeds and get pardoned from their Master and amended their ways they would have been well treated by the Master and he would restate them even to the dignified position of 'cornerstone'.

That is what Jesus wants us to do. Everything we handle in this world belongs to God as its one and only Owner. As we hear from Isaiah, God delights in all of them and sings a romantic love song about his Vineyard of the Universe. (Is. 5: 1) He has elevated all humans as his favorite 'stones' and entrusted the Vineyard as a lease. Though we are responsible in all these creative works, we are accountable to him because he is the sole proprietor of creation. Unfortunately most of us ignore this fact and take everything of it in our hands and do according to our whims and fancies. Besides, when the Lord stands inside of us and warns us or admonishes us through conscience and his Prophets, especially his beloved Son Jesus, we begin to react against him and perform many misdeeds pernicious to ourselves and the entire humanity.

As the inevitable result of this violent and imprudent reaction, whatever we perform and manage brings forth only bitter fruits at the harvest: *God looked for the crop of grapes, but what it yielded was wild grapes.* (Is. 5: 2-4) Those fruits can be the twisted and bad behaviors of our own sons and daughters, the family feuds, the immoral situation of our nation, and all social evils pervading the entire universe. When God finds the endresults of our creations are not according to his expectation he gets outraged. He dashes us out of his Vineyard. *Yes, I will make it a ruin.* Jesus echoes God's words: *'Therefore, I say to you, the kingdom of God will be taken away from you and given to a people that will produce its fruit."*

At the same time, even if we have been rejected by God, Jesus encourages us today saying that in whatever painful situations we are held we have the capacity to rise up and reclaim the same dignity in the Vineyard of the Lord. In this he indicates by his life and teachings that in those horrible moments of being rejected, we should humbly surrender to the Supreme God. Though he was a beloved Son to God, he encountered such painful moments of rejection from humans, surprisingly even from God. That is why he could cry aloud on the cross, *"Eli, Eli, lema sabachthani?"* which means, "My God, my God, why have you forsaken me?" (Matt. 27: 46) His patient endurance brought to him the highest position in God's Kingdom. He, *the stone, rejected by humans, which has become the cornerstone.* (Acts 4: 11)

History testifies that so many people, who experienced such rejections as Jesus, have been readmitted into the Kingdom and bestowed the 'cornerstone-position'. In the process from being rejected to reclaiming 'cornerstone-dignity' the Spirit through Paul advises us to perform some spiritual exercises: Never stop *making our requests known to God in everything by prayer and petition, with thanksgiving;* plus, *keep on doing whatever is true, whatever is honorable, whatever is just, whatever is pure, whatever is lovely, whatever is gracious.* (Phi. 4: 6-9) Thus we will get peace and not reacting we will be proacting according to the will of the Landowner.

FORTY SEVENTH WEEKEND

Twenty Eighth Sunday in ordinary time

Let us enjoy Qualitylife participating in God's Banquets

> *Jesus again in reply spoke to them in parables, saying, "The kingdom of heaven may be likened to a king who gave a wedding feast* for his son. He dispatched his servants to summon the invited guests to the feast, but they refused to come... Then he said to his servants, 'The feast is ready, but those who were invited were not worthy to come. Go out, therefore, into the main roads and invite to the feast whomever you find.' The servants went out into the streets and gathered all they found, bad and good alike, and the hall was filled with guests...Many are invited, but few are chosen."* (Matt. 22: 1-14)

We love to attend parties as well as to host them. Happy are the days of a good celebration, when we can forget our worries for a while, enjoy one another's company and laugh and sing, dance and be happy. We are lucky to have such a day now and then, a day of feasting and real joy. It is about one of such parties the Spirit bids us to meditate this weekend. It is a party hosted by God in Jesus not only after our death but even in our daily life.

God's entire life consists in simply hosting parties; he offers sumptuous meals for his creations: *On this mountain the Lord of hosts will provide for all peoples a feast of rich food and choice wines, juicy, rich food and pure choice wines"* (Is. 25: 6). As Jesus proclaims, God is a King who hosts continuous heavenly wedding banquet for his Son: *The kingdom of heaven may be likened to a king who gave a wedding feast for his son* (Matt. 22: 2); God also, as a loving Father, hosts splendid parties at the return of his prodigal children: *Take the fattened calf and slaughter it. Then let us celebrate with a feast, because this son of mine was dead, and has come to life again; he was lost, and has been found.' Then the celebration began.* (Lk. 15: 23-24).

Jesus, our Redeemer, too was a partyperson. He loved to participate such parties. *John came neither eating nor drinking and they said, 'he is possessed by a demon.' The Son of Man came eating and drinking and they said, 'look, he is glutton and a drunkard'* (Matt. 11: 18-19). Do you know that Jesus did not allow his disciples fast, while others in his community were fasting? He questioned his enemies, *"Can the wedding guests mourn as long as the bridegroom is with them?"* (Matt. 9: 14-15) Gospels prove most of his beautiful sayings came out of his mouth while he was dining. Above all, he chose Paschal Feast Dinner time to institute the greatest miraculous banquet of the Eucharist.

When the Scriptures talk about God and his Son hosting a banquet for all of us they indicate a deeper meaning to it: The Lord God offers us lively banquet of his salvation, liberation and redemption; his banquet provides us all that we need physically, emotionally, mentally and spiritually; God's party is a banquet of joy and forgiveness because he would destroy death forever and would wipe away the tears from every face. It is a banquet of rest and peace. All of us know well enough that in a well-hosted genuine party we feel all our inhibitions are gone. We feel one with each other. We too are ready to help and assist other persons in a way possible. In other words we are out of ourselves. The same kind of feeling that God in his Son wishes for all of us, not just in one or two banquets but throughout our lives. Like a caring Parent he provides us a beautiful life with all its resources. We can name it as 'qualitylife'. As the Psalmist sings, he feeds us like a shepherd to green pastures; he leads us beside restful waters; he goes on feeding us, nourishing us with his power and love. (Ps. 23)

This 'qualitylife'-menu of God's banquet contains also the capsules of contentment, fullness, and sportive spirit. Paul, being so nourished in God's daily parties, writes how he felt the post-effect of them: *I know also how to live with abundance and in all things I have learned the secret of being well fed and of going hungry, of living in abundance and of being in need.* (Phil. 4: 12-14).

God in Jesus invites us daily to this sort of Banquet. Very surprisingly not all of us are ready to take it. Though God as the host would cook, prepare the table, serve at table and even do the dishes, he never compels us to come and join the party. He simply invites us and leaves to our discretion. But according to God's survey for the past millions of years, '*many are called but a few choose to be chosen* to participate in the dinner. We, humans with our free will, can reject this invitation. Let us never lose sight of God's banquet of love, mercy and providence even in difficult times. His dinner party is eternal, no interruption. Those who are serious about God's invitation go and attend and fill their heart and soul and body.

FORTY EIGHTH WEEKEND

Twenty Ninth Sunday in ordinary time
Let God let go

> *Then the Pharisees···sent their disciples to him, with the Herodians, saying, "Teacher, we know that you are a truthful man and that you teach the way of God in accordance with the truth. And you are not concerned with anyone's opinion, for you do not regard a person's status. Tell us, then, what is your opinion: Is it lawful to pay the census tax to Caesar or not?" Knowing their malice, Jesus said, "Why are you testing me, you hypocrites? Show me the coin that pays the census tax." Then they handed him the Roman coin. He said to them, "Whose image is this and whose inscription?" They replied, "Caesar's." At that he said to them, "Then repay to Caesar what belongs to Caesar and to God what belongs to God." (Matt. 22: 15-21)*

In the Gospel passage taken for our today's meditation we notice the Pharisees and his enemies plan to trap him in his words and attitudes as a religious Jew; plus to make him politically incorrect and get into the bad book of Romans. Jesus responds: *Give to Caesar what is Caesar and to God what is God's.* Through this statement Jesus, with all his God-given Jewish smartness brings out very clearly his continued theme of life, namely: 'God and God only.' According to him there can be other political and social priorities in life, like paying taxes, but it is God who should be 'number one' in our attitudes and actions. This saying of Jesus is reflected in his entire life and teaching, thus restoring the right relationship between the Creator and the creature.

Educated Jews like Pharisees, Sadducees and Scribes knew very well what Jesus was referring to. It was the supreme command of God: *Love your God with your whole heart, whole mind, whole soul, whole body and strength;* and the addition to it was: *love your neighbors as yourself.* Scriptures profusely proclaim the 'supremacy of God'. Repeating the assertion that *I am the LORD, there is no other, there is no God besides me,* God makes Prophet Isaiah write: *I have called you by name, giving you a title, though you do not know me. It is I who arm you, though you do not know me, so that all may know, from the rising of the sun to its setting, that there is none besides me.* (Is. 45: 4-6)

Psalmist therefore exhorts the people to *Give the Lord glory and honor due to his Name.* (Ps. 29: 1-2) Paul continued to live in the same spirit of faith in the sovereignty of God and never ceased to preach about it in all his Letters. *We give thanks to God always knowing, brothers loved by God, how you were chosen. For our gospel did not come to you in word alone, but also in power and in the Holy Spirit and with much conviction.* (1 Thess. 1: 2-5) That conviction was nothing but the sole faith and hope Paul had for the Lord God alone.

As the disciples of Jesus our first and deepest loyalty must be allocated to God. Any of our attitudes, any of our plans, any of our opinions, any of our suggestions and any of our personal, social, religious and political activities regarding the development, management and maintenance of our life must be generated, influenced and presented and implemented on the basis of the truthful fact. If not, our Master would be reprimanding us as he did to Peter: *Get behind me, Satan! You are an obstacle to me. You are thinking not as God does, but as human beings do.* (Matt. 16: 21-23)

Therefore we should 'give to God what is God's'; God is the Lord, and that there is no other; we are to worship him alone. Let God, let go, meaning: Our whole body, whole soul, whole mind, whole strength and whole life; not just 5% or 10% or 50%; but 100% of everything we own and do should be handed over to our Creator. This is the challenge, God presents to us now.

FORTY NINTH WEEKEND

Thirtieth Sunday in ordinary time

Jesus' Love Command is Three in One

> *When the Pharisees heard that he had silenced the Sadducees, they gathered together, and one of them a scholar of the law tested him by asking "Teacher, which commandment in the law is the greatest?" He said to him, "You shall love the Lord, your God, with all your heart, with all your soul, and with all your mind. This is the greatest and the first commandment. The second is like it: You shall love your neighbor as yourself. The whole law and the prophets depend on these two commandments."* (Matt. 22: 34-40)

God places before us three lovers whom he orders to love, of whom two are mentioned directly and the third indirectly. He wants us first to love him: *You shall love the Lord, your God...*; and secondly to love our neighbors: *You shall love your neighbor;* and the third is to love ourselves: Love your neighbor *as yourself.* We know it is very hard to love three as God demands.

By experience we know it is difficult to love our neighbors in the same way we love ourselves. To love oneself is the norm of survival for every human being. 'Loving our neighbors' becomes an extra fitting into our lives. As long as others feed our self-love it is ok to love them. But it is something beyond our self to love anyone who is different than ourselves, who are pain in our neck, who are strangers, who are useless to us, to our family and to the society as widows, orphans, refugees, enemies and older people. Yet God expects us to love our neighbors as ourselves. This is what God has been commanding from the beginning of Adam and Eve. *You shall not oppress or afflict a resident alien...you shall not wrong any widow or orphan.* Besides, he too, as Champion for these vulnerable and needy people, threatened his people with curse and death if they violate his order of neighborly and compassionate love. (Ex. 22: 20-26)

Since God knew our inability to love ourselves and others in an integrated way according to his will, he, out of compassion and mercy, designed his Law in such a way that he places himself as the first Lover who grabs our 'first love' for him and by such divine love and agape, he makes it easy for us to integrate both loves. He says to us today: "Love yourself for my sake and love your neighbors too for my sake." This sounds like a mother directing her child to love his siblings for her sake even though he does not like them. If that boy possesses a true love for his mother surely he would forget the prejudices against his brothers and start loving them for the love of his mother.

This is why God points out that loving him should be our priority in life and it should be total. Once it is well set, on this foundation we can build up our home of love for others and ourselves. When God is worshipped and loved in a right perspective and at his terms, we begin to love our body, our soul and our very life with all its joys and sorrows and added to it we will include our neighbors into our lives with right motivation and sincere concern. What will happen is we start seeing God in every one we meet. A Hindu proverb sums up the above: *"The narrow minded ask, 'Are these people strangers or are they members of our tribe? But to those in whom love dwells, the whole world is but one family."*

The Jewish spiritual writer, Rabbi Harold Kushner, when he was asked "Where is God?" corrected their question saying 'you should ask, "When is God?" Then he added: "God is present when we love him and when we love our neighbor." In the grip of total love of God we can feel the remarkable dignity of every human, as our Catholic Catechism expresses: *Being in the image of God the human individual possesses the dignity of a person, who is not just something, but someone.* (#357) A journalist visiting Saint Mother Teresa in Calcutta watched her dressing the wounds on a man with gangrene in his leg. The journalist was appalled by the wound but was full of admiration for the Mother who seemed to show no disgust as she was cleaning the suppurating wound. 'I wouldn't do that for million dollars.' said the journalist. 'Neither would I,' said Mother Teresa, 'I do it for love of God.'

Saints, like Mother Teresa, who tried their best to follow the three-to-be loved command of God testified that they had not reached to its success. Christian life is not a done deal. It is not a product but a process. The poet Maya Angelou was once asked what her lifetime goals were. Maya Angelou was Christian. Yet she answered that she wanted to become a Christian. Her point was that Christianity is an ongoing 'process of becoming'. Every day we take steps to becoming a Christian. It is much true in the case of fulfilling the love-command of God.

FIFTIETH WEEKEND

Thirty First Sunday in ordinary time
Puffed-up self will pull us down to the Pit

Then Jesus spoke to the crowds and to his disciples, saying, "The scribes and the Pharisees have taken their seat on the chair of Moses. Therefore, do and observe all things whatsoever they tell you, but do not follow their example. For they preach but they do not practice. They tie up heavy burdens hard to carry and lay them on people's shoulders, but they will not lift a finger to move them. All their works are performed to be seen... They love places of honor at banquets, seats of honor in synagogues, greetings in marketplaces... The greatest among you must be your servant. Whoever exalts himself will be humbled; but whoever humbles himself will be exalted. (Matt. 23: 1-12)

We hear in the Gospel reading used for today's meditation that all things that are occurring now and at the end of our lives as well are coming from God's hands either as his blessings or curses. People, who are in glory will be humbled one day and those who lead today a life of humiliation and brokenness will be exalted in future.

Throughout our lives we have been watching and witnessing many of our neighbors and friends shining in public as very good politicians and diplomats and many priests, preachers, teachers and elders honored and esteemed popular and glamourous at the pulpits, podiums, and in front of the audience. But we too have noticed some of them being cursed and humiliated in public. Surely all of these spotlight people were once started well their carrier and they were counted as blessings from the Lord. But at one time they can be turned out to be curses and contemptible in the eyes of God. How does it happen?'

In course of our lives God has been sidelined and our puffed-self took our priority. We have created our petty kingdom and form our own laws for which we become strongly opinionated. Our unaccounted supremacy replaces God's own and we use even God's authority, his podium, his words, for our vain glory. We forget God is only one Father, one Source, one Parent, one Master and one Superior. Many times we abuse our titles and recognitions to delete God's power and glory. This is why we read in OT that the Lord became very angry against those whom he chose and appointed as priests and teachers to his people because he noticed they had turned aside from his way and caused many to stumble; corrupted their covenant; and shown partiality in their teachings. Therefore he threatened them with sending curses upon them; turning their blessings into curses; and made them contemptible and base before all the people. (Mal. 2: 2-9)

Secondly as the time goes on we begin to learn the tricks of survival and so most of the time our words do not correspond to our actions. We say one thing in the public and do another thing in private. Jesus calls those persons hypocrites. Hypocrites in Greek means actors. It is like our kids who with their Halloween costumes play Trick-a-Tree. God expects us to do our part in building up his world but not merely acting. Jesus observed there was no integrity between the preaching and life of the Scribes and Pharisees; so he exhorted his followers: D*o and observe all things whatsoever they tell you, but do not follow their example. For they preach but they do not practice.*

Thirdly we always go against the will of God who always advises us to be humble. It is pride that breaks the bond we have with God. It is pride which keeps us stony hearted. It is pride that leads us to exploit and cheat others, especially those who are ignorant and weak. Sometimes this pride takes a different ugly shape of patronizing others and bring them under our control. If we have humility, truth and obedience to God we will respect others' rights.

Disciples, like Paul, were fully aware of the holy admonitions of God and learned from the Master Jesus' life and teachings, behaved gentle among their people as a nursing mother caring her children; but they shared with people not only the gospel of God but also their very self; and they never imposed bigger burdens though they could have done it but they earned their livelihood by working night and day. Due to such attitude and conduct, people received from them not human words but those of God. (1 Thess. 2: 7b-9, 13) To be always getting blessing from the Lord and walk as a blessing in the midst of our friends and relatives we need to be obedient to God, truthful to our words and to be humble servant to others only for the sake of God.

FIFTY FIRST WEEKEND

Thirty Second Sunday in ordinary time

Fear is useless, what is needed is trustful life of charities

Then the kingdom of heaven will be like ten virgins who took their lamps and went out to meet the bridegroom. Five of them were foolish and five were wise. The foolish ones, when taking their lamps, brought no oil with them, but the wise brought flasks of oil with their lamps. Since the bridegroom was long delayed, they all became drowsy and fell asleep. At midnight, there was a cry, 'Behold, the bridegroom! Come out to meet him!' Then all those virgins got up and trimmed their lamps. The foolish ones said to the wise, 'Give us some of your oil, for our lamps are going out.' But the wise ones replied, 'No, for there may not be enough for us and you. Go instead to the merchants and buy some for yourselves.' While they went off to buy it, the bridegroom came and those who were ready went into the wedding feast with him. Then the door was locked. Afterwards the other virgins came and said, 'Lord, Lord, open the door for us!' But he said in reply, 'Amen, I say to you, I do not know you.' Therefore, stay awake, for you know neither the day nor the hour. (Matt. 25: 1-13)

The Scriptural passage we have taken for our today's meditation is very salutary; it reminds us to be on our guard, to have our priorities right and to expect to be called to face God at any time. Be prepared for the worst? No. This is how many of us misinterpret the Scriptures and getting ourselves ready to face any casualties as people were preparing themselves at the eve of the year 2000 to face 'Y2K' and Millennium Bug. Jesus invites us to be prepared for the best. He compares it to the wedding. Any wedding invitation makes us feel joyful as it summons us to join in one of the happiest celebrations in human life. Jesus invites us today to a heavenly wedding reception, a feast beyond our wildest dreams.

Jesus' parables about 'the reign of God' are his admonishing words to prepare us well for that great day, when we shall 'see him face to face'. Our Christian faith and its practices are the means by which we anticipate that day without fear. Only the authentic Christians who have been gifted with the fullness of truth can face that most terrible of days without trepidation. The fullness of truth that comes from Jesus exhorts us that we are responsible, in the first place, for our own salvation. The ten bridesmaids in the parable, equipped with their torches alight and waiting for the bridegroom, are a lesson by which we examine our own lives. The five foolish virgins did not prepare adequately, did not bring oil along with them. They could not predict how long the waiting period might be. This why Jesus ends his parable saying: S*tay awake, for you know neither the day nor the hour.*

When Jesus urges us to be awake as our preparation for the 'that Day', he means we need to live our Christian faith fully and consciously every day. Our worry is always about our human sleep of death which may be either the effect of our own sinfulness or that of our neighbors. We too are anxious about how all of us would be withstanding and scoring on 'that Day'. Paul encourages and consoles all of us as he describes about the happenings of 'that Day': *The Lord himself, with a word of command, with the voice of an archangel and with the trumpet of God, will come down from heaven, and the dead in Christ will rise first. Then we who are alive, who are left, will be caught up together with them in the clouds to meet the Lord in the air. Thus we shall always be with the Lord.* (1 Thess. 4: 13-18)

One thing is certain: Those of us who, as the Wise Virgins, love, seek and watch diligently and prudently for the arrival of Jesus, the Eternal Wisdom (Wis. 6: 12-16), and busy ourselves in our daily tasks of loving and merciful deeds, will meet the Bridegroom on 'that Day' and will be taken *into the wedding feast with him.*

FIFTY SECOND WEEKEND

Thirty Third Sunday in ordinary time

*Let us risk ourselves with the Lord
for attaining our Destiny*

*It will be as when a man who was going
on a journey called in his servants and
entrusted his possessions to them. To
one he gave five talents; to another, two;
to a third, one—to each according to his
ability. Then he went away...After a long
time the master of those servants came
back and settled accounts with them.
The one who had received five talents
came forward bringing the additional
five. He said, 'Master, you gave me five
talents. See, I have made five more.' His
master said to him, 'Well done, my good
and faithful servant. Since you were
faithful in small matters, I will give you
great responsibilities. Come, share your
master's joy.' Then the one who had
received two talents also came forward
and said, 'Master, you gave me two
talents. See, I have made two more.' His
master said to him, 'Well done, my good
and faithful servant. Since you were
faithful in small matters, I will give you
great responsibilities. Come, share your
master's joy'...The one who had received
the one talent came forward and said,*

'Master, I knew you were a demanding person; so out of fear I went off and buried your talent in the ground. Here it is back.' His master said to him in reply, 'you wicked, lazy servant... Should you not then have put my money in the bank so that I could have got it back with interest on my return? Now then! Take the talent from him and give it to the one with ten (Matt. 25: 14-30)

The Spirit once again calls us to meditate today in the light of Jesus' Parable of the Talents about passing through the most remarkable Day of the Lord. First of all, Jesus wants us to be aware of the fact happening after death, namely the accounting we have to submit to our Creator and Proprietor regarding how we made use of his talents, gifts and blessings. Our loving God, being a just Master, expects us to be wise enough in making use of all that he has given us not in maximum possible but in the best possible way. This means every use of every talent, God has provided us with, should most likely have or near to the desired outcome. How to achieve this goal?

Through his parable Jesus also indicates that our heavenly Father bestows to every one of us plentiful gifts to trade with, in his Kingdom. We should know in Jesus' time a 'talent' was a large sum of money, the equivalent of six thousand *denarii* or the equivalent of the wages of a day laborer for fifteen years. One denarius was the wage of a common daily laborer. God distributes such enormous gifts according to his plan of action. We have no say in it or we can murmur and frustrated over the matter and do nothing about the gifts being offered to us. Jesus expects us to use whatever gifts we are endowed with as best as we can.

There are also people among us who find excuses for their laziness as the third person mentioned in the parable by saying: *'Master, I knew you were a demanding person; so out of fear I went off and buried your talent in the ground. Here it is back.'* In other words, some of us think that since our God is very good and kind and therefore will surely save us, no matter what we do. And thus do nothing to improve, to multiply or to apply the available gifts for better use. We too hold another wrong notion about the 'fear of God' by which we think the merciful Father will waive his punishment against us.

On the other hand, God instructs us today from the Book of Proverb (chapter 31) pointing out an industrious lady whom he praises highly and presents to us as a rolemodel in handling the 'fear of the Lord' in a wise way. Her fear is not merely a fright; rather reverential awe and respect for God. It is her human consciousness about the existence and intervention of a Supreme God who is for her the sole Giver of the talents and blessings she possesses; and she tries to use every bit of her talents as an opportunity for acknowledging God and serving others.

God's revelation also instructs us today that we must be conscious of our risky but only available present moment: *As children of light, you are not in darkness,* insists Paul (1 Thess. 5: 1-6), who uses verbs in the present tense, indicating that the life of the future for which we wait begins here and now. Jesus will indeed come again, but let us not lose sight of the fact that he has already come and moved among us, incarnating in his words and works the loving mercies of God. The life that we long to live forever has already begun in us at baptism. Therefore, our belonging to Christ and to God should be evident in words and deeds, in thoughts and motivations so transparent they reflect the goodness and grace of God. We should uphold in daily enterprises: *All of you are the children of light and children of the day.*

Feast of Christ the King

*Let us make a life by what we give as
we make a living by what we get*

*"When the Son of Man comes in his glory,
and all the angels with him, he will sit
upon his glorious throne, and all the
nations will be assembled before him. And
he will separate them one from another,
as a shepherd separates the sheep from
the goats. He will place the sheep on his
right and the goats on his left. Then the
king will say to those on his right, 'Come,
you who are blessed by my Father. Inherit
the kingdom prepared for you from the
foundation of the world. For I was hungry
and you gave me food, I was thirsty and
you gave me drink, a stranger and you
welcomed me, naked and you clothed
me, ill and you cared for me, in prison
and you visited me.' Then the righteous
will answer him and say, 'Lord, when
did we see you hungry and feed you, or
thirsty and give you drink? When did we
see you a stranger and welcome you, or
naked and clothe you? When did we see
you ill or in prison, and visit you?' And
the king will say to them in reply, 'Amen,
I say to you, whatever you did for one of
these least brothers of mine, you did for*

me.' Then he will say to those on his left,
'Depart from me, you accursed, into the
eternal fire prepared for the devil and his
angels. For I was hungry and you gave
me no food, I was thirsty and you gave
me no drink, a stranger and you gave me
no welcome, naked and you gave me no
clothing, ill and in prison, and you did
not care for me...And these will go off to
eternal punishment, but the righteous to
eternal life."* (Matt. 25: 31-46)

Today we celebrate the feast of Christ the King, who
invites us today to meditate and to reaffirm our Christian
acceptance of the unique leadership of Jesus of Nazareth,
not as a Jewish, Galilean Rebel, who lived some 2000 years
back, and who founded his own 'Better Way' to reach the
Supreme Being, or as a feudal king who emerged in the
beginning of 3rd century to counteract and topple down all
then-existed rulers of the world.

Rather, at this celebration we proclaim: That we
encounter Jesus Christ personally and communally today
as the resurrected Lord in his Spirit moving and leading
at his will around the globe; that this leader cannot
be contained or restricted only to a few, even to the so-
called Christians, but to every living creatures with no
discrimination or labeling or profiling; that *"In Jesus,
who was raised from the dead as firstfruits,* (1 Cor. 15:
20) *we all have redemption by his blood, the forgiveness
of transgressions;* (Eph. 1: 7) *God set forth in Christ, as a
plan for the fullness of times, to sum up all things in him,
in heaven and on earth.* (Eph. 1: 9-10); and that we are so
proud of being inducted into this Jesus' Church and share

the same power and dignity of being assigned as the proxies of his leadership, plus the assurance of entering into his heavenly mansions of eternity.

While we feel so happy about our sharing with Christ his leadership, leading others to our true and complete destiny, today God reminds us to reflect over the handling of such dignified leadership. In the kingdom of God the one and only definition for leadership is 'imitating Jesus, loving others with justice, loving with truth and serving them with love.

Matthew uses Jesus' words as the ultimate advice for every leader how and why they should imitate God in Jesus in managing their leadership with loving others in justice, truth and in action. Jesus Christ whom we acknowledge as God-appointed Leader with the ultimate power of, sitting on the Throne of his Father, even judging all humans at their Endtimes. The one and only benchmark with which he is going to measure our lives is nothing but love-saving love, life-giving love, truthful love, justice-based love and surely action-packed love. This act of charity toward the needy and the neglected will be properly handled by us only when we unite ourselves with the Spirit of resurrected Christ and see his presence in others as if they are the proxies of Christ.

Jesus actually echoes how the heavenly Father considers our leading task. Through Prophets God declared the unique style of his leadership: *I myself will look after and tend my sheep. As a shepherd tends his flock, when he finds himself among his scattered sheep, so will I tend my sheep. The lost I will seek out, the strayed I will bring back, the injured I will bind up and the sick I will heal.* (Ez. 34: 11-17) As the foremost authority on today's gospel was Saint Mother Teresa who is quoted saying: *Undoubtedly we will be judged at the end by the words of Jesus "I was hungry and you gave me to eat. I was naked and you clothed me. I was homeless and you took me in". However Jesus wants me to add: "Hungry, not only for bread, but hungry for love; naked not only for clothing, but for human dignity and respect; homeless not only for want of a room of bricks, but homeless because of rejection. This is Christ in distressing disguise."*

HILLTOP MEDITATIONS

For Year B Weekends

FIRST WEEKEND

First Advent Sunday

Living in the spirit of catchy Word: 'Watch'

But of that day or hour, no one knows, neither the angels in heaven, nor the Son, but only the Father. Be watchful! Be alert! You do not know when the time will come. It is like a man traveling abroad. He leaves home and places his servants in charge, each with his work, and orders the gatekeeper to be on the watch. Watch, therefore; you do not know when the lord of the house is coming, whether in the evening, or at midnight, or at cockcrow, or in the morning. May he not come suddenly and find you sleeping. What I say to you, I say to all: 'Watch!' (Mk. 13: 33-37)

All of us have so much trouble to keep up our interior rest due to fretting over too many worldly matters and consequently being unable to settle down in serenity. The Spirit invites us today to go deeply into this perennial problem and try to salvage the genuine rest by meditating on Jesus' emphatic advice: *Watch*.

What does he mean by the catch word, 'Watch'? He means that we must not be ignorant or careless or complacent or cold and indifferent to God, his design for us and our responsibilities in this world; also, positively Jesus advises us to be aware of the significance of this earthly life. It is so important in God's eyes that every moment is very precious to him. He has designed so much to accomplish for the entire universe and his creatures. Also as Christians we are blessed by God with abundant gifts.

Acknowledging those blessings gratefully, Paul writes that in Jesus we were enriched in every way with all discourse and all knowledge; not lacking in any spiritual gift during our lifetime of waiting; and since God is faithful, he will keep us firm to the end, helping us to be blameless on the day of the Lord's coming. (Ref. 1 Cor. 1: 3-9)

God the Creator, together with his gifts, also has entrusted to us certain responsibilities to be performed and accomplished according to His marvelous design. The main vision and goal in his mind is to make his creation better for his creatures to live and ultimately come to their destiny. Every one of God's creatures, especially his human children must live in peace, joy and fullness of contentment. This is why our human hearts often dream about a beautiful world without worries or pain. We know that our world will never be such a paradise. Imperfection is the mark of our world and of every human being. Nonetheless, if we let God come into our world and if we let him enter our individual life, we will find our settlement in him, then everything will get better.

Undoubtedly this is possible if we begin to pray ceaselessly during our 'waiting time' in this passing world, as Isaiah prayed to God in the name of Israel. First of all we should be fully aware of our priveledge to demand from God to come and help us as Isaiah prayed: *Lord, why do you make us wander from your ways? Return for the sake of your servants. Would you please rend the heavens and come down to help us!* (63: 17-19) While we do this, we too must be humble enough, like the Prophet, to uphold our firm faith and hope in his merciful and almighty love as his children. *LORD, you are our father; we are the clay and you our potter: we are all the work of your hand.* (64: 7)

In fact we know God did come already; he is here with us in Jesus. Only thing we have to do is to be fully aware of this redemptive fact. With him we can make this world not yet a paradise but at least much better if we learn to bear with him the pain of the evil in this world and fight it with all our might. Then it may become a sign of the paradise of heaven.

There are many among us who are healthy, wealthy, energetic, and much more with enlightened mind and spirit by Christ. Many are parents who cooperated with God in multiplying his humanity. Many are gifted with very good IQ, sharp mind, creative talents and physical, moral and spiritual power. We should never forget that these blessings are all given to us to rise up, not just to walk in our own way but take with us all those pushed backward in the community. Unfortunately we see around us millions of weak and very fragile people like the elderly, like babies and vulnerable children, emotionally –immature adults, teenagers-always living-in feelings, people with defects and terminal diseases, poor people living in poverty and ignorance and slavery by social injustice and by sophisticated people's exploitation. Unfortunately we don't apply this truth in our lives; we behave like wanderers, worse than this, as sleepwalkers. This is what Jesus meant by his clarion call: *Be watchful! Be alert!*

....

SECOND WEEKEND

Second Sunday of Advent

As it is written in Isaiah the prophet: "Behold, I am sending my messenger ahead of you; he will prepare your way. A voice of one crying out in the desert: 'Prepare the way of the Lord, make straight his paths.'" John the Baptist appeared in the desert proclaiming a baptism of repentance for the forgiveness of sins. People of the whole Judean countryside and all the inhabitants of Jerusalem were going out to him and were being baptized by him in the Jordan River as they acknowledged their sins. John was clothed in camel's hair, with a leather belt around his waist. He fed on locusts and wild honey. And this is what he proclaimed: "One mightier than I is coming after me. I am not worthy to stoop and loosen the thongs of his sandals. I have baptized you with water; he will baptize you with the Holy Spirit." (Mk. 1: 2-8)

Every time we open our ears and hearts to the Lord in a spiritual way, he proclaims his good news appropriate to that situation, to that need and to that time. That is what he has been performing in our weekend hilltop meditation times. Today he offers us some tips for how to go through in the 'delay of the Lord' we discover during our life of waiting for his triumphant interaction among us.

Through John the Baptizer God proclaims today a most striking good news that reclaims and affirms the true identity of the Person Jesus for whose arrival we are waiting: That he is none other than Jesus, Son of Mary; and that, though he lived like an ordinary carpenter's son, though still he is judged by majority of humans as one among many religious leaders and teachers, he is the one appointed by God to represent him at the end time endeavors. He is none other than the Son of God, the one whom we have taken in our lives as our mentor, leader and Master. This Jesus is mightier than any prophet, any king, any judge and any leader ever lived.

As OT Prophets have foretold, when Jesus arrives, he would comfort our hearts with the assurance of the Shepherd's tender compassion and patient love for us, the cherished sheep of God's flock; he would feed us, console us, educate us, inspire us, and blesse us with abundant riches and talents and especially he will direct us in right path so that we can escape, as much as we can, from imprisonment, and from losing good name respect from our family and community. The same Lord is knocking at our doors. He is not sleeping and indifferent to our daily ups and downs. He is always ready and alert more than we to intervene in our lives. He is indeed waiting to enter into our lives with full power, with his rewards, and with his shining glory. (Ref. Is. 40: 1-5; 9-11)

Asking us to wait for the coming of the day of God, Peter portrays the endresults of his coming: *The heavens will be dissolved in flames and the elements melted by fire. But according to his promise we await new heavens and a new earth in which righteousness dwells.* (2 Pet. 3: 12-13)

Jesus' coming will be like a 'big bang' factor, tremendous power will be unleashed to judge and to transform the human race and the entire creation.

We too hear from the Spirit through John that if we desire to meet this powerful, lucky, redemptive, and loving person at his coming and to get all that he has promised, what we have to do is '*to prepare the way of the Lord.*' For this preparation work, John exhorts us first we need to be baptized in water of repentance. The Spirit comes forward to add one more magnificent advice to us, namely as Jesus was baptized, we should be baptized with the Holy Spirit of fire, love, justice, and faith, hope and joy. By receiving these two baptisms we will be enabled to observe when and how our Master arrives in our daily life and we too will be strengthened in listening to his admonitions for 'fuller life'.

While we wait for God's interventions in life, there is one thing that disturbs us. It is his 'delay' in coming. The Spirit tells us today that we need not worry about God's delay because with the Lord *one day is like a thousand years and a thousand years like one day.* We are told, the reason for our God's delay is that he patiently waiting for his children to come back home. He does not wish even a single person of his family to be perished.

Following the above-mentioned advices of the Spirit we become the living good news of God. We begin to act as messengers and heralds of God's good news. As Jesus, John and the Apostles, we will announce the Good News of Hope, joy and peace to our needy spouses, children and friends; by sharing our love, our food, our money, our service and our smile with those who are in need. Above all, let us announce this good news by forgiving others, our enemies, those who despise us by their prejudices. This is the way to prepare the way of the Lord.

THIRD WEEKEND

Third Sunday of Advent

Blissful Life is possible in this world provided...

...When the Jews from Jerusalem sent priests and Levites to him to ask him, "Who are you?" he admitted and did not deny it, but admitted, "I am not the Messiah." So they asked him, "What are you then? Are you Elijah?" And he said, "I am not." "Are you the Prophet?" He answered, "No." So they said to him, "Who are you, so we can give an answer to those who sent us? What do you have to say for yourself?" He said: "I am 'the voice of one crying out in the desert, "Make straight the way of the Lord,"' as Isaiah the prophet said." John answered them, "I baptize with water; but there is one among you whom you do not recognize, the one who is coming after me, whose sandal strap I am not worthy to untie." (Jn. 1: 19-27)

Joining with all religions of the world Christianity accepts the experience of joy as its ultimate goal. Justice, peace, love and any other virtues spoken in Scriptures and by spiritual authors are simply the components of that sparkling spectrum of joyous life. The eternal life which the Lord speaks about and promises to his disciples is simply a blissful life forever. 'Bliss' is another way of saying the' complete joy'. We also profess this 'blissful life' starts already here on earth. What makes even our earthly life blissful is the one important factor that differentiates Christianity from all other religions. And that is a person, Jesus born in Bethlehem 2000 years ago. On this unthinkable truth the Spirit invites us today to meditate and pray.

God created us to be as he is, namely as he is joyful. Therefore our human life is totally a celebration of joy in this world to be continued in heaven. It is for this reason, we believe, Jesus of Nazareth was born, lived, died and rose. The core of our Christian faith is Jesus Christ is the true source of our complete joy. Prophet Isaiah fittingly acknowledged the right reason for Jesus' coming into this world: *The spirit of the Lord GOD is upon me, because the LORD has anointed me; he has sent me to bring glad tidings to the poor, to heal the brokenhearted, to proclaim liberty to the captives and release to the prisoners.* (Is. 61: 1-2)

We should never forget that merely knowing and accepting Jesus as the source of joy would in no way offer us the 'complete' joy. True it is, when we accept Jesus our Lord and Savior the joy begins to dwell in us. However that joy can be faded away or dwindled by our carelessness in course of our life. The only way to keep this joy getting its completeness is that Jesus must be allowed to interact in us and we should develop an intimate relationship with him; in other words, not by simply adhering to certain doctrines and practices but more by an experiential life with God in Jesus. Isaiah wrote how he was leading a joyful life: *I rejoice heartily in the LORD, in my God is the joy of my soul; for he has clothed me with a robe of salvation and wrapped me in a mantle of justice, like a bridegroom adorned with a diadem.* (61: 10-11) The same thing was true in Mary's life: *My spirit rejoices in God my Savior,* she sang, *for he has looked upon his lowly servant.* John the Baptizer, describing about his amazing relationship with Jesus, admitted that 'he was only a messenger, a witness, a forerunner, a humble herald, and a friend to the Bridegroom. He recognized his worth as the Best-man to Jesus who is the Bridegroom.'

There is one more way to preserve our joy growing: We should try our best to make others joyful. We are very grateful to Jesus proclaiming in his Sermon on the Mount that we are *the light of the world.* Each one of us, by our Baptism, has been sent to be the light in the world but with difference-not obviously as the original Light Who is Jesus; but only we are to give witness to this Light. John the Baptizer, stressing vehemently about his genuine role in front of Christ, has testified, as the Gospel Writer portrays: *John was sent from God. He came for testimony, to testify to the light, so that all might believe through him. He was not the light, but came to testify to the light. And this is the testimony of John.* Obviously, we are supposed to be the light of Christ in the same way as the moon is in its reflection of the sun. There are so many people out there who live in darkness, feeling lonely, rejected, and marginalized. They are sincerely waiting for the light of Christ shine on them and to turn their lives into experiences of joy. Jesus has entrusted that work to us so that our joy may be complete. Our dream of this blissful joy will be withered away or never become complete unless and until we share that joy with others who need it as our Master expects.

Let us remember the great Apostle Paul who lived upto our Master's demand. This is why, even while he was persecuted, imprisoned and waiting for his final end, he could encourage his fellow-Christians: *Rejoice always. Pray without ceasing. In all circumstances give thanks, for this is the will of God for you in Christ Jesus... The one who calls you is faithful, and he will also accomplish it.* (1 Thess. 5: 16-24)

FOURTH WEEKEND

Fourth Sunday of Advent

Waiting imposes heavy weight of faith, hope and charity

In the sixth month, the angel Gabriel was sent from God to a town of Galilee called Nazareth, to a virgin betrothed to a man named Joseph, of the house of David, and the virgin's name was Mary. And coming to her, he said, "Hail, favored one! The Lord is with you." But she was greatly troubled at what was said and pondered what sort of greeting this might be. Then the angel said to her, "Do not be afraid, Mary, for you have found favor with God. Behold, you will conceive in your womb and bear a son, and you shall name him Jesus. He will be great and will be called Son of the Most High, and the Lord God will give him the throne of David his father, and he will rule over the house of Jacob forever, and of his kingdom there will be no end"...And behold, Elizabeth, your relative, has also conceived a son in her old age, and this is the sixth month for her who was called barren; for nothing will be impossible for God." Mary said, "Behold, I am the handmaid of the Lord. May it be done to me according to your word" (Lk. 1: 26-38).

Once being irritated by my friend's attitude of failing in his reciprocal friendly relationship, I reproached him pointing out, *when he comes to me he expects what I will give him and when I go to his home he says: 'What do you bring to me?'* This is how we selfishly behave in our dealings with God. While we expect from God numerous benefits and gifts we behave indifferent and sluggish toward his demands or try to blame him for our inability. In this regard the Spirit today desires to offer more insight to us during our reading and meditating of his Words on how to maintain well our reciprocal relationship with God.

Indeed God had promised us so many blessings and unthinkable benedictions. All his gifts are bundled and packaged in the form of Scriptural Promises. They are concerned with a fuller life- 'qualitylife', as I love to say, which is filled with true justice, joy, peace, love and healing. Those numerous promises have been fulfilled among Israelites both individually and socially as they are recorded in OT Books.

We interpret most of God's promises made individually to his Kings, Judges, and Prophets, and socially to Jewish clans, especially Judah, as those proposed to us. We got this insight largely from NT Writers. In this vein, we hear Angel Gabriel reminding Mary that those OT promises of God very well applied to her Baby Jesus. In the second Book of Samuel we read God promising to King David: *I will raise up your offspring after you...I will establish his kingdom...and I will establish his royal throne forever. I will be a father to him, and he shall be a son to me...I will not withdraw my favor from him.* (7: 12-16)

Apostles, like Paul, continued to profess this realization of OT promises happened in Jesus of Nazareth. He esteems such factor as a unique historical revelation of the mystery kept secret for long ages. (Rom. 16: 25) In addition, he exhorts us to believe and totally place our trust in the God with the confirmed thought that all the promises we uphold are according to the gospel and the proclamation of Jesus Christ; the only intention of God for such manifestation is, as Paul underscores, *to bring about* (in us) *the obedience of faith.* (Rom. 16: 26) The cardinal virtues of faith, hope and charity are intrinsically intertwined and therefore if we neglect one of them in our application the other two lose their identity and vigor. This why Paul includes all three in his remarkable song about charity (1 Cor. 13) he does the same in his discussions about faith and hope. Hence when he writes about God's intention of 'bringing about the obedience of faith', he means we should relate to God's promise about Jesus in faith, hope and charity as well.

There are millions of God's children, like Mary, lived in history as rolemodels in living the 'obedience of faith'. God asks us today to do the same in our lives. Our life with God should be like that of Mary, who respected and loved all God's promises; despite of many hurdles and odds in her personal life and very sadly not even seeing the total fulfillment, she gave gifts to God in the form of rituals, religious practices and loving services like performing her role in the family and society sincerely and gladly. She totally surrendered to the Giver of the Gifts. Her unceasing heartbeat was: *Behold, I am the handmaid of the Lord. May it be done to me according to your word.*

As long as we live in this world we carry not only all fulfilled promises of the Lord in our lives but also many unfulfilled ones; The Christian act of waiting for God's promises fulfilled in every one of us demands heavy weight of faith, hope and charity. Let's wait with that weight for tomorrow of joy, peace and powerful coming of God to take care of our unfair lifesituation.

FOURTH WEEKEND-SPECIAL

Feast of Christmas

Only the poor in spirit eligible for
Christmas Gifts from God

When the angels went away from them to heaven, the shepherds said to one another, "Let us go, then, to Bethlehem to see this thing that has taken place, which the Lord has made known to us." So they went in haste and found Mary and Joseph, and the infant lying in the manger. When they saw this, they made known the message that had been told them about this child. All who heard it were amazed by what had been told them by the shepherds. And Mary kept all these things, reflecting on them in her heart. Then the shepherds returned, glorifying and praising God for all they had heard and seen, just as it had been told to them. (Lk. 2: 15-20)

On this happiest day of Christmas let us go into Bethlehem Crib and meditate on the messages of God to us through his marvelous deeds done on this Day 2000 years ago. In particular, let us go deeper into the messages he has delivered through the poor and rustic shepherds. These shepherds were the first evangelists to preach his Good News of Christ. Undoubtedly their choice to be first messengers was no accident; it was totally providential. Throughout the history of God's involvement with his people he God declared himself to be their Shepherd. Actually he preferred to be called Shepherd more than any other names because he knows the intrinsic and intense tender loving relationship existing between a shepherd and his sheep. He claimed himself so. He loved therefore to delegate his kingly power to humans to shepherd boy like David. He wanted shepherding should be the model for leaders of his Kingdom on earth. Very sadly those leaders whom he chose failed him in this regard. He took the whip in his hands and tried to straighten out. However he didn't see any change in humans' behavior. Hence when he decided to become Emmanuel in the form of Jesus to demonstrate his principle and policy of human behavior in his Kingdom, he was very choosy in bringing shepherds as his first visitors, admirers, and companions.

Those shepherds' routine tasks for centuries most clearly reflect God's own. Their daily life has been consisting of watching over their flocks; defending them from the prowling predator; leading them into good pasture; rescuing the lost and foolish stray; tending the wounds and bringing them safe home to the fold. That is what God willed that his Son Jesus should testify to, behaving as Good Shepherd in his life. He too demanded all his followers, especially those who are chosen to lead his flock, to perform their ministries in his Church as genuine shepherds as he is.

There are some more splendid messages God wanted to convey to us through these shepherds' activities at the birthday of Jesus. During the hours of Jesus' birth he, Mary and Joseph were alone except a few animals. At that moment, we find God seeking out simple people as their companions who were none other than those poor and humble shepherds. As one preacher commented, the reason for such choice by God is that they, living in poverty, would not be dismayed at finding the Messiah in a cave, wrapped in swaddling clothes. More than this, we can understand this move of God as to proven his prophecies being fulfilled at his Son's coming: *See, your savior comes! See, his reward is with him...And you shall be called "Cared For," "A City Not Forsaken."* (Is. 62: 11-12) Plus, *the people who walked in darkness have seen a great light...You have brought them abundant joy and great rejoicing.* (Is. 9: 1-2) By the coming of Christ, his Son, any humans, socially-neglected as the shepherds, will never again be despised as having a menial task, or as being vagabonds, A whole new dignity will descend upon them.

The next turning point in the story was, after seeing the 'historical scenario' with their own eyes exactly as they were told by the angels, Gospel says: *the shepherds returned, glorifying and praising God for all they had heard and seen, just as it had been told to them.* In other words, they started looking at the world they lived in with new eyes; they understood the real meaning of events that looked, though outwardly, ordinary. And finally, let us also remember what the shepherds did next: *They made known the message that had been told them about this child. All who heard it were amazed by what had been told them by the shepherds.*

As the shepherds were invited by God, we are chosen by Christ and his Church to be sent out into the world to share the awesome truth God brought through his Son. Jesus reveals himself to us in the midst of the ordinary incidents of each day. We have to be alert so as to discover Jesus in the simplicity of ordinary life and he wants us to proclaim him to the world only through our simple, and humble shepherding those whom God sent to us for our caregiving. *The shepherd should smell of the sheep* (Pope Francis).

....

FIFTH WEEKEND

Feast of Holy Family

Give respect and get respect

When the days were completed for their purification according to the Law of Moses, they took him up to Jerusalem to present him to the Lord...When they had fulfilled all the prescriptions of the law of the Lord, they returned to Galilee, to their own town of Nazareth. The child grew and became strong, filled with wisdom; and the favor of God was upon him. (Lk. 2: 22-40)

We, in Christianity, are fortunate enough being brought up from early childhood with many golden rules and resourceful sayings and proverbs which staying permanently in our hearts direct us to walk in right path. Not as old religions which proclaimed some hateful sayings such as 'tit for tat, an eye for an eye and a tooth for a tooth, our Teacher Jesus gave us many precious love-based sayings. One among them is: "Do to others whatever you would have them do to you." (Matt. 7: 12) In simple words we can say this: "Give respect and get respect." This is what we meditate today in the light of the Gospel passage and some other related Scriptural verses.

Paul gives a detailed description of the term 'respect': *Put on then, as God's chosen ones, holy and beloved, heartfelt compassion, kindness, humility, gentleness, and patience, bearing with one another and forgiving one another, if one has a grievance against another; as the Lord has forgiven you, so must you also do. And over all these put on love, that is, the bond of perfection.* (Col. 3: 12-14)

God expects us to give this kind of respect to our family members. Knowing the importance of such relationship he inserted it into his Commandments. *Honor your father and mother,* which is the fourth commandment of God, very surprisingly he placed it just after the three commandments that are to be followed in our relationship with God; and this being the first commandment among all the other commandments that are to be followed in our relationships with our neighbors. Expounding it the Teacher Sirach wrote: *God sets a father in honor over his children; and a mother's authority he confirms over her sons.* (Sir. 3: 2) He too talked about its endresults: *Those who honor their father atone for sins; they store up riches who respect their mother. Those who honor their father will have joy in their own children, and when they pray they are heard. Those who respect their father will live a long life.* (Sir. 3: 3-6)

We witness this sort of magnanimous and respectful behavior among the members of the Holy Family at Nazareth. Joseph who had a dream at midnight and admonished by the angel of God to flee to Egypt got up immediately, woke Mary and child Jesus who were in deep sleep, rose and took the child and his mother by night and departed for Egypt. Surely Joseph, being a person of justice, would have explained about his dream to Mary; so respecting each other they managed to adjust to the critical situations they were in. Though their son Jesus was longing to stay in his Father's House, as Luke confirms, *he went down with them and came to Nazareth, and was obedient to them.* (Lk. 2: 51)

Certainly this sort of behavior is not possible for any human person. Human nature always is prone to judge others; to put down others; to seek self-gratification; to compare and contrast with others. These are all human techniques for survival of the fittest. But this kind of self-oriented relationship never bring forth any peace or joy; rather only fight, war, separation and hatred. Therefore Scriptures recommend to us first and foremost to give respect to the Lord and then automatically the element of true respect will be present permanently in our human relationships.

As the Gospels underline, the entire family of Nazareth lived and moved on the basis of God's word and will. They were respecting God as their supreme Sovereign and Master. Mary and Joseph and Jesus had more than their share of problems and woes, especially that the very reason and heart of this family was Jesus, this bewildering son. They did everything for him. What is typical of the Holy Family was that in everything they sought God's will; this will be characteristic too for Jesus, God's will was to be his food and drink.

Most of the time, we lose our respect for each other, mostly at times of crisis-problems of job, sickness, weaknesses of individuals and so on. If we follow the footsteps of Holy Family Members, honoring God as our priority, respecting and honoring our family members, we will preserve and sustain our peace and joy. Let us never forget: For a Christian, the Golden Rule is a three-way process: *Give respect to God and automatically the mutual respect among the members of the family starts existing.*

....

FIFTH WEEKEND-SPECIAL

New Year Day/Feast of Mary, Mother of God
Love our life as it is now

> *But when the fullness of time had come,*
> *God sent his Son, born of a woman, born*
> *under the law, to ransom those under the*
> *law, so that we might receive adoption.*
> *As proof that you are children, God sent*
> *the spirit of his Son into our hearts, crying*
> *out, "Abba, Father!" So you are no longer*
> *a slave but a child, and if a child then also*
> *an heir, through God.* (Gal. 4: 4-7)

It is said, when a young man asked 'what should I do to be happy for life?' a sage told: 'Just love your life as it is.' Though it sounds good, the answer seems unsatisfactory for many of us as we begin the New Year. When we reflect over our life, lived and experienced over the past years, especially last year, though it might have been somewhat productive and creative, perhaps more sentimental and pleasurable and in addition a little bit exciting, for most of us life has seemed very vulnerable, demanding, risky, unfair, and unpredictable. Hence our mind bubbles with question: Have I to love such a life, which is a blending of these ups and downs, negative and positive and a life, which is transient and temporary? However the Spirit asks us today to fathom the deep truth contained in the answer of the wise man and meditate on it.

Let us go back again to the sage's answer: To make ourselves happy we have to love the life not the life as it looks like but as it is. Many a time human life is misinterpreted and misunderstood by all of us. This is why we do not truly love it. We pretend to love it. But as Christians through the revelation we got from God through Jesus Christ the human life is not as it appears. First of all, our life in this world is a gift from God. We are his creatures, created in the likeness and image of the Word, which existed already in the beginning. We have been predestined by the Triune God to enter into relationship with him and stay with him eternally. We, as his special creations, possess abundant gifts and resources for our living in this world to know, to love and to serve him.

In order to safeguard us, nourish us and make us move forward fearlessly and happily at every step of our life, he offered us abundant and powerful promises of blessings; he even delegated his power of blessing to his elders: *The LORD bless you and keep you! The LORD let his face shine upon you, and be gracious to you! The LORD look upon you kindly and give you peace! So shall they invoke my name upon the Israelites, and I will bless them."* (Num. 6: 22-27)

Unfortunately such a beautiful and gratified and blessed life has been utterly damaged by our frequent and stupid disobedience. Sin spoiled the image of the 'amazing image' in us. So God sent his beloved Son to us to heal that image of God in us and redeem it to its original status of beauty, power, wisdom and godliness. Our life has been again renovated by our covenant with the Son of God, Jesus. Paul gratefully testifies to the immeasurable grace we have received through the Son's coming: *God sent the spirit of his Son into our hearts, crying out, "Abba, Father!" So you are no longer a slave but a child, and if a child then also an heir, through God.* In one of the Church Morning

Prayers we recite as its concluding prayer: *Lord God, you restore our human nature to a dignity higher than you gave it at creation.*

Plus, the life we live today is truly face-lifted and supported by so many sources of grace in the Church: graces from sacraments, from the Scriptures, from the traditions, from the entire Body of Christ and from the communion of saints, especially our connections with the Mother of Jesus, Mary our Mother. She has offered her womb as a spotless abode for the Word becoming flesh; she has become our rolemodel in how we should treat our life both its past and future. We find her not throwing the past as useless, as some people advise us; rather as we hear in Luke's Gospel, she treasured all the events of the past and their messages in her heart and continually pondered over them. This does not mean she was regretting and killing herself by self-pitying and depressed, rather she was always glorifying God for his past deeds (Ref. Lk. 1: 46-55): *The Mighty One has done great things for me, and holy is his name. His mercy is from age to age to those who fear him.* And about her dream of future she sang: B*ehold, from now on will all ages call me blessed.*

We are not to be depressed discovering in life the fact of *'I am not ok and you are not ok.'* We should rather be fully convinced our life is worth living because Jesus is ok. Also, in our journey of life we have around me, God as a Father, Jesus as a Brother, Sprit as a Lover and Mary as a Mother. W*hen all of them are with us who will be against us?* So let us love our life as it is as of today.

....

SIXTH WEEKEND

Epiphany of the Lord

Christian life is as if moving-in-settlement

If, as I suppose, you have heard of the stewardship of God's grace that was given to me for your benefit, namely, that the mystery was made known to me by revelation...which was not made known to human beings in other generations as it has now been revealed to his holy apostles and prophets by the Spirit, that the Gentiles are coheirs, members of the same body, and copartners in the promise in Christ Jesus through the gospel. (Eph. 3: 2-6)

One of the mind-boggling dimensions of God's mystery, which has been finally revealed in Jesus' coming, is that a life lived with Jesus in this world is a thrilling experience of 'move-in-settlement.' This is what the Spirit invites us today to meditate and pray over on the feast day of Epiphany when God's mysteries ushered in a new phase.

As we hear from Paul, God the Creator slowly and gradually revealed his identity and nature throughout the Ages and generations of mankind. The core of his revelation was that Christianity puts before us God as the complete and total settlement of our human life on earth. Our life started from him and will find its end in him also. Paul writes: ...*it is he who gives to everyone life and breath and everything...For In him we live and move and have our being...* (Acts 17: 25-28) God is the biggest dream of our life toward which we all travel in this world. We are not entirely wanderers or entirely settlers. We have settled in God already but we to move toward him and with him. We accept fully that we are truly wanderers and pilgrims walking and running toward our eternal settlement, namely God. All other settlements we have in this world as tents, religions, homes, societies, and countries are merely temporary ones on the road. They have to be experienced and enjoyed as 'move-in-settlement' of mobile homes and trailer houses.

In continuation of Paul's contention we read that 'when the fullness of time came', God revealed the stunning climatic dimension of his mystery that while our life must be settled with him, we too must be settled in Jesus of Nazareth who is the Way, the Truth and the Light as prophesied in OT: *Arise! Shine, for your light has come, the glory of the LORD has dawned upon you...Upon you the LORD will dawn, and over you his glory will be seen. Nations shall walk by your light...* (Is. 60: 1-3)

The Epiphany story, told by Matthew, proclaims that the three Magi were settled in the historical fact of the birth of Emmanuel, God-with-us who was none other than Jesus who was the would-be King of the Jews and the universe. This they founded out by their intense reading and interpreting of the available Scriptures and Traditions. *But you, Bethlehem-Ephrathaha, least among the clans of Judah, from you shall come forth for me one who is to be ruler in Israel; whose origin is from of old, from ancient times...He shall take his place as shepherd by the strength of the LORD, by the majestic name of the LORD, his God.* (Mic. 5: 1-3) Being convinced of the amazing event, they began their journey of their goal-finding; they traveled through deserts and many obstacles to reach this grand goal.

They too settled well with the 'means' God bestowed to them to reach Jesus. That was the 'star'. But the story tells us in between they missed it; perhaps the Supreme God would not have relished their effort of getting some help from certain criminal-minded persons like Herod; however being merciful to them, God permitted his star appear again to them and lead them to the place where the Child Jesus was with Mary and Joseph.

There are too many stars moving in the sky glittering. There are too many means at our assistance in searching and finding our eternal Goal, God. But we have to choose proper ones and settle with them. They are different religions, different denominations, different authorities, preachers, teachers and prophets in media and Internet. We have to choose the appropriate stars for us and take them as our means to realize our Dream. The Star that took the wise men to the Baby Jesus is a symbol of his Body, the Church, which we all believe will take us to our settlement. It is the sacrament of love and God. Sometimes we may not see its light fully because of the unholy leaders and fellow Christians. But if we are really and sincerely settled in that means surely it will come back and lead us to the goal and settle us in the crib of peace, love, joy and fulfillment.

SEVENTH WEEKEND

Second Sunday in ordinary time

Come, let us go and see his whereabouts and howabouts

> *The next day John was there again with two
> of his disciples, and as he watched Jesus
> walk by, he said, "Behold, the Lamb of God."
> The two disciples heard what he said and
> followed Jesus. Jesus turned and saw them
> following him and said to them, "What are
> you looking for?" They said to him, "Rabbi"
> (which translated means Teacher), "where
> are you staying?" He said to them, "Come,
> and you will see." So they went and saw
> where he was staying, and they stayed
> with him that day. It was about four in the
> afternoon. Andrew, the brother of Simon
> Peter, was one of the two who heard John
> and followed Jesus. He first found his own
> brother Simon and told him, "We have found
> the Messiah" (which is translated Anointed).
> Then he brought him to Jesus. Jesus looked
> at him and said, "You are Simon the son of
> John; you will be called Cephas" (which is
> translated Peter). (Jn. 1: 35-42)*

When I read the inviting words of Jesus 'Come and See'
in today's Gospel picked up for this weekend meditation I
am reminded of the invitations we hear and read in many
TV or social media ad jingles to allure us to go and buy
their products or their values and thoughts.

Unquestionably Jesus didn't intend that way of promoting his project or any of his product as consumeristic promotion tactics. When he invited the seekers with these words he was very faithful to their references God had used in his Scriptures whenever he invited humans in different ways to have home with him. For example, God invited Samuel for his purpose, though he was not matured enough to understand that it was God's calling, but at the advice his mentor Eli, he responded to the Lord in surrender and obedience *Speak, for your servant is listening.* (1 Sam. 3: 3-19)

In the New Testament Books we are told this was the customary way for Jesus. From the moment of his coming into the world upto his death, he continuously responded to God the Father's invitation: *"Sacrifice and offering you did not desire, but a body you prepared for me; holocausts and sin offerings you took no delight in. Then I said, 'As is written of me in the scroll. Behold, I come to do your will, O God.'"* (Heb. 10: 5-7) He behaved like an obedient and innocent lamb, even ready to be taken to slaughterhouse. Surprisingly John the Baptizer introduced Jesus to his would-be disciples at the start of his public ministry saying: *Behold, the Lamb of God.*

This outstanding Lamb of God was fully aware of God's appreciation of his childlike obedience by hearing God's attestation from heaven that: *This is my beloved Son, with whom I am well pleased.* Therefore he demanded the same kind of obedient lamblike attitude from his disciples. When he invited his new disciples with the words 'come and see' that is what he reminded: "I am sent by the Father to fill you with the same blessings I am filled. For that first and foremost you have to come out of your selfish darkened tombs of sins, getting out of your slumbers; don't remain lying there as couch potatoes. Come to me."

The word 'see' he used pointed out very clearly that those who seek his values and blessings must see through his very life. "Watch keenly, probe intelligently and absorb and uphold truth, nothing but the truth. This is because Jesus is the way, the truth and the life. Everything you seek for is found in him."

Jesus goes on inviting all humans, especially the true seekers of genuine life proposing 'Come and See.' It is a factual truth most of us are willing to go to him, sit with him at his feet or even walk with him wherever he goes; but very sadly not all of us find it easy to see the truthful facts of his life. When we closely watch him and his life we can see what the true reality of life; what it means to be child of God; how a man or woman can rise up from the dunghill and downhill of human life; where and when we can encounter him very intimately; what is our Creator's intention when he created us in our mother's womb and surely what an admirable body we possess; we too get in touch with the new stature we have been bestowed with by the grace of God in Jesus. Paul loudly proclaims this unfathomable position we, as Christians are settled in: *Do you not know that your bodies are members of Christ? ...But whoever is joined to the Lord becomes one spirit with him... Do you not know that your body is a temple of the Holy Spirit within you, whom you have from God, and that you are not your own? For you have been purchased at a price. Therefore, glorify God in your body.* (1 Cor. 6: 15-20)

Come, let us accept his invitation to "come and see" what he has to offer us and what he is asking of us. Let us ask Jesus to show us where he lives, who he is, and what he expects of us.

EIGHTH WEEKEND

Third Sunday in ordinary time

To err is human; to repent divine; but to persist devilish

> *After John had been arrested, Jesus came to Galilee proclaiming the gospel of God: "This is the time of fulfillment. The kingdom of God is at hand. Repent, and believe in the gospel." As he passed by the Sea of Galilee, he saw Simon and his brother Andrew casting their nets into the sea; they were fishermen. Jesus said to them, "Come after me, and I will make you fishers of men." Then they abandoned their nets and followed him. He walked along a little farther and saw James, the son of Zebedee, and his brother John. They too were in a boat mending their nets. Then he called them. So they left their father Zebedee in the boat along with the hired men and followed him.* (Mk. 1: 14-20)

I think the most central theme and message of our Religion and surely of the entire Bible is that human life in this world is short-lived and therefore every one of us must repent. This was the theme of the first but most bewildering homily of Jesus. The Spirit summons us to reflect on it in prayer. In OT we see God sending his messengers to his people with the one and only message of repenting as he did in Jonah's life. Jesus knew the mind of his Father so he even started his public ministry with that message: *This is the time of fulfillment. The kingdom of God is at hand. Repent, and believe in the gospel.* Though it was a very short one, it contained superb and brilliant exhortation; unfortunately it was a message perennially hurting all of us; but being the one and only Word that came out of his Father's heart, he knew his Father's mind in this regard.

We notice how logically and wisely Jesus put forth his message of repenting. First he starts with a positive reason for repenting: *This is the time of fulfillment.* By this he points out that "you should grow adults; never play your life a childish game; your fulfillment in life depends on some other thing; be matured and think matured and do matured." The second thought in his preaching is certain positive thinking about human life. He adds: *The kingdom of God is at hand.* In other words he means that "you are not alone; God is with you; He is Emmanuel. So don't be afraid of your own limitations and weaknesses. Join together as a group of my disciples; and I will be with you till the end of the time." The third part of his preaching is *repent.* That means he expects us to <u>recognize</u> our wrongdoings <u>and</u> be <u>sorry</u> <u>about</u> them; to <u>feel</u> <u>regret</u> <u>about</u> a <u>sin</u> or <u>past</u> <u>actions</u> <u>and</u> <u>change</u> <u>our</u> <u>ways</u> or <u>habits</u>.

From the Scriptures we can discover the full meaning of Jesus' admonition. Repenting means that we should *come out of* living only on our past spiritual and religious accomplishments. We need to be growing in our salvation daily. There is no place in this life where we can be content to say, "I have arrived; I'm mature enough." Jesus wants us to repent of our self-satisfaction: In the Book of Revelation Jesus says: *"You say, 'I am rich; I have acquired wealth and do not need a thing.' But you do not realize that you are wretched, pitiful, poor, blind and naked."* (Rev. 3: 19) We must never be lying satisfied with our status quo.

According to Jesus repenting includes of our growing lukewarm and complacent and we should rise up and change our mind-setup, either detouring or taking U-turn start again another new life. Being tepid and self-righteous is perhaps the most dangerous mindset for a Christian. In the Book of Revelation we read Jesus telling us: *"I know your works; I know that you are neither cold nor hot. I wish you were either cold or hot. So, because you are lukewarm, neither hot nor cold, I will spit you out of my mouth."* (Rev. 3: 15-16)

There is one more element contained in Jesus short homily and that is *believe in the gospel.* He never left us with no other tips for what we should do after our repenting. He says we should accept all his Gospel values of justice, forgiveness, love, truth and peace and start living and abiding by them. Then he promises that we will reach our fulfillment as our human spirit longs for in this world and the world to come.

As we read in OT that the Ninevites, both the Israelites and pagans, responded to Jonah's call for repenting, we should do the maximum possible with an urgency; we should follow the footsteps of the first disciples who responded promptly to Jesus' call to follow him and his preaching; they even abandoned their nets; their family and friends for the sake of eternal Kingdom. In this 'repenting' matter, Apostle Paul urges us pointing out, *I tell you, brothers, the time is running out...act using the world as not using it fully. For the world in its present form is passing away.* (1 Cor 7: 29-31) The spirit of Jesus exhorts us to begin our detour or U-turn today toward Jesus' Gospel, choosing the Kingdom of God as number one priority in life.

NINETH WEEKEND

Fourth Sunday in ordinary time
The restored and enhanced human authority

> *Then they came to Capernaum, and on the Sabbath he entered the synagogue and taught. The people were astonished at his teaching, for he taught them as one having authority and not as the scribes. In their synagogue was a man with an unclean spirit; he cried out, "What have you to do with us, Jesus of Nazareth? Have you come to destroy us? I know who you are— the Holy One of God!" Jesus rebuked him and said, "Quiet! Come out of him!" The unclean spirit convulsed him and with a loud cry came out of him. All were amazed and asked one another, "What is this? A new teaching with authority. He commands even the unclean spirits and they obey him." (Mk. 1: 21-28)*

Our Scriptures, being inspired by God's Spirit, make us understand the supremacy and sublime sovereignty and immense power of God among his creations. At the same time they too offer very reasonable arguments for the human authorities we hold in the family, in the society. It is about this Biblical truth we are called by the Spirit to meditate today.

All great leaders in history try to articulate their plans as promises about how they would be using their power and authority for the future continuation of their mission or work for the welfare of the society. Very sadly most of these leaders-political and religious as well, fail in their promises. God knows the limitation of humans in this regard. Hence, through his Son he offered some guidelines for how to apply our God-given power and execute it.

We read in the Gospel about Jesus' handling of his authority. *The people were astonished at his teaching, for he taught them as one having authority.* The words he uttered were not empty ones; they had power even to drive out the evil spirits; his words got powerful and forceful because he made the wavelength of his relationship with his Father very intimate. Unquestionably Jesus was the realization of God's promise through Moses: *I will raise up for them a prophet like you from among their kindred, and will put my words into the mouth of the prophet; the prophet shall tell them all that I command.* (Deut. 18: 18) Nonetheless we find in Jesus' life a sincere and faithful commitment to God's expectations of his prophets. He knew God demanded from his messengers to speak in his name only his words and not theirs. But if the prophets didn't obey as he willed, he cursed them. *If a prophet presumes to speak a word in my name that I have not commanded, or speaks in the name of other gods, that prophet shall die.* (Deut. 18: 20)

Jesus delivered not merely his authoritarian speech, but they were accompanied with deeds of exemplary life, deeds of healing others and surely concentration on targeting to cast out evil spirits from others. People therefore testified on this saying to each other, *what is this? A new teaching with authority. He commands even the unclean spirits and they obey him.*

All of us, in our families, communities and around the globe, are possessed at one time or another by various types of evil spirits: jealousy, pride, anger, grudge, partiality, revenge, laziness and many others. To expel these from our hearts, we still need the powerful and authentic words of Jesus which surely transmitted from his committed disciples.

When we are healed by his authoritative words we become stronger and more powerful. We can speak and act as wounded healers. We will be chosen as God's prophets in our limited milieu and either he would be glad to bless us if we in our executing power of ordering or disciplining speak the balanced truth as God proposes to us and never rely on human authorities or power-centers' influences; or he would punish us as he has cautioned through Moses.

When we are attuned to the good Spirit of God, we can surely discern the difference between good and unclean spirits. As Jesus we may be bestowed with spiritual power to cast out those demons around us. Nonetheless, we know we cannot all the time turn out to be miracle workers of healing the sick. Jesus tells us we have power to make our people whole and wholesome; that means, he wants us to make everyone around us become like him, that is, completely human, good and whole persons, not only physically but in every way. If we want to enrich our prophetic power, as Paul advises, we must try our best to be free of worldly anxieties, instead we must be spiritually anxious about the things of the Lord, and how we may please the Lord with no distraction whatsoever. (Ref. 1 Cor. 7: 32-35)

TENTH WEEKEND

Fifth Sunday in ordinary time

How to make our burden light and our yoke easy?

> *Is not life on earth a drudgery, its days
> like those of a hireling? Like a slave who
> longs for the shade, a hireling who waits
> for wages. So I have been assigned
> months of futility, and troubled nights
> have been counted off for me. When I
> lie down I say, "When shall I arise?"
> then the night drags on; I am filled with
> restlessness until the dawn...My days are
> swifter than a weaver's shuttle; they come
> to an end without hope. Remember that
> my life is like the wind; my eye will not see
> happiness again.* (Job 7: 1-7)

Many times I am approached by my parishioners as their spiritual mentor exposing their life's burdens and drudgeries. Whenever I hear those groanings, my inner spirit reminds me of the Scriptural passage we are summoned today to meditate on.

All humans born in this world-holy or unholy, weak or strong, prudent or imprudent, are undergoing such miseries and desolations. Suffering will always remain a scandal or at least a mystery. We can try to act as if it doesn't affect us, denying that it exists or running away from it, but there is no real escape from it for a Christian. It is written into our existence since Christ died on the cross. Though we will never understand it fully, we know in the light of God's revelations that all human sufferings are meaningful and saving, if we would bear them as God expects us.

The first and foremost advice God offers us is first to listen to his Son's counsels on this matter; and try to spend each and every day of our life as Jesus has spent the last three years of his life. Jesus the best of his exhortations on pulling through our life's drudgeries is: *"Come to me, all you who labor and are burdened, and I will give you rest. Take my yoke upon you and learn from me, for I am meek and humble of heart; and you will find rest for yourselves. For my yoke is easy, and my burden light."* (Matt. 11: 28-30)

We know well the nature of his 'yoke'. He was literally a vagabond walking under the Palestinian hot sun; hilly and deserted locations; thickly populated villages and towns; through the dusty roads, and in the midst of many of his enemies; foxes had holes but he had no room to lay down and take rest; plus with no big bag of savings accounts; he and his disciples were always waiting for somebody to invite them for dinner. He was literally like one of us in undergoing life's burdens worse than that of Job. However Jesus never lost his peace, serenity, dignity, hope and joy. He left with us a paradigm of how we should live day today life of pains and sufferings. The daily chores of Jesus is marked by his three primary preoccupations:

First, he immersed himself in prayer with his heavenly Father. Mark writes, *'rising very early before dawn, he left and went off to a deserted place, where he prayed'.* (Mk. 1: 35) There are references in the Gospels about Jesus praying throughout the night. In between those prayer hours, Jesus never missed before and after any event or scheduled programs of healing and doing good people.

Thus Jesus started every activity from prayer and ends it in prayer. Jesus preferred to stay among the people throughout the day. In the Gospels we hear that when it was evening, after sunset, needy people brought to him all who were ill or possessed by demons. The whole town was gathered at the door. ((Mk. 1: 32-34) All kinds of people, especially those who were downtrodden and poor, reached him out and he extended his healing and loving hands to them with no discrimination whatsoever.

Following the Master's footsteps, his disciples, like Paul, would untiringly take the burdens of others and alleviate their maladies. The great Apostle asserts: *I have made myself a slave to all so as to win over as many as possible. To the weak I became weak, to win over the weak. I have become all things to all, to save at least some.* (1 Cor. 9: 19-22) Followers of Christ understood well how to make the life's burden light by holding one conviction of sharing the blessings of the Gospel they proclaim. (1 Cor. 9: 23)

We are like Job at one time or another...miserable, depressed, negative, discouraged, desolate, and gloomy. But Jesus gives us his very life as for our example to be followed and change the whole dark and negative aspect of sufferings. Plus we learn from Jesus that the brokenhearted people should not stop upholding this positive attitude in their sufferings but also they should encourage others in their suffering times as well. There are many wounded in spirit waiting for us to heal them from their pains and sorrows and liberate them from the demons that plague them. These wounded people may be in our homes, neighborhoods, and in and around the globe. We must be ready to go beyond our likes and dislikes. That is the only way for a Christian to be a merrygoer and a jollygoodfellow even in pains, sufferings and perils.

ELEVENTH WEEKEND

Sixth Sunday in ordinary time

Condescend toward the needy as Jesus to us

A leper came to him [and kneeling down] begged him and said, "If you wish, you can make me clean." Moved with pity, he stretched out his hand, touched him, and said to him, "I do will it. Be made clean." The leprosy left him immediately, and he was made clean. Then, warning him sternly, he dismissed him at once. Then he said to him, "See that you tell no one anything, but go, show yourself to the priest and offer for your cleansing what Moses prescribed; that will be proof for them." The man went away and began to publicize the whole matter. He spread the report abroad so that it was impossible for Jesus to enter a town openly. He remained outside in deserted places, and people kept coming to him from everywhere. (Mk. 1: 40-45)

The Spirit of the Lord, through the Gospel passage, bids us today to meditate on the lovely nature of Jesus' encounters in our daily life. In the Gospel event we notice a miraculous contact happening between Jesus and a human person afflicted by an incurable and abominable disease.

The actions of the sick person in his encounter with Jesus are remarkable. He kneels down bending himself with respect and humility. With the sense of trust he beggs

Jesus to cure him. He too communicates to Jesus what is bothering in his mind, namely he is unclean. We can notice in his communication certain faith and recognition of Jesus' independence and dignity. *If you wish, you can make me clean.*

As for the actions of the other party, Jesus, in this lovely event are very awesome. He reacts, acts and reciprocates immediately to his lover: First he was moved with pity. The word pity, in its genuine meaning, points out one's feeling for others, particularly sentiments of sadness or sorrow. Many people, when they help the needy, hold certain voluptuous agenda behind. But with Jesus his only attention was in reciprocating the needy person with sincere love. He stretches out his hand and touches his needy partner. In human communications, gestures (body languages) are better than mere words. Being fully aware of our human capacity Jesus shows his love to the needy as his Father does in his love affairs with humanity only in actions.

Finally Jesus offers a beautiful and amazing gift to his love-partner, the leper. Using his power of the Word becoming flesh, he cures the sick person by uttering the miraculous words: *I do will it. Be made clean.* The leper was then and there made clean.

And when we observe what happened in the life of the healed leper, we find him unmistakably obeying Jesus' first demand. He would have gone and showed himself to the clergy of the Temple and offered the due offerings prescribed by Moses. He would have got his license to go out of his ghetto and walk freely in open places with the crowd. However he was so taken up and overwhelmed with joy, gratitude and love for Jesus, the one who healed him, that he overlooked Jesus' second demand of not publicizing the happenings between him and Jesus. Gospel says that he publicized what had happened to him in his historical contact with Jesus and showing everybody his license of being cleansed by the great healer, Jesus.

By this miraculous deed, Jesus, besides demonstrating his compassionate nature of encountering with any needy humans, brings home to his disciples that God in him never denies his friendship to all humans, even they be depreciated or excluded by other fellow humans. In Jewish culture the disease of leprosy was considered very abhorring and abominable one given by God as a curse or punishment for sins. (Deut. 13: 44-46) Though Godly justice and mercy had been misused in this way, the Spirit takes it as a prophetic warning to our own unjust misdeeds. Because of abused cultures, many may suspect us and throw us out of their nearness as scums and craps and personification of evils; but if we preserve our right judgment about God's love in humility, he will surely bend himself down to us. We should never be put down or discouraged by others' remarks and attitudes and behaviors against us. We should rather march on with Jesus every moment of our life. He will never let us down.

Jesus, by his loving interactions with us recreates us, renews us, molds us, shapes us, grooms us, heals us, fills us and surely in a mysterious and stunning way, he begins to use us for his glory and for humans' eternal life. Being grateful of all his breathtaking encounters, let us also go around the world proclaiming those deeds in the form of our own condescending charitable deeds to the needy. Being healed by the merciful encounter of Jesus, Apostle Paul imitated his Master in all possible ways. Whether he ate or drank, or whatever he did, he did everything for the glory of God. We too must do the same and consequently we can daringly say to our friends as Paul does: *be imitators of me, as I am of Christ.* (1 Cor. 11: 1)

TWELFTH WEEKEND

First Sunday of Lent

Settled in the Covenantal Ark of the Spirit we can win

> *At once the Spirit drove him out into the desert, and he remained in the desert for forty days, tempted by Satan. He was among wild beasts, and the angels ministered to him. After John had been arrested, Jesus came to Galilee proclaiming the gospel of God: "This is the time of fulfillment. The kingdom of God is at hand. Repent, and believe in the gospel."* (Mk. 1: 12-15)

Our life in this world is a battlefield between God and Satan. Today the Spirit asks us to get some tips for winning the battle as we meditate on one of the warfare-events happened in Jesus' life, namely his forty days experience in the desert. Mark writes that *he remained in the desert for forty days, tempted by Satan.*

During those days, besides feeling the absence of relationships, Jesus would have been feeling lonely, gazing out at a wilderness and its emptiness and surely suffering out of its inclement climate. Together with such evils the devil joint company to give him hard time. As Biblical scholars say, this story of three temptations is the summary of Jesus' entire life which was an intense warfare between the Good and the Evil.

Through Mark's Gospel passage the Spirit ascertains to us that Jesus passed through his life's warfare successfully as he went through the forty-day struggles against Satan. As the result of his remarkable success, as we read in Hebrews, he was made a rolemodel, a sympathizer, and even the source of eternal salvation to all humans. (Ref. Heb. 4: 15-16; 5: 1-10) Like Jesus we too are tempted, we are tossed around, we are broken to pieces, we are wounded, we are crucified, we are misunderstood, we are diagnosed with different kinds of unheard, brand new diseases, and we are struck down by natural calamities and other social and political problems as wars and terrorism. Besides all these we as Christians join with Christ to fight against Satan who deploys his legion of evil spirits that are inside and outside of us. In order to cope with this hectic lifesituation and to live in peace and joy in the midst of problems and temptations, to win our life's battle the Spirit of God today suggests some ammunitions.

As Jesus and God's messengers stayed put to the movement of God's Spirit we are told to choose willingly and remain faithfully in the Ark of God's covenantal love and Spirit wherever our life situates us. As Noah and his family were saved from deluge by staying in the Ark (Ref. Gen. 9: 8-15), we will be saved and reach our victory. Our God is proclaimed in the Bible as the guaranteed covenant partner to humans. He always desired to build his relationship with us through a covenant of love. The OT Ark of the covenant is the symbol of such love-based relationship. As Jesus was always led by the Spirit even to the desert-encounters, the Spirit wants us to be led to enter freely and stay firmly inside the Ark, Jesus has built for us, the Church. (Ref. 1 Pet. 3: 18-22)

The Spirit summons us also to believe in the Gospel of Jesus and follow it faithfully. As soon as Jesus came out of the desert and hidden life to the public he preached the first sermon on the belief in the Gospel. According to his Gospel the kingdom of victory is sure and within reach. It is also within us. Especially after our Baptism the kingdom established by God within us at our creation has become solid and enterprising. We turn out to be the moving Ark built on God's covenant in which we offer accommodation, shelter and if need be our very life. Thus we should feel fulfilled and satisfied at every moment of our Christian life. We shouldn't be doubtful of the authenticity of the Gospel we believe or the Ark we stay in. The Gospel of Jesus is the one and only Gospel of fulfillment in human life and the Church of Jesus is the only place which can be called 'the Ark of fulfillment.' It is where we can find our safety and security plus great strength to win our battle against evils.

Today's world where we are led in to reside is a sort of desert milieu worse than Jesus was led into by the Spirit. We are shattered by war, poverty, homelessness, violence, unemployment, famine, flood, greed, apathy, crime, global warming, flash mob vandalism, an out-of-touch hierarchy, child abuse, spousal abuse, elder abuse, earthquakes, and more. Undoubtedly our life is a warfare. It is a never-ending struggle and tension. Simply we are torn between bad and good spirits. Some of us put the blame for this 'broken world' on 'those people' as scapegoats. However we should keep in mind that just as the sins of a society begin with one individual, so the renewal and transformation of society begins with each individual. Therefore let us constantly repeat the old cry: *Lord, send a revival, and let it begin with me.*

THIRTEENTH WEEKEND

Second Sunday of Lent
Walking in the Land of the Living

*I shall walk before the LORD in the land
of the living. I kept faith, even when I said,
"I am greatly afflicted!"...How can I repay
the LORD for all the great good done for
me? I will raise the cup of salvation and
call on the name of the LORD. I will pay
my vows to the LORD in the presence
of all his people...LORD, I am your
servant, your servant, the child of your
maidservant; you have loosed my bonds.
I will offer a sacrifice of praise and call on
the name of the LORD...* (Ps. 116: 9-19)

By all the poets and authors, especially by Judeo-
Biblical Writers, Christian authors and teachers, human life
is considered as a journey from womb to tomb. Every town
has got two graveyards: One is literally a yard outside the
town where dead are buried; the other unfortunately inside
the town many live and move as if dead humans walking
with no sap in life. The Spirit calls us today, through Psalm
116 and with some inspiring Scriptural passages, to know
more about this journey and the way to walk through it
energetically and fruitfully.

The Psalmist vows that he will walk in the land of the
living. He means it is a land where his relatives and friends
including their cattle live together joyfully and productively
as a bonded community and as a nation where humans live

and move consciously as the people of God. However we are tempted to ask ourselves 'how can we go through this life, the valley of tears and darkness?' The Spirit beckons us to see through and learn from the lives of Abraham and Jesus and his Apostles.

The main lesson from these great persons' lives is that our God is a 'living Lover' to them and demands our covenantal response to his love. When God called Abraham (Ref. Gen. 22: 1-18), the great patriarch immediately responded, "Here I am." Then God asked the unthinkable! Abraham's enthusiasm for doing God's will was put to the ultimate test. Nevertheless, when God called a second time, the answer was the same: "Here I am." Even though he knew what was being asked of him, Abraham was able to maintain his fervor, and he was willing to surrender to an action that appeared to quash his hopes for the future.

Jesus on his part, behaved like Isaac and obeyed as his Father asked to do: He emptied himself, came down from heaven, took the form of a slave and underwent ignominious death. At the onset of his journey of redeeming mankind Jesus willingly replied to his Father, "Here am I Lord, I am ready to do your will." He was very firm in his answer and lived upto it till his last breath. Throughout his journey in this world Jesus went through terrible trials and tribulations. Yet he accepted them and consciously lived as an obedient Son of God. For such a remarkable fervor and faith God *elevated him to sit at his right hand.*

We are fortunate enough to be disciples of Jesus, who, through his life and words showed us the way of surviving and succeeding in the land of the living. As he got a remarkable recognition from his Father he longed his disciples too would receive such appreciation. He constantly advised them to take up their own crosses and follow him. They truly accepted it first as they started their journey of life but during it they occasionally, but some very frequently, drifted away from his values. He tried to convert them into his side and strengthen them in their decipleship by many miraculous deeds, personal discussions, and even through showing a little glimpse of his true divine personality on the hilltop of Tabor (Mk. 9: 2-10)

Indeed like any other humans, they were struggling to cope with the 'faith-demand' from heaven as shared by Jesus. We know, after being empowered by the risen Lord's Spirit, they were renovated. They truly walked in the land of the living despite dungeon and fire. They smiled with interior joy to suffer for the sake of Jesus. The world would have maligned them saying they were scum, foolish and spectacle to the world. But, because of their staunch faith they never let themselves downspirited. Their hearts were constantly uttering what Paul writes: *If God is for us, who can be against us? God who did not spare his own Son but handed him over for us all-how will he not also give us everything else along with him?* (Rom. 8: 31b-32)

We had started our journey with Christ in Baptism. If we browse our life-journal, we would realize that most of us started it well, but on the way we have failed when we faced our life's challenges and when things we handle become too difficult. The spirit asks us: Are we today walking in front of God and in the land of the living? Or still lying in the graveside of the dead humans? A legitimate question indeed!

FOURTEENTH WEEKEND

Third Sunday of Lent

The right scale for right judgement about us

Since the Passover of the Jews was near, Jesus went up to Jerusalem. He found in the temple area those who sold oxen, sheep, and doves, as well as the money-changers seated there. He made a whip out of cords and drove them all out of the temple area, with the sheep and oxen, and spilled the coins of the money-changers and overturned their tables, and to those who sold doves he said, "Take these out of here, and stop making my Father's house a marketplace." His disciples recalled the words of scripture, "Zeal for your house will consume me." At this the Jews answered and said to him, "What sign can you show us for doing this?" Jesus answered and said to them, "Destroy this temple and in three days I will raise it up"...While he was in Jerusalem for the feast of Passover, many began to believe in his name when they saw the signs he was doing. But Jesus would not trust himself to them because he knew them all, and did not need anyone to testify about human nature. He himself understood it well. (Jn. 2: 13-25)

Very frequently people around judge us but most of the times we know they are wrong because they don't use proper yardstick or criterion in their half-baked judicial enterprise. The same is true also about our own judgments of our life. Most of the times we are incorrect in our judgments because we use improper yardsticks, and even in a pharisaical way we interpret those yardsticks according to our convenience. Today Jesus' Spirit calls us to revisiting our way of judging ourselves and pondering over some appropriate benchmarks, through which we can honestly reach right conclusion about our life.

We often say to ourselves 'am I leading a proper life pleasing to God?' The question arises from the way we have been brought up, formed and groomed, nourished and developed by the society which is disorderly, unjust, and dishonest in so many ways, especially making every human, every nature's creations as mere commodities for buying and selling and worth for nothing besides. Even the name of God, his religion, his Scriptures, his Traditions, and all that had been erected as his house of prayer and divine interactions. A sample of such millions of commercial brutalities is seen in the Gospel event of Jesus cleaning up God's Temple by whips of anger and zeal. We hear him shouting out those sellers: *"Take these out of here, and stop making my Father's house a marketplace."*

As God is good and holy, he expects his creation too to be so. Anything that goes beyond or below his will must be either riveted or punished by him. God knew what is human and what is in human as Jesus understood: *Jesus would not trust himself to them because he knew them all, and did not need anyone to testify about human nature. He himself understood it well.* Hence in order to safeguard the holiness and goodness of his creations, especially human creatures, God proposed his laws as our best touchstones for assessing our handling of life. Those are the Ten Commandments he handed down through Moses to his chosen ones and those who came after. (Ref. Ex. 20: 1-17) These laws are to govern humans' attitudes and actions toward God and one another as the terms of their covenantal relationship with God. These precepts challenge our efforts at honesty, uprightness, justice and fairness. They safeguard us and our communities.

This is why Jesus applied those Ten Yardsticks very faithfully and by the same he judged his own life as well as the lives of his disciples. He emphasized: *"Do not think that I have come to abolish the law or the prophets. I have come not to abolish but to fulfill.* He confirmed that: *Amen, I say to you, until heaven and earth pass away, not the smallest letter or the smallest part of a letter will pass from the law, until all things have taken place.* He too following his Father, highlighted the efficacy of those laws bringing either blessings or curses: *Therefore, whoever breaks one of the least of these commandments and teaches others to do so will be called least in the kingdom of heaven. But whoever obeys and teaches these commandments will be called greatest in the kingdom of heaven.* (Matt. 5: 17-19)

While he was totally in alliance with God's Commandments, he observed how badly God's people desecrated and damaged those commandments and heavenly values in their application. Hence taking his own revelatory whip of wisdom and power he enhanced those Laws. We notice this in all his sayings, in particular in his Sermon on the Mount and in his newly-packaged and synthesized law of love and ordered us to love God totally and to love our neighbor as he did. This means: Our love for God should be the zeal that consumed Jesus; and our love for neighbors must be the sign of the Cross and the only media to proclaim to the world 'Christ crucified as the power and wisdom of God'. (Ref. 1 Cor. 22-25) Our Master averred this is the only way to get into the heavenly mansions: *I tell you, unless your righteousness surpasses that of the scribes and Pharisees, you will not enter into the kingdom of heaven.* (Matt. 5: 20)

Fourth Sunday of Lent
Cross is not sign of a deathwish but of a lifespring

> *And just as Moses lifted up the serpent in the desert, so must the Son of Man be lifted up, so that everyone who believes in him may have eternal life." For God so loved the world that he gave his only Son, so that everyone who believes in him might not perish but might have eternal life. For God did not send his Son into the world to condemn the world, but that the world might be saved through him. Whoever believes in him will not be condemned, but whoever does not believe has already been condemned, because he has not believed in the name of the only Son of God. And this is the verdict, that the light came into the world, but people preferred darkness to light, because their works were evil...But whoever lives the truth comes to the light, so that his works may be clearly seen as done in God. (Jn. 3: 14-21)*

In our churches and in most of our homes the crucifix is given a place of honor. Does that mean that we have to love our sufferings? No, but it indicates that we love the love it points out; we love the Lover who is hanging there for us; we love the One who so loved us that he sent us his own beloved Son and made him die on the cross. He saved us by his cross and resurrection. He is the sign that God loved us so much that he gave us his only Son to bring us forgiveness and life and love. Today in our Scriptural meditation the Spirit injects in us more appreciation and gratitude toward the crucified Lord, the symbol of God's love.

In the Gospel passage taken for our today's reflection, we hear Jesus explaining splendidly to Nicodemus about the unfathomable goal of his life: *"For God so loved the world that he gave his only Son, so that everyone who believes in him might not perish but might have eternal life."* We are indeed surprised when Jesus affirms that we are loved—unconditionally, everlastingly—by God. Though the God of wisdom is fully aware of our sinful condition, surmounted by so many transgressions and blunders doing against God's love, he proves his identity and worth as a great lover. Paul in his Letter elaborates this unfathomable mystery of God's love. *"God, who is rich in mercy, because of the great love he had for us, even when we were dead in our transgressions, brought us to life with Christ by grace you have been saved...*(Eph. 2: 4-7)

If we browse our daily life-schedule we can discover how terribly we hurt God by our sins. The Hebrew root for 'sin' means 'to miss'. In sacred Scriptures therefore sin is described as "missing the mark," and "turning away from God." It also refers to "moral blunder," "rebellion," "evil intent and actions," and as a "debt." Our act of sinning, more than anything else is an event or action of missing God and His Love through our *misconduct, misbehavior, and mistake.* It makes the bond of love, existing between the Divine and humans, broken and a few times null and void. Sin is something like death we bring to ourselves. Surprisingly we are bestowed the Good News by Jesus that our God, due to his condescending love, brings us always back from the endresults of our sins.

It is an uninterrupted human history that while, on one side humans slap in the face of a loving God, he on the other side continues to reach out to them trying to liberate them from all the evil repercussions of sin. In OT we hear about the Good Lord's covenant of love with his people and how easily they ignored it and lived careless about it. As they were reaping the bad consequences of their blunders he came again to their rescue. God's love was far-reaching. He proved His greatness and power even by the help of a foreign pagan king Cyrus. He freed his people from their exile and he also arranged for the rebuilding of the Temple in Jerusalem. (Ref. 2 Chr. 36: 14-23) However humans never yielded to his love-demands. Hence, this is what God ultimately did when the fullness of his time arrived. He sent his beloved Son to save us.

Unquestionably we are torn between two factors of our humanness: We have been called to be holy but we are susceptible to fall low to be sinful. As one modern spiritual leader stated most of our sins are both personal and social, namely against the love-family of God. We are used to make eight blunders: *"Wealth without work, pleasure without conscience, knowledge without character, commerce without morality, science without humanity, worship without sacrifice, politics without principles and rights without responsibility."* Despite these blunders of modern generation, God loves humankind and graces us with the immeasurable riches of salvation. For this reason, blundering sinners need not fear to approach God for forgiveness. In the forgiveness we experience from God, we learn the love that enables us also to forgive one another. Forgiveness calls forth forgiveness, just as love calls forth love. This is the history and story retold time and time again as we face the Cross on which the crucified Lord hangs.

SIXTEENTH WEEKEND

Fifth Sunday of Lent

*Let us make our life a perfect sacrifice
of covenant with God*

*See, days are coming—oracle of the
LORD—when I will make a new covenant
with the house of Israel and the house of
Judah. It will not be like the covenant I
made with their ancestors the day I took
them by the hand to lead them out of the
land of Egypt. They broke my covenant,
though I was their master—oracle of the
LORD. But this is the covenant I will make
with the house of Israel after those days. I
will place my law within them, and write
it upon their hearts; I will be their God,
and they shall be my people. They will no
longer teach their friends and relatives,
"Know the LORD!" Everyone, from least to
greatest, shall know me; for I will forgive
their iniquity and no longer remember
their sin.* (Jer. 31: 31-34)

Our entire life as humans is fully based and centered
on promises; this is hundred percent true in our deals with
other human beings. It includes also our dealings with God.
The Spirit moves us today to dwell in those promises God
proposed to us and challenges our own reaction to them.

In the Scriptures our Christian life is described as a
covenantal journey to reach our destiny of glory. It depends

solely on the covenant God made with us and mutually on how we freely respond and be committed to it in our daily life. This historical covenant is of three dimensions. The first dimension is the fact that it was the Creator who took the initiative in making the covenant with his human creatures and substantiated it through his mighty deeds in their midst. *"I will be your God; you will be my people,"* he pronounced, *"It was I who called you forth from Egypt to give you a land"* (19:4-6; 20:2). Secondly through the gift of commandments he gave to humans directions to govern the relationship between him and humans (Ex. 20: 3-23:33); and as the third dimension of the remarkable covenant, we are told that covenants between God and Israel were often confirmed as a seal by the sacrifice of an animal, whose blood was offered to expiate sin and whose flesh was cooked and shared as a sign of communion between him and his people (24: 9-11).

We know the sad fact that several such covenants were made and broken throughout Israel's history. However as we hear today from Jeremiah, God's Prophets dreamt of the covenant of God was *unconditional and everlasting.* Unlike the stipulations of previous covenants, which were carved in stone, the terms of the covenant envisioned by Jeremiah *would be recorded in the human heart,* and all, from least to greatest, would be privileged to know God. This covenant would also *bring forgiveness of sins.* Humankind would be forever free of guilt, for God would remember their sins no more.

Those promises remained only as mere dreams until Jesus came. It was only through Jesus and through his embrace of the cross that this covenant was realized. Jesus in the Gospel has been emphatic in confirming the fact that his entire life together with its challenges had only one *raison d'être*, namely to establish, solidify and ratify the new and eternal covenant that the Prophets had dreamed and promised centuries before. Jesus did this amazing covenant coming true by revealing God in human flesh and blood and by enunciating, in his every word and deed, the love God has for sinners. Love of God and love for one another became the law by which this covenant would stand. To guarantee this unending love relationship, Jesus used his bleeding and death, as a grain of wheat falling to the earth and dying, for sprouting new life. He offered himself to be lifted up on the cross so that sinners would be forgiven. (Ref. Jn. 12: 20-33)

Attesting to the historical contribution of Jesus toward the renewal of God's covenant with humans, the Letter to the Hebrews announces that it is not just the moment and act of death of Jesus that has great effect on God's covenant with us but it is his entire life in which he obeyed God's will every moment of his life. He was conceived in obedience; he was born poor in obedience; he was tempted in obedience; he earned his daily bread by sweat and blood in obedience; he encountered trouble after trouble daily in obedience; thus he made himself as a perfect sacrifice that was most fitting seal for the covenant made between God and humans. (Ref. Heb. 5: 7-9)

Like Jesus, we have to become a fitting sacrifice in the covenantal life with God. This is the goal of every Christian as we travel this earthly journey of covenant. Like him we have to grow in wisdom and grace; we should grow in obedience by suffering the flings and arrows of unpredictable life. We gradually grow in grace by traveling the dusty road of everyday events. That is the way to make our filthy, vulnerable, fragile life a perfect sacrifice of covenant with God.

SEVENTEETH WEEKEND

Palm Sunday

The rare Blend of Christian Life

On the next day, when the great crowd that had come to the feast heard that Jesus was coming to Jerusalem, they took palm branches and went out to meet him, and cried out: "Hosanna! Blessed is he who comes in the name of the Lord, even the king of Israel." Jesus found an ass and sat upon it, as is written: "Fear no more, O daughter Zion; see, your king comes, seated upon an ass's colt." His disciples did not understand this at first, but when Jesus had been glorified they remembered that these things were written about him and that they had done this for him. (Jn. 12: 12-16)

While our Master Jesus was living physically in our world, he had been frequently giving surprises to his disciples-many times in his speeches, sometimes in his performing miraculous deeds, but most of the times in his very life shattering and shocking the people by his controversial behavior in public. One of them is the event of Palm Sunday. The Spirit summons us today to meditate over this event. At any time in life Jesus never wished to be honored or glorified as a celebrity; he never permitted any one to call him good (Mk. 10: 18) nor to make him king (Jn. 6: 15). Though this kind of behavior of Jesus was not welcomed by the disciples, yet his attitude of humility was commendable to them when he said: F*or the Son of Man did not come to be served but to serve and to give his life as a ransom for many.* (Mk. 10: 45) Jesus too commanded his disciples they should differ from other leaders: *Let the greatest among you be as the youngest, and the leader as the servant.* (Lk. 22: 25-27) John discovered this Jesus' attitude not only from his lips but in action of washing the disciples' feet at the Last Supper. (Jn. 13: 1–20)

Nonetheless, they were bewildered to see Jesus, who was a humble and unostentatious person, accepting a pompous welcome from the public. Besides, they couldn't find any meaning of his desire of a funny and deriding way to ride on an ass with its colt. This was because, *his disciples did not understand this.* Also, they viewed by the natural light of humanness anything they came across in life-be it becoming disciples of Jesus or the dreams about their future by staying in the team of the Messiah. Jesus indicated it to Peter: *You are thinking not as God does, but as human beings do.* (Matt. 16: 23) Our compassionate Master never left them in that same state of grim darkness. He promised before he left them that they would understand all his words and deeds through the Spirit. *The Advocate, the holy Spirit that the Father will send in my name—he will teach you everything and remind you of all that told you.* (Jn. 14: 26)

There is a different connotation about what the Lord promised and did to his disciples. In his narration about the Palm Sunday event John writes that at first the disciples didn't understand what was going on that day, but later they did. W*hen Jesus had been glorified they remembered that these things were written about him and that they had done this for him.* Here is the most striking factor the Spirit invites us to reflect what John contributes to our spiritual life. According to the Biblical scholars, John's Gospel is highly literary and symbolic, interpreting all the deeds and words of Jesus as 'heavenly signs' for revealing the glory of God's only Son, who came to reveal the Father and then returned in glory to the Father. As closing remark, John writes: *Now Jesus did many other signs...But these are written that you may come to believe that Jesus is the Messiah, the Son of God, and that through this belief you may have life in his name.* (Jn. 20: 30-31)

On this background, John interprets the passion and death of Jesus as the sign of his glorification as the Son glorifying his Father. Jesus' being lifted up on the Cross was an ascending in glory. In it 'everything was fulfilled'; by it he would be the owner of entire humanity. *When I am lifted up from the earth, I will draw everyone to myself.* (Jn. 12: 32) As he was a paradoxical entity of rare blend of humanity and divinity, he demonstrated how we, his disciples should cope with and succeed in maintaining our own duality of body and soul; rare blend of social and personal dimensions; going through earthly life which is again another shocking blend of ups and downs, glory and infame, joys and sorrows, darkness and light and certainly death and life.

His disciples, being subdued by natural order, couldn't grasp this 'blend-factor'. Only after being enlightened by the Spirit they understood everything in details. They then were ready to descend even to the hellish life for the sake of God's kingdom because they were convinced they were after all ascending to heavenliness; they were rejoicing to be persecuted, because it was a part of the rare blend of Christian life. We learn such an astounding fact from Jesus not only just on Palm Sunday, not only during the Holy Week but every day as we sit down before the Lord on the Hilltop.

235

EIGHTEENTH WEEKEND

Easter Sunday

*Walking as if empty tombs but truly
carrying the risen Lord*

*When the Sabbath was over, Mary
Magdalene, Mary, the mother of James,
and Salome bought spices so that they
might go and anoint him. Very early when
the sun had risen, on the first day of the
week, they came to the tomb. They were
saying to one another, "Who will roll back
the stone for us from the entrance to the
tomb?" When they looked up, they saw
that the stone had been rolled back; it was
very large. On entering the tomb they saw
a young man sitting on the right side,
clothed in a white robe, and they were
utterly amazed. He said to them, "Do not
be amazed! You seek Jesus of Nazareth,
the crucified. He has been raised; he is
not here. Behold, the place where they laid
him. But go and tell his disciples and Peter,
'He is going before you to Galilee; there
you will see him, as he told you.'" Then
they went out and fled from the tomb,
seized with trembling and bewilderment.*
(Mk 16: 1-8)

The postmodern society is horribly bombarded by
thousands of opinions on millions of issues- legal, political

and religious, tearing the entire world. In the Church surely we are well aware how we are divided by opinions. In all matters of faith every Christian has got our personal opinions and die with them. From the Gospels we gather the same kind of rifts and dissensions occurred among the primary team of Jesus, especially after his resurrection. On this Easter weekend the Spirit brings us before the empty tomb of Jesus and meditate intensely on our opinion on the incredible fact of his resurrection.

It's true that the first appearance of the risen Lord, as narrated by Gospel writers was to Mary Magdalene, who later went and announced this good news to other apostles and disciples. It's true also that Apostles could not digest the opinion of a woman. They thought she was hallucinating. But this woman's opinion became popular and accepted finally by the entire global Church.

In the realm of God human opinion matters very little. Whatever be the talent of a person who generated that opinion unless it is connected to the risen Lord and his Spirit it will never become popular and eternal. It was not the talented proclamation of Mary Magdalene that gave continuity to her opinion about the risen Lord. Rather it was the Spirit of the risen Lord that influenced and possessed her that made all possible. This was the truth, which Gamaliel, a teacher of the law, contended before the Sanhedrin about the unrivaled post-effect of Jesus' resurrection-factor: For if this endeavor or this activity is of human origin, it will destroy itself. But if it comes from God, you will not be able to destroy them; you may even find yourselves fighting against God. (Acts 5: 34-39) And so is with the 2000-years-old proclamation of the Church about Jesus' resurrection.

The risen Lord has truly risen and with his Spirit he is pervading the hearts and minds of millions of people of this world. They have experienced him and his intervention in their lives. They encountered him in prayer, Scriptures and Tradition. Due to the effective influence of the risen Lord, sinners like Mary Magdalene and many other disciples died truly in their sinful past and rose to new virtuous life. They are convinced now that, 'the old life is comfortable; the new life is demanding. Yet the new life is rich and the old life is barren.'

These disciples, enlightened and enlivened by the risen Lord, emptied their entire body, their mind and heart, became liberated from all kinds of evil thoughts, words and deeds and began walking seemingly as 'empty tombs' but truly carrying the risen Lord. Whoever saw their lives and not just heard their opinions became energized by the same risen Lord. Being the disciples of Jesus today, our opinion about the risen Lord should also become our life. Consequently our present life becomes a celebration of the reality that Jesus lives! As Paul exhorts us on this day of 'SONrise' we need to demonstrate our faith through our daily living. If then you were raised with Christ, seek what is above, where Christ is seated at the right hand of God. Think of what is above, not of what is on earth. For you have died, and your life is hidden with Christ in God... (Col 3: 1-4)

We too should try our best in ripping of our old sinful lifestyle and upholding a new order of life. Do you not know that a little yeast leavens all the dough? Clear out the old yeast, so that you may become a fresh batch of dough, inasmuch as you are unleavened...Therefore let us celebrate the feast, not with the old yeast, the yeast of malice and wickedness, but with the unleavened bread of sincerity and truth. (1 Cor 5: 6b-8) This is our genuine Easter proclamation.

NINETEENTH WEEKEND

Second Sunday of Easter

Weird behavior but workable solution for economic crisis

> *The community of believers was of one heart and mind, and no one claimed that any of his possessions was his own, but they had everything in common. With great power the apostles bore witness to the resurrection of the Lord Jesus, and great favor was accorded them all. There was no needy person among them, for those who owned property or houses would sell them, bring the proceeds of the sale, and put them at the feet of the apostles, and they were distributed to each according to need.* (Acts 4: 32-35)

During this Easter season, the Spirit summons us to go deep into the startling interactions of the risen Lord in our midst. This weekend we are asked to enter into the life of the first community of Jesus' disciples and meditate on their quality life in the risen Lord. We read in the Book of Acts that the early Christians were *of one heart and mind.* Their oneness of heart and mind was testified in their hysterical behaviors such as: No one claimed that any of his possessions was his own; they had everything in common; they would sell all their properties, brought and put the proceeds of the sale at the feet of the apostles and they were distributed to each according to need. The obvious result was that there was no needy person among them.

Such bewildering behavior may be either not well understood by today's Christians or simply rejected and nullified by modern skeptics. But, we should never forget the economic values these early Christians held were those of Jesus Christ preached by his Apostles. They followed exactly what the Lord commanded them: *"If you want to be my disciples sell all your possessions, give to the poor and then follow me."* It was indeed a hardest saying of Christ; yet the first Christians lovingly followed it because of their inner encounter with the risen Lord. As John wrote in his Letter, they esteemed their faith in the resurrected Lord as their victory and based every bit of their earthly steps and enterprises on that belief that they were the children of God who is love. (Ref. 1 Jn. 5: 1-6) They obeyed very meticulously word by word God's loving command that we should love our neighbors as our brothers and sisters. This command to them, seemingly a utopian dream, was not burdensome because as John says, *whatever is begotten by God conquers the world.*

Today, more than ever before, we are indeed very much frightened at the looming financial crisis around the globe. Our society soon has to deal with the difficult situation of being populated by more than 3 billion of humans among whom there are too many elderly citizens; and the immoral and Godless solution, promulgated by many, is to lessening the number of older people. The "right" to die is quickly becoming the "duty" to die, especially when the millennials feel how costly it is to keep older people alive and regrettably some of them viciously state, *'you've lived a full life, but now you cost too much. Time to step aside.'*

This kind of cold and ungrateful attitude is the result of wrongly handling our social and economic values. It is here we see the good old values followed by our early

Christians. Esteeming every citizen born in this world is the child of God as we are and in the spirit of risen Lord we should rise up to solve the impending problems in our own way. It need not be called as any isms, like communism, socialism, totalitarianism or capitalism but simply let us call it Christianism. We must start our life again from our initial faith on the risen Lord. Like Apostle Thomas, who initially did not want to believe in the resurrection of Jesus (Jn. 20: 24-28), we may be wavering in our faith holding; But as he finally bent down to the risen Lord and responded in faith loudly, *"My Lord and my God!,* we should soon reconcile with it and get stronger in that faith.

In this way all that the qualitylife the Scriptures promise will be ours. The early Christians bore powerful witness to their contemporaries by this kind of quality life consisting of unity, oneness, forgiveness, peace, truth, justice and love. This was possible not by their human natural power and abilities but only by their close connection with the risen Lord in their strong belief in his presence among them As John writes in the Gospel, *"through this belief we may have life in his name."*

Undoubtedly with the impact of our formidable faith in the risen Lord, we would be energized to follow, what the early Christians did, in our efforts of solving our current financial problems: We begin sharing what we own with our needy family members; sharing willingly with senior citizens a portion of what we earn and save in life; and the last but not the least, sharing what we possess with the needy citizens of today, the downtrodden sections of the global society. This is the only way to solve our global economic problems.

TWENTIETH WEEKEND

Third Sunday of Easter

Forgiveness and peace are the gifts
of Jesus-crucified but risen

...While they were still speaking about this, he stood in their midst and said to them, "Peace be with you." But they were startled and terrified and thought that they were seeing a ghost. Then he said to them, "Why are you troubled? And why do questions arise in your hearts? Look at my hands and my feet, that it is I myself. Touch me and see, because a ghost does not have flesh and bones as you can see I have." And as he said this, he showed them his hands and his feet...And he said to them, "Thus it is written that the Messiah would suffer and rise from the dead on the third day and that repentance, for the forgiveness of sins, would be preached in his name to all the nations, beginning from Jerusalem. You are witnesses of these things. (Lk. 24: 35-48)

'Save us, Savior of the world, for by your cross and resurrection, you have set us free'. This is what we proclaim during the Eucharistic celebrations as the mystery of our faith. Unquestionably this sort of faith holding may sound new and weird to many modern minds. Today the Spirit moves us to reflect on this incredible factor of human salvation.

But the Church never hesitates to recognize this salvific fact and its valuable contribution to humans. The central message of apostolic preaching has been that Jesus of Nazareth, who died and rose, continues to resurrect the all humans and offers them salvation and liberation. Their message came out of their vivid memory about what the Lord proclaimed to them: *Thus it is written that the Messiah would suffer and rise from the dead on the third day and that repentance, for the forgiveness of sins.* And as John testifies, *Jesus is expiation for our sins, and not for our sins only but for those of the whole world.* (1 Jn. 2: 2) While so many in this modern Age continue doubting about this redeeming action of Jesus, the Lord reveals to us this new teaching is the most necessary message for our life.

First of all, Jesus' death liberates us from all our sins. This assertion was made by the risen Lord himself to his Apostles when he appeared to them before he left for heaven. And he wanted them to be faithful witnesses to this truthful fact. *...that repentance, for the forgiveness of sins, would be preached in his name to all the nations, beginning from Jerusalem. You are witnesses of these things.* This is why Jesus' disciples had been making their continuous appeal to people exhorting: *Repent, therefore, and be converted, that your sins may be wiped away.* (Acts 3: 19) Scripturally, sin is a denial of the Triune God, and excluding him from our life as our forebears did in human history. As Peter pointed out in his addresses, we deny Jesus, *the Holy and Righteous One*; even sometimes, we plan *to put him to death* in and around our life, acting out of ignorance, as our forebears did. (Acts 3: 14-15)

Church upholds that Jesus redeemed us from such sins, by shedding his blood as 'scapegoat'.

In tandem, Jesus initiated also another dimension of our salvation, namely through his resurrection from the dead, he liberated us from dark and gloomy situation of our life, being buried in the murky tomb. Our earthly life imposes us too many troubles and frustrations. Everywhere pain and death; no one is exempted from worries. No peace and therefore no sleep. To gain true peace, God tells us his Son is the source of liberation and peace. Gospels narrate that the risen Jesus stood in the midst of Apostles, even the doors were locked and greeted them: *Peace be with you.* He understood their fear and trouble. He encourages them not to feel so and as a plan of action he exhorts them to look at his life which had been totally damaged by his enemies; he showed them his scars of crucifixion and wanted them to believe his risen presence and interaction. That was the Gospel message God offered us: Jesus is source and guide in our life's challenges.

The fact of getting forgiveness for sins and liberation from peacelessness has happened first to the disciples. Our Master commanded them to be witnesses of the amazing things happened to them and in their midst. He also wanted them to witness to the transformation they experienced: after getting plentiful repentance for their sins, they experienced relief from distress; true joy settled in them; and as the Psalmist sings, as soon as they lied down in bed, they fell peacefully asleep. (Ps. 4) Today we are called to be his living witnesses. When our manner of witnessing becomes a way of life, and when our manner of living becomes itself a credible witness, then we will be able to offer the worthy testimony that will enable others to recognize and accept the truth of the good news by which we are saved.

TWENTY FIRST WEEKEND

Fourth Sunday of Easter

*Our unique Claim: Jesus' Way of Sacrificial
Love is the only way to attain fuller life*

*I came so that they might have life and
have it more abundantly. I am the good
shepherd. A good shepherd lays down his
life for the sheep. A hired man, who is not a
shepherd and whose sheep are not his own,
sees a wolf coming and leaves the sheep
and runs away, and the wolf catches and
scatters them...I am the good shepherd,
and I know mine and mine know me, just
as the Father knows me and I know the
Father; and I will lay down my life for the
sheep. I have other sheep that do not belong
to this fold. These also I must lead, and they
will hear my voice, and there will be one
flock, one shepherd...* (Jn. 10: 10b-18)

Whenever Christians point out that Jesus Christ is
the only Savior of humanity, the world is outraged. That
sort of zero-tolerance attitude regarding salvation has
been contemptuously scorned by most of humans both
outside and inside of the Church. However the Spirit
today asks us to meditate on this critical issue with the
relevant Scriptural verses and renew our faith. This kind
of assiduous claim was preached viva voce by Apostles
like Peter proclaiming that *there is no salvation through
anyone else, nor is there any other name under heaven*

given to the human race by which we are to be saved. (Acts 4: 12) He meant plainly that the *only way* to be saved and enter into Heaven is through Jesus Christ. Apostles held such seemingly 'intolerant' claim because our Master Jesus claimed so. He is quoted stating that he is the good Shepherd and the human race is his sheep; and all the others who claim to be so are simply thieves, hired men and many times wolves in sheep clothes. He ascertains also one day all humans would be one flock under Leadership.

Such an unwavering claim posted in the NT Books as well as in Church Tradition upto this day didn't begin overnight nor does it belong to a genre of historical conspiracy theory as some friends propose. It blossomed out of personal experiences of early Church members with the risen Lord's Spirit. Peter, for example, who had sinfully denied his Master, was radically changed by his encounter of the Risen Lord. No longer was he focusing on himself. In Acts (3: 1-19) we read about a healing Peter performed to a crippled man. *Peter said, "I have neither silver nor gold, but what I do have I give you: in the name of Jesus Christ the Nazorean, rise and walk." Then Peter took him by the right hand and raised him up, and immediately his feet and ankles grew strong.* However Peter was resolute in making the crowds know that this was not his work but entirely the work of risen Jesus. *And by faith in his name, this man, whom you see and know, his name has made strong, and the faith that comes through it has given him this perfect health, in the presence of all of you.* There were numerous miraculous encounters happened between Apostles and their risen Master. It is surely from those factual encounters came their astounding statement that their Master is the sole Savior and Lord of the Universe.

Jesus claimed himself as the only way of truth for living fuller life. It is undebatable to state that he is the foundation of our salvation. *He is the stone rejected by you, the builders, which has become the cornerstone.* (Acts 4: 11) If Jesus is not the foundation of our lives, we have no foundation. However we should remember that in his bewildering claim he adds: *I came so that they might have life and have it more abundantly.* This is what our faith statement is all about Jesus. If we add anything to or subtract from this creed we betray Jesus and his Gospel. All the practices that we perform in the name of the Church, all the doctrines and dogmas we formulate or interpret and promulgate must be totally focused on only Jesus and his values of love. Because we firmly hold that it is in Jesus we *see what love the Father has bestowed on us that we may be called the children of God.* (1 Jn. 3: 1)

There is indeed some valid reasons why the modern people reject such claim. They point out, due to this exaggerating exclusive claim, too many wars and deaths happened. Thanks to Vatican II's renewal spirit, most of us try not to repeat those past blunders. However some, instead of eradicating the abused forms of this claim, make another blunder of completely erasing the centrality of Christ in human life and proclaiming a gospel of humanistic love with no reference to Christ's love. Such a distorted attitude has had its repercussions such as violence, atrocious killing of babies, family broken to pieces by divorces, glorifying homosexuality, euthanasia, mercy-killing and so on. One thing must be underscored: Our style of proclaiming that Jesus is the one sent by God to liberate humans from maladies, might have been wrongly botched, but its content and goal are still persevered vivid and truthful: Jesus' Way of sacrificial and compassionate love is the only truthful way for humans to enjoy fuller life here and in heaven.

Fifth Sunday of Easter

*Remain in Jesus to live lively and
to bear fruits abundantly*

*"I am the true vine, and my Father is
the vine grower. He takes away every
branch in me that does not bear fruit, and
every one that does he prunes so that it
bears more fruit. You are already pruned
because of the word that I spoke to you.
Remain in me, as I remain in you. Just
as a branch cannot bear fruit on its own
unless it remains on the vine, so neither
can you unless you remain in me. I am
the vine, you are the branches. Whoever
remains in me and I in him will bear much
fruit, because without me you can do
nothing. Anyone who does not remain in
me will be thrown out like a branch and
wither; people will gather them and throw
them into a fire and they will be burned. If
you remain in me and my words remain
in you, ask for whatever you want and it
will be done for you. By this is my Father
glorified, that you bear much fruit and
become my disciples.* (Jn. 15: 1-8)

There are so many references in the Bible to explain
to us, through metaphors and images, what kind of
relationship God longs to keep up with us. Most of them

are concerned with our external encounters with him. Today the Spirit takes us to another important realm of relationship that occurs interiorly between ourselves and God in Jesus. Let us join him today in our meditating moment.

Jesus is quoted uttering to the disciples: *'I am the vine, you are the branches.'* It is all about an ontological connection, very intrinsic relationship between him and us. The branch cannot be separated from the parent vine and continue to live. Jesus is right when he says: *"Just as a branch cannot bear fruit on its own unless it remains on the vine, so neither can you unless you remain in me. "Apart from me you can do nothing."* He too adds: *"Whoever remains in me and I in him will bear much fruit."* The words *'much fruit'* refer to a qualitylife of fulfillment and a life-saving life. When we believe in Jesus Christ, partake of his mysteries, and keep his commandments, his person becomes, through the Spirit, the living and interior rule of all our activities. John, referring to this fact, exhorts us, *Children, let us love not in word or speech but in deed and truth.* (1 Jn. 3: 18)

Undoubtedly loving through words is a part of love. Often many of us find it easier to express our love by doing something than by speaking directly to a person. Parents, for instance, often feel they show their love by providing the best education they can afford for their children, by showering them with gifts and pocket money. Yet, those same children may seldom hear real words of love and affection spoken by their parents. In that and similar cases, loving by deeds becomes an escape for the more direct love expressed in sincerely meant words. We have an excellent example of what we have been talking about in the experience of Paul who used his words to witness that he was a disciple of Jesus and no longer a persecutor of Christians. Unfortunately they just did not believe him; his life was threatened by them and his friends had to send him away to a safer place. Only later, when he really proved his love of Jesus by his total service of the community the world was ready to accept him, plus accepted his faith proclamation. (Acts 9: 26-31)

Only when we love in deed can we know that Jesus lives in us. God's love is in some way similar to electric power which cannot go through us if first it doesn't go into us. It is an eternal fact that God does not love us because we are good; rather, we are good because God's love is working in and through us to others. Jesus says: *By this, is my Father glorified, that you bear much fruit and become my disciples.* Many times Jesus has emphasized that he is the only person who is sent by the heavenly Father to offer us the qualitylife of fulfillment and lifesaving life. Today he emphatically reiterates that he is the sole God-grown true vine. Even though there may exist some competing vines looking to be true Jesus is the true vine which is the most life-giving, the most nourishing, and the most dependable.

As his intimately-connected branches we are challenged, nourished, encouraged, and advised by his life and words. God, being the faithful gardener, would prune us for helping us to channel all that is life-giving into our lives and actions: Selfless love, sacrifice, voluntary cross-carrying, feeding others, clothing others, visiting others, comforting others, serving others, forgiving others, healing others, reaching out to the marginalized, protecting defenseless life, and even giving up our lives for others. It is for this much-fruit-bearing life we are summoned by the Spirit.

TWENTY THIRD WEEKEND

Sixth Sunday of Easter

Complete joy is the result of total love

As the Father loves me, so I also love you. Remain in my love. If you keep my commandments, you will remain in my love, just as I have kept my Father's commandments and remain in his love. "I have told you this so that my joy may be in you and your joy may be complete. This is my commandment: love one another as I love you. No one has greater love than this, to lay down one's life for one's friends. You are my friends if you do what I command you... It was not you who chose me, but I who chose you and appointed you to go and bear fruit that will remain, so that whatever you ask the Father in my name he may give you. This I command you: love one another. (Jn. 15: 9-17)

Many disciples of Jesus find hard to listen and practice many of Jesus' demands from us, specifically his new command: *Love one another.* Today as we stand on the hilltop in praying and meditating the Spirit encourages us to reread the reasons and the results of Jesus' demand of love through some Scriptural passages.

The world knows our Master led a paradoxical life on earth that spelt out a bewildering fact: He lived to die but died to live as a grain of wheat which dies and disappears so that from it a newer life can be sprout. He wanted the same order of life to be lived by his followers. In the history of Christianity we notice that all disciples, committed to Jesus' paradoxical Way of Life, lived a life of death but finally died a victorious death that led them to eternal joy and bliss. The more they died in life to sin and other imbalanced ways of humanness they were the happiest people in the midst of trials and persecutions.

As a matter of fact, such a paradoxical life is not that easy to lead in this world. Therefore Jesus offered us a strategy that is very close to our hearts. *As the Father loves me, so I also love you. Remain in my love...This is my commandment: love one another as I love you.* He wants us to remain in the way he loves us; in the way he died to live in love; in the manner he lived to die in and for love. He emphasized: *No one has greater love than this, to lay down one's life for one's friends.* Inhaling Jesus' breath of love, Apostle John writes: *Beloved, let us love one another, because love is of God... Whoever is without love does not know God, for God is love... not that we have loved God, but that he loved us and sent his Son as expiation for our sins.* (1 Jn. 4: 7-10)

When Jesus 'asks us to remain in his love,' there are two criteria that will help us to distinguish true love from the fake one. The first criterion of true Christian love is one that always proceeds from and ends with the recognition of our priveledge to have been chosen by Jesus who categorically stated: *It was not you who chose me, but I who chose you and appointed you to go and bear fruit that will remain.* True love does not remain isolated, being puffed up with proud individualism that forgets God and Jesus our Master who have been remaining with us as Emmanuel. Jesus cannot bear with any sort of 'spiritual form of egoism', staying closed up in oneself and searching for one's own advantage. Therefore, to remain in Jesus' love means being able to communicate and dialogue uninterruptedly both with God and our neighbors.

The second criterion is that love is more in deeds than in words. It is not a saga of love, a fantasy, or that which make our hearts beat a little, but nothing more. True love is not soap-opera love, or a whim or something that makes our heart beat a little faster and then nothing more. Rather, it is found in concrete actions which we discover from the Apostles' love-in-actions. Peter, though he was aware of the biased attitude and custom of early Christians' relationship with the Gentile as unlawful, went to pay a friendly visit to Cornelius and his friends. The main reason was, as he stated, that *God of love has shown him that he should not call any person profane or unclean.* The astounding result of such love-in-action was, while Peter was still speaking these things, the Holy Spirit fell upon all the Gentiles who were listening to the word. (Ref. Acts 10: 25-48) True love is not a simple enthusiasm; many times it can be a painful act which must be borne as Jesus carried the cross.

Unquestionably, only by remaining in Christ's love and keeping his commandment of love in attitude and in action the disciples will find the remarkable joy our Master has promised: *I have told you this so that my joy may be in you and your joy may be complete.*

TWENTY FOURTH WEEKEND

Ascension of the Lord

The paradoxical but majestic life of Jesus' disciples

> *But grace was given to each of us according to the measure of Christ's gift. Therefore, it says: "He ascended on high and took prisoners captive; he gave gifts to men." What does "he ascended" mean except that he also descended into the lower regions of the earth? The one who descended is also the one who ascended far above all the heavens, that he might fill all things. And he gave some as apostles, others as prophets, others as evangelists, others as pastors and teachers, to equip the holy ones for the work of ministry, for building up the body of Christ, until we all attain to the unity of faith and knowledge of the Son of God, to mature manhood, to the extent of the full stature of Christ.*
> (Eph. 4: 7-13)

This weekend the Spirit invites us to meditate on our faith in Jesus' ascension to heaven, which has become historically a paradoxical event consisting of an ending and a beginning: The abruptly ending of the 33 years-life of Jesus on earth plus the startling beginning of the final era of salvation history, in which we still live: the period of the Church.

If we go deeper into this mystery of ascension with Paul we discover an unthinkable factor occurring inside this event. Namely very surprisingly it contains a rare blend of both acts of Jesus-descending and ascending as well. Referring to Psalm 68, Paul writes: *What does "he ascended" mean except that he also descended into the lower regions of the earth? The one who descended is also the one who ascended far above all the heavens.* He surely would have meant that as God was triumphantly leading Israel to salvation in Jerusalem, Jesus too ascending to a status of mystical presence, becoming the head of the church and the source of our spiritual gifts through his incarnation of descending to the earthly life (Ref. <u>Phil. 2: 6</u>–<u>8</u>) consisting of poverty, pain, suffering, death and burial.

Such an awesome mystery of Jesus' descending and ascending is the base and core of our Christian life. It is completely built on three paradoxical factors from which Jesus' disciples cannot escape even a single moment. The faith we uphold is paradoxical, blending of 'already and not yet' and of 'ascending and descending'. We are already saved but not yet fully; already we enjoy God's peace and joy but not yet complete. The higher we ascend with and in Jesus through prayer, meditation and disciplined life the deeper we are urged to be involved in earthly affairs. A true and genuine disciple of Jesus cannot stay all the time looking up to heaven as the disciples did. If we are truly praying and intensively connecting ourselves to the heavenly Lord we would be asked as the angel told the disciples to go down to our own family, our business, our community and our lifesituation to be his witnesses. (Acts 1: 9-11)

With firm faith in the heaven-focused earthly life and with persistent hope of reaching it at his second coming as angels reminded, *This Jesus who has been taken up from you into heaven will return in the same way as you have seen him going into heaven,* we live together as Jesus' team of disciples at present Age on the basis of his command of love. As he promised us, we would be bestowed with powerful and authoritative gifts to eradicate and cast out all social and spiritual evils from humanity. This miraculous enlargement of the team of Jesus is nothing but his own ascension in which we too have the privilege of being ascended with him. Paul proclaims about this remarkable goal of our Christian ascending with Jesus in this world: *That Jesus might fill all things for building up the body of Christ, until we all attain to the unity of faith and knowledge of the Son of God, to mature manhood, to the extent of the full stature of Christ.*

As the famous theologian Karl Rahner explains, Jesus, in ascending to God, has taken us with him. He ascended to heaven with the human body, with the human nature and this means with the entire humanity. Because he wanted to come close to us, definitively, he has gone away and taken us with him. Because he was lifted up on the cross, in his resurrection and in his ascension, he and everything in him have become near. The reason for this is that Jesus' Spirit is already in us now. Since something of our humanness already dwells in glory with Jesus, he summons the rest of ourselves to a greater, deeper, holiness, here and now, not only at liturgy but in the course of our daily existence. To put it more bluntly, we are to live in accord with the gift that we are heaven-sent, rather than hell-bent.

Feast of Pentecost

*Victory between our two inner spirits
is possible only with Spirit*

*I say, then: live by the Spirit and you will
certainly not gratify the desire of the flesh.
For the flesh has desires against the Spirit,
and the Spirit against the flesh; these are
opposed to each other, so that you may not
do what you want. But if you are guided
by the Spirit, you are not under the law.
Now the works of the flesh are obvious:
immorality, impurity, licentiousness,
idolatry, sorcery, hatreds, rivalry,
jealousy, outbursts of fury, and acts of
selfishness, dissensions, factions, and
occasions of envy, drinking bouts, orgies,
and the like. I warn you, as I warned you
before, that those who do such things will
not inherit the kingdom of God. In contrast,
the fruit of the Spirit is love, joy, peace,
patience, kindness, generosity, faithfulness,
gentleness, self-control.* (Gal. 5: 16-26)

We are natural born weak, coward, barbaric, self-centered, self-interested and with some survival kits and possessed with many diplomatic and cunning First Aid Tools. At the same time, we are gifted by God in creation with many natural talents such as wisdom, understanding, counsel, fortitude, knowledge, piety and fear of God.

Unfortunately as we decide many times to abuse these marvelous gifts, not only they bear fruits that are very temporary, but also they bring havoc to ourselves and others. This is our perennial problem. On this day of Pentecost the Spirit summons us to accept some of his admonitions to solve this human crisis.

Our forebears believed and taught us in their limitations that our spiritual enemies are three: world, devil and body, of which the first two reside out of us and the third is part of us. Their teaching is both right and wrong. It is right in the sense that all the three create lots of spiritual and moral problems in our life but they forgot to tell us these three evildoers cannot win in their attacks against us unless and until the fourth enemy which is existing within us yields to them. Paul very well explains about our inner evil source by exposing the fact our human spirit, breathed by God when we were created, had been damaged by the First Sin and thus broken into two spirits, *fleshly* and *spiritual. For those who live according to the flesh are concerned with the things of the flesh, but those who live according to the spirit with the things of the spirit. The concern of the flesh is death, but the concern of the spirit is life and peace… and those who are in the flesh cannot please God.* (Rom. 8: 5-8)

It is about this fleshly spirit Paul warns us to be careful. Our (spiritual) spirit is open to God; desires him and is drawn to him; is attracted by goodness, beauty and truth, which yearns for completion in God and to see his face; whereas our 'fleshly' spirit is inner part of us that alienates itself from God, being rebellious and obstinate; can become the gateway to sin; the arena in which sin embeds itself it; and to the extent it can turn out to be sinful itself. Paul therefore uses the term 'flesh' in his Letters to denote such as: physical flesh, human body, humanity as a whole, human descent and human relationships, in order to make us understand our human physical life is transient, frail, and provisional in contrast to the eternal, unchanging and powerful realm of the Spirit which is the only sphere of salvation. However since a part of our inner spirit became so damaged, twisted that it became so weak to be failing with our spiritual enemies from outside. Thankfully our weak spirit, assisted by the Holy Spirit draws us to desire what is best, what is upright, good and helpful.

As we hear in the Gospel (Jn. 20: 19-23), before Jesus was taken up to heaven, he breathed on the disciples reminding them by receiving his Breath of the Spirit, the already residing spirit of the Creator within them, though it be a damaged one, will be renewed and rejuvenated. He emphasized that the Spirit, through whom he would be going to stay with them, would act like an Advocate and a Counselor, a Peace-maker like a dove; a purifier like fire; a mover like strong wind; a productive strong glue that bonds all diversified people together under his wings like an eagle.

Paul reminds us today it is possible to win the battle against our spiritual enemies by living in and by Jesus' Spirit. *I say, then: live by the Spirit and you will certainly not gratify the desire of the flesh.* When we make use of our natural gifts most of the time we join in hands with evil spirit. Our talented undertakings with intelligence, IQ, diplomacy, cunningness, etc. are planned and executed with evil intention and motivation such as self-gratification, vengeance, jealousy, pride, fake self-prestige; and consequently we know the results are too bad. But when we connect every move of ours with and to the Holy Spirit all that we think, speak and do making use of our God-given talents bear excellent and solid fruits as Paul enlists. *Come Holy Spirit! Heal our wounds. Renew our strength. Give us the virtue's sure reward.*

TWENTY SIXTH WEEKEND

The Feast of Holy Trinity

We are connected to the Triune Family Tree of God

> *The eleven disciples went to Galilee, to the mountain to which Jesus had ordered them. When they saw him, they worshiped, but they doubted. Then Jesus approached and said to them, "All power in heaven and on earth has been given to me. Go, therefore, and make disciples of all nations, baptizing them in the name of the Father, and of the Son, and of the Holy Spirit, teaching them to observe all that I have commanded you. And behold, I am with you always, until the end of the age."*
> (Matt. 28: 16-20)

According to God's desire, his humans must worship only him and him alone. That is prerogative and sovereign proposal to his human creatures as he placed it as number one of his Ten Commandments. Being by nature a jealous Person, he too repeatedly detailed it of how his humans should love him: *Hear, O Israel! The LORD is our God, the LORD alone! Therefore, you shall love the LORD, your God, with your whole heart, and with your whole being, and with your whole strength.* (Deut. 6: 4-5) Knowing also his humans are reasonable in their taking obedience steps to his will, he offered proper reasons for demand of total love. He explained to his people through Moses (Ref. Deut. 4: 32-40) that first he demonstrated his immense love and concern for them in the past by his marvelous deeds of choosing, saving and guiding them to reach their Promised Land. Hence, remembering his parental, undivided love, he wanted them to love him in return with filial devotion.

However at the fullness of his time he performed another unfathomable love-deed for the same humans who had been arrogant, self-centered and very stubborn in fulfilling his love-will. Scriptures and Church Tradition say that he sent his beloved Son to the world and made him make reparation for all human sins by his bloody death and in addition he raised his dead Son from the tomb as a resurrected Spirit in order to stay with us permanently. We celebrate this fact today as the Feast of Holy Trinity of which the Spirit calls us to meditate and confirm our faith in this precious dogma with all our mind of reason and heart of love.

Christian life starts, proceeds and ends in the name of the Triune God-Father, Son and Holy Spirit. Before Jesus ascended to heaven, he commanded his disciples to baptize us in that mysterious Name. 'Baptizing' and 'becoming Christians' means 'sinking' deeply into a marvelous religious faith in the Triune God. Most of the humans, in the past and present as well, especially non-Christians, consider God as a powerful person, residing far away, in his high heaven, and very remote from our everyday life, as someone we fear to make angry. Whereas we, Christians, honor a God who lives in the community of a covenant relationship with us; that means, a God who makes us like his blood relatives, a God as close to us as a marriage partner, a God who preferred us to his own Son as he let Jesus give his life for us, a God who keeps stirring us through the Spirit with the inspirations of love and tenderness, of compassion and courage.

Paul therefore could state this truth with no qualms about it: *For those who are led by the Spirit of God are children of God. For you did not receive a spirit of slavery to fall back into fear, but you received a spirit of adoption, through which we cry, "Abba, Father!"* (Rom. 8: 14-15) According to Paul, we are chosen by God; it is true, but there is more to it, we are the sons and daughters of God; we have a great advantage to call God, 'Daddy'; and because of this we have the right to possess God's inheritance as Jesus did. We too will be glorified with Jesus by our Father God provided we endure all the sufferings this earthly life offers.

As a marvelous result of being baptized in the faith of the Trinity, we are privileged not only to be inducted as a member into the community of God, the Church, but also to be inserted into the Family Tree of Father, Son and the Spirit. Triune God, in himself is a unified Family of Three Persons. What makes our Christian community so exceptional, so unique is the belief that we, though divided in various ways, are unified as one family, which founded on the love of our Triune God which 'has been poured into our hearts by the Holy Spirit which has been given to us' (Rom. 5: 5). Therefore we are to live in and by the same love as our 'sharing God'. He is the rolemodel for how we are to be in relationship with one another.

Dwelling continuously in this noble mystery of Trinity, let us greet every one we meet in our life, saying: *"May the grace of Our Lord Jesus Christ, and the love of God, and the communion of the Holy Spirit be with you all."*

TWENTY SEVENTH WEEKEND

The Feast of Corpus Christi
The breathtaking Eucharistic Transformation

*While they were eating, he took bread,
said the blessing, broke it, and gave it to
them, and said, "Take it; this is my body."
Then he took a cup, gave thanks, and
gave it to them, and they all drank from
it. He said to them, "This is my blood of
the covenant, which will be shed for many.
Amen, I say to you, I shall not drink again
the fruit of the vine until the day when I
drink it new in the kingdom of God." Then,
after singing a hymn, they went out to the
Mount of Olives. (Mk. 14: 22-26)*

Our Lord Jesus before he left from this world he
handed down to his disciples the ritual of celebrating his
Passover of redemption in the Sacrament of the Eucharist,
Scriptures and Church Tradition teach us that this ritual,
containing some awesome and very powerful actions and
words, becomes a remarkable source of our divine and
spiritual experience. The Spirit in our today's meditation
takes us to the Eucharistic Table to confirm in, and conform
to, this mystery of mysteries. From Church Catechism we
have learned about so many effects happening through
the Eucharist. Postmodern Age theologians, like Karl
Rahner, summing up all those benefits of the Sacrament of
Eucharist, underline the awesome incidence occurring in

every faithful communicant. They label it: The 'Eucharistic Transformation'.

The primary dimension of transformation is that we become so conscious and positive about the life we have been gifted with in this world. Despite its odds and challenges, this life has become the starting point of enjoying eternal life and that is what Jesus promised. *I am the bread of life...Amen, amen, I say to you, unless you eat the flesh of the Son of Man and drink his blood, you do not have life within you. Whoever eats my flesh and drinks my blood has eternal life, and I will raise him on the last day.* (Jn. 6: 35-53) Eucharist therefore is true food and drink which nourishes us and helps us share in the eternal life of Jesus already. This thought makes our participation in this ritual energizing us to live today's life to the brim.

By fully living the qualitylife of eternity we are transformed o be 'persons of self-giving'. The Sacrament of the Eucharist shows how Jesus gives himself, in total love, to be eaten by us. His self-giving was perfected and completed on the cross when he died, shedding the last drop of his blood for our salvation. Jesus, thus, gives himself totally for us. (Ref. Heb. 9: 11-15) He gives until nothing is left to give. He loves his own as much as to sacrifice everything for his loved ones. In this celebration of the Eucharist Jesus acts not only priest and the altar but also the victim of the new Passover, more perfectly and more realistically, as his Father willed it to be performed by his people (Ex. 24: 3-8). Our conscious and willful participation in the Eucharist would make us less selfish and more self-giving, loving, caring, forgiving and compassionate.

When we consume Jesus' Body and Blood, we are transformed like unto him. St Augustine heard the words of the Lord in his prayer: *You will not change me into yourself as you would food of your flesh; but you will be changed into me.* We become what we eat! Our participation of the Eucharist, challenges us to love, to promote, to uphold and to defend life in all its forms, from the moment of conception to natural death. Just as the Lord shares himself in the life-giving sacrament, we need to share our own lives, our talents, time and resources with the needy. This makes our Eucharist more meaningful and transforming.

Moreover by participating in the Eucharist we would possess an amazing ability to see dualities -- the pros and cons of situations as change approaches -- and to quickly and efficiently think them through before making any decisions. We would dare to look deeply into our desires, regenerate self-awareness and recognize psychological ambiguities. This will bring balance into our home and family life. We would pay attention to the details as we bring our inner and outer life into unity and harmony. Surely we will enjoy the changes occurring within us!

As we come to terms with ourselves, we would be able to see a more fulfilling purpose in life, and our field of experience broadens. We would focus on matters that affect us most deeply and, like magic, our life will become easier and things will seem to take care of themselves. We will have all the necessary resources and motivation to make tangible changes and achieve results in all our endeavors. We will become unique persons of self-giving, life-giving and surely unifying. In every step of our lives we will develop into a peacemaker and peacelover. We will be energized to live like a true champion of Eucharistic unity at home, in the community and around the nation.

TWENTY EIGHTH WEEKEND

Tenth Sunday in Ordinary Time

Are we inside or outside?

Jesus came home. Again the crowd gathered, making it impossible for them even to eat. When his relatives heard of this they set out to seize him, for they said, "He is out of his mind." The scribes who had come from Jerusalem said, "He is possessed by Beelzebul," and "By the prince of demons he drives out demons." ...His mother and his brothers arrived. Standing outside they sent word to him and called him. A crowd seated around him told him, "Your mother and your brothers and your sisters are outside asking for you." But he said to them in reply, "Who are my mother and my brothers?" And looking around at those seated in the circle he said, "Here are my mother and my brothers. For whoever does the will of God is my brother and sister and mother." (Mk. 3: 20-35)

As there are two sides in a coin, our life, related to God in Jesus, is made of both its inside and outside. The Spirit taking us today to the hilltop to meditate with the passage from Mark's Gospel and other Scriptural words related to it, underscores Mark's inclusion in his narration, that

'Jesus' family *standing outside*', as the core theme for our prayertime.

From the start of his public ministry Jesus preached his Gospel truths in so many ways, especially by his life and miraculous charitable deeds of healing and casting our demons from the needy people in order to offer to them a qualitylife in this world. Through the same ways he demonstrated the establishment of God's promised Kingdom among humans. Very regrettably many people around him didn't accept his sincere intentions and performances even though they considered themselves residing inside God's realm. Some named him as a 'disciple of Beelzebub'; many others considered him 'mad', quite out of his mind. Due to such callous arrogance and sheer ignorance, many rejected him till his death; some others joint first to his team but then left him; while many others conspired against him to the extent they caused him to die on the cross.

In the eyes of Jesus such self-righteous people are not only standing outside of God's Kingdom but also their sins will not be forgiven by God. He stated they were sinning against the Holy Spirit, namely they turned their backs on God by rejecting God's teaching and guidance. In other words, they totally fit to be 'inside' God's Kingdom. These people were like our first parents living and enjoying God's Garden of Life, yet refusing to listen to his word and disobeying him by eating the forbidden fruit. (Gen. 3: 9-15) This resulted in their being expelled from the garden. They were then on the outside and subject to all kinds of distress and suffering, left, by their own choice, on their own.

Jesus was aware of our human weakness that can make us deaf to hear his continuous knocking at our inner spirit and indifferent and stubborn to recognize him and his words of Truth, Life and Way. Hence he used the event Mark narrates in the Gospel to teach us a positive lesson for living fruitfully always inside his Kingdom both before and after our death. Pointing out those who were sitting at his feet like Mary of Bethany, around him like all his beneficiaries and listening to him, namely, those who are 'inside', with him sincerely being ready to commit themselves to his Gospel, said: *"Here are my mother and my brothers. For whoever does the will of God is my brother and sister and mother."*

What Jesus meant was that the new way he established by his coming in their midst was the source of valid and fruitful relationship his disciples should hold between each other; he was inaugurating a new family. In this family disciples are brothers and sisters to each other not on the basis of blood, or culture, or race, or nationality, or any other conventional group but solely on their faithful commitment to God's will- acknowledging him as our Lord and Brother and God as our Father.

Paul reminds us frequently in his writings about our human fragility and weakness: our gradual decline as we grow older; and we can be weighed down by many troubles. However, he advises us not to be groaning and mourning endlessly; rather we must be filled with hope; as long as we keep listening to Jesus' word of God's will coming to us at all time, our 'inner self is being renewed day by day' (Ref. 2 Cor. 4: 13; 5: 1). The million dollar question is: Are we on the outside or the inside of the Kingdom? To what extent do we listen to, accept and fully assimilate Jesus' call to belong to his family?

Eleventh Sunday in Ordinary Time

*The Word is sown in our conception
but rejuvenated by Sacraments*

Jesus said, "This is how it is with the kingdom of God; it is as if a man were to scatter seed on the land and would sleep and rise night and day and the seed would sprout and grow, he knows not how. Of its own accord the land yields fruit, first the blade, then the ear, then the full grain in the ear. And when the grain is ripe, he wields the sickle at once, for the harvest has come." He said, "To what shall we compare the kingdom of God, or what parable can we use for it? It is like a mustard seed that, when it is sown in the ground, is the smallest of all the seeds on the earth. But once it is sown, it springs up and becomes the largest of plants and puts forth large branches, so that the birds of the sky can dwell in its shade..." (Mk. 4: 26-34)

Jesus came to us to establish the Kingdom of God. We are led by the Spirit today to meditate on the Scriptural exhortations regarding how God works in that kingdom, with us and without us. This means, God's work will be carried out whether we cooperate or not. If we choose not to cooperate, God's plans will not be frustrated but we ourselves will be the losers. Let us start praying about this stunning factor.

God has sown the seed of his power, his love, his wisdom, his holiness, his sanctity, his joy, his peace already inside humanity. We are not fully sure how many centuries back he began this marvelous work. It was hidden; it was buried; it was watered, it was enlightened; it was nourished by the same Gardener for centuries. In general, Bible names this seed as God's Word. He has sown his Word in all the environments of the universe-mountains, oceans, planets, stars, and particularly every human heart. When each creature grows from that Word as it is designed, he can transplant it, break or prune it if need be, as he desires.

A benevolent time came in his eternal creative works, God revealed that the Word he has sown in his creations is none other than his Beloved Son Christ. He made this mysterious truth be manifested to humanity through Jesus of Nazareth. Mark underscores it throughout his Gospel, especially explaining it through Jesus' parable of the seed. Jesus, the God's Seed, was hidden, simple and humble in appearance like the mustard seed, but always was in God and with God. (Jn. 1: 1-5)

As any seed takes its proper duration for its maturation, so does the seed God had sown take its own course of growth-sprouting, blossoming, flowering, and fructifying. While this God's Seed took so many centuries to grow to its full structure at one point of human history, as the Bible loves to proclaim through Prophets and Apostles, it was none other than Jesus of Nazareth, Mary's Son. Ezekiel's prophetic words in his Book (17: 22-24) certainly target to picturize the unique action of God wrought in Jesus.

The historical process of the Word becoming incarnate has become a model for every human being for how to make the seed of God sown in our birth sprout and bloom and grow to its full stature. The amazing factor in human creation is the unthinkable potential discovered in every human. If any individual cherishes the Word sown by God within oneself with loving tender care, they will, as trees portrayed in the Bible, put forth branches and bear fruit, and become a majestic cedar. Birds of every kind shall dwell beneath it, every winged thing in the shade of its boughs. (Ez. 17: 23) And as the Psalmist sings, *he/she shall flourish like the palm tree, like a cedar of Lebanon shall grow and shall bear fruit even in old age being vigorous and sturdy.* (92: 13-15)

When Jesus said 'the kingdom of God' he meant it was the power or glory or status or realm or environment of God that is present within us, in our midst, and is near us. He has emphasized through his parabolic teaching that this realm, environment of God, sown as a tiny little mustard seed at our conception and then watered, nourished by the Sacraments, will grow and bear solid and valid fruits if we remain with him always. Paul is never tired of advising us that those of us who earnestly work hard to manage our inner gardening of the God's Seed, should be always courageous, although we know that while we are at home in the body we are away from the Lord, for we walk by faith, not by sight; and we should be ready to face the judgment seat of Christ so that each may receive recompense, according to what we did in the body, whether good or evil.

THIRTIETH WEEKEND

Feast of Nativity of John the Baptist

*True witnessing to Christ is by our life
and death, other efforts extra!*

*When the time arrived for Elizabeth to
have her child she gave birth to a son. Her
neighbors and relatives heard that the
Lord had shown his great mercy toward
her, and they rejoiced with her...All who
heard these things took them to heart,
saying, "What, then, will this child be?"
For surely the hand of the Lord was with
him. The child grew and became strong in
spirit, and he was in the desert until the
day of his manifestation to Israel.* (Lk. 1:
57-80)

Only three times during the year does the Church
celebrate a birthday: for Jesus, for his mother Mary and for
John the Baptist. How does John's birthday get speciality
in joining into the company of those two illustrious persons
in salvation history? The main reason for the celebrity-
position given to John is his intense and honest life of
witnessing to God's graciousness revealed in Jesus. It is
on this phenomenal fact the Spirit summons us today to
meditate.

John's first witnessing started at his conception and
birth by strange happenings that directed the public's
attention to the mysterious and transcendent presence
and interaction of the Almighty. They were the miracles of

Angel announcing the good news of his birth; old parents conceiving him; his father having been punished to be dumb but then stunningly recovers his power of speech; and leaping for joy at the presence of Messiah's mother, while John was still an infant in his mother's womb. Above all, he witnessed to the Almighty by the name 'John' given by the Angel as well as being accepted finally in an awesome way by his parents and relatives. John literally means: 'God is gracious'.

As an adult, John witnessed through his choice of milieu for his entire living which bore witness to a different 'otherworldly' reality. He became a man of the most austere desert; totally separated himself from the world in order to give testimony of another world; and within his solitude he was able to hear the voice of God. His simple and unglamorous dressing bore witness as well. Both his preference of location and food and dress-code demonstrated a counter-culture, going against the prevailing wisdom of his day. He testified by his unobtrusive lifestyle to how important it is to be simple and detached from the things of this world. Being aware of John's unrelented life of witnessing to God's Kingdom values, praised him in public: *What did you go out to the desert to see—a reed swayed by the wind? Then what did you go out to see? Someone dressed in fine garments? Those who dress luxuriously and live sumptuously are found in royal palaces. Then what did you go out to see? A prophet? Yes, I tell you, and more than a prophet. This is the one about whom scripture says: 'Behold, I am sending my messenger ahead of you, he will prepare your way before you.' I tell you, among those born of women, no one is greater than John; yet the least in the kingdom of God is greater than he.* (Lk. 7: 24-28)

Beyond all the above-listed elements of his witnessing, John's message was the most intriguing factor that placed him as the third person with Jesus and Mary in God's salvific history. His message was all about Jesus, whom he pointed out to people as the Messiah, the Lamb of God who would take away their sins. He too verified to them Jesus' glorious and powerful identity. And he underlined that every action of Jesus was the one and only source of salvation. In this regard, he witnessed his unworthiness and limitation before Jesus. *One mightier than I is coming after me. I am not worthy to stoop and loosen the thongs of his sandals. I have baptized you with water; He will baptize you with the Holy Spirit* (Mark 1: 7-8). John not only preached a message, he was the message. He was an authentic witness because he himself was authentic. That was why people couldn't resist a witness like him. As Paul would proclaim about his contribution to God's salvific plan, *John heralded his coming by proclaiming a baptism of repentance to all the people of Israel...* (Acts 13: 24-25)

John's ultimate witness came in his death and that too was caused by his unrelented testimony to Jesus' Gospel value of truth and fidelity in human relationships. King Herod personified those human beings who from the beginning of time until the end of time, choose to live a lie, rather than the truth. From the depths of the dungeon, John's martyrdom is a testimony that every disciple of Jesus must never be afraid to proclaim the truth.

John reminds us on his birthday that we are called to be witnesses like him, especially in this modern Age of total secularism and worldliness. We must witness like him that our identity is centered on true spirituality, and that our morality derives from that spirituality.

Thirteenth Sunday in Ordinary Time
The right approach to Faith-Healing

Because God did not make death, nor does he rejoice in the destruction of the living. For he fashioned all things that they might have being, and the creatures of the world are wholesome; there is not a destructive drug among them nor any domain of Hades on earth, for righteousness is undying. For God formed us to be imperishable; the image of his own nature he made us. But by the envy of the devil, death entered the world, and they who are allied with him experience it. (Wis. 1: 13-15; 2: 23-24)

While we are proud of our heritage of Enlightenment and Independence, through which human life has been blessed with technology, science and material possessions and all sorts of human pleasures, we also should acknowledge the dark side of our lives. We are now in a culture of death, depression and anxieties; we are experiencing a culture of reverse values; a culture of disbelief and violence; a culture of poverty of spiritual contentment. As Job we cry aloud to our Creator 'where are you God?' and 'why have you done this to us?' Today the Spirit warmly invites us to listen in meditation to God's response to our question through Scriptures.

God indicates to us that he is not the source of evils we experience. *God did not make death, nor does he rejoice in the destruction of the living... For God formed man to be imperishable; the image of his own nature he made him. But by the envy of the devil, death entered the world.* The evils we encounter are all human-made perversions to a beautiful structure of creation God intended to be good and life-giving. This message echoes what we read in the Book of Genesis.

The death, spoken here, refers not only to what we face at the end of life but also the semi-deaths we undergo in daily life, such as illness-chronic and terminal, temporary sicknesses like cold, stomachache, and the hurt feelings of anxiety, discouragement and chronic sadness. All these deaths-little or huge, are the wages of our human sins and not from the hands of our Creator. However our Creator God as a Parent, never left us in that grim situation. He came to us in the form of Jesus Christ in order to liberate us and show us the right way to cope with our awkward creatureliness. In all the Gospels we come across how Jesus paved the way of healing our perverted situation. He demonstrated it by his miraculous deeds.

All Mark's narrations of Jesus' miracles, especially the two miracles the Spirit presents to us today (Mk. 5: 21-43), clearly demonstrate Jesus' power over life and death of humans, who mess up the order of creation. The woman in the crowd simply touches Jesus' cloak, and immediately power flows from him into her and she is restored. Jesus arrives at the bedside of the girl, who is already dead; but when he touches her hand and summons her, she is alive again. Whatever God of the living touches comes alive. The woman in the crowd believed so deeply in Jesus that, even without his choice, she was able to tap into the life force that sprang from him. When he touched the child's hand, life leaped through him into her.

This sort of healing from Jesus is possible by our strong faith in Jesus' power. Faith means staying in touch with Jesus, even if we must push through the curious but unbelieving crowds and the mockery of the professional mourners who discount religion or the promise of resurrection. When we falter in our faith, Jesus says to us, *don't be afraid, just have faith*. When we struggle to find Jesus, he encourages us to persevere. Once healed, he declares in appreciative tone, *your faith has saved you*.

According to our 'Faith-Healer' we too must share our healing faith and love with one another by nursing, encouraging, consoling, strengthening and assisting when others are ridden by various maladies. These gestures of healing, as the Spirit points out to us through Paul (2 Cor. 8: 7-15), need not only to our relatives and friends but also any strangers whom even we don't know about their identities. We are reminded of how Jesus, rich though he was, became poor for our sake, *to make you rich out of his poverty*. Interestingly, Paul writes that in sharing with others we are not expected to give away what we genuinely need ourselves but only from our surplus. And, when we share our surplus today with someone in greater need, ourselves can hope to be treated in the same way in our own hour of need.

All of us, in some way or another, are constantly in need of God's healing. The Spirit tells us that God wills fullness of life for us and therefore there is no circumstance or condition to which God cannot be present. The human challenge is to have the courage to believe that what looks like death does not have the final word. This is the exact definition of 'Faith-Healing'.

THIRTY SECOND WEEKEND

Fourteenth Sunday in Ordinary Time
No gain for a prophet without any pain

He departed from there and came to his native place, accompanied by his disciples. When the Sabbath came he began to teach in the synagogue, and many who heard him were astonished. They said, "Where did this man get all this? What kind of wisdom has been given him? What mighty deeds are wrought by his hands! Is he not the carpenter, the son of Mary, and the brother of James and Joses and Judas and Simon? And are not his sisters here with us?" And they took offense at him. Jesus said to them, "A prophet is not without honor except in his native place and among his own kin and in his own house. So he was not able to perform any mighty deed there, apart from curing a few sick people by laying his hands on them. He was amazed at their lack of faith. He went around to the villages in the vicinity teaching. (Mk. 6: 1-6)

As we experience the wear and tear and struggles of daily living, we are bound to pick up some scars along the way. Some of these are physical and of little consequence, as in the little bumps and scrapes of childhood's rough-and-tumble play. Others are more severe, as in the bruises of the abused or the wounds suffered by victims of war, injustice and illness. There are other scars that go more than skin-deep. Emotional and psychological and even spiritual traumas can create lasting mementos of suffering that are difficult to heal. These experiences are written on the faces and on the souls of those who suffer them and often come back to haunt them with uncanny freshness. In this regard, we as disciples of Jesus are not exempted at all. Today the Spirit calls us to meditate on our Master's trail of tears in his life and be inspired by his example of how he handled his sufferings in his Prophetic life.

Jesus has borne ignominious sufferings and finally experienced horrible death for the sake of the Gospel. Despite the wonders he had done and all the healings and the conversions he had effected, we notice the people, who thought they knew him best, rejected Jesus. While they *were astonished at his wise teachings and miraculous charitable deeds, they took offense at him.* Indeed his people were astounded at his doctrine yet they were offended at his person, namely they were prejudiced against him and looked upon him with contempt; and for that reason would not receive his proposal that they should accept him sent by God as their Way, Truth and Life.

Undoubtedly Jesus found it hard to cope with such a blind and arrogant rejection from his own people. But from the onset of his earthly life Jesus was fully aware of his call to act as God's Prophet. He was convinced that the Spirit of the Lord anointed him and sent him to preach God's Kingdom values. He too cherished vivid memory of what he read about the deplorable lives of Prophets like Jeremiah who wrote in his Book God already warned him about the horrible things he would face in his Prophetic ministry: *I am sending you to the Israelites, a nation of rebels who have rebelled against me; they and their ancestors have been in revolt against me to this very day. Their children are bold of face and stubborn of heart—to them I am sending you.* (Ez. 2: 3-4)

Hence he faced all those odds and obstacles triumphantly, putting up with his people's denunciation not only as a 'human thing' but also mainly it belongs to any Prophet's territory. It is not surprising, as Mark indicates, he performed some healings among them; setting aside the snubs they put upon him, he exhibited his graciousness even to the evil and unthankful. Also, being smarty, he didn't permit himself brooding, groaning and mourning on his failure in the town; rather he went round about the village, and continue his teaching.

As Christians, being baptized and anointed by God's Spirit to live as the disciples of Jesus, we are called to be 'Prophets' in this world. Prophet means to be a person for God. As one spiritual author puts it very well it is a ministry of reaching out to the world in and through and with and for God in Jesus. Imitating our Master, as Paul did ((2 Cor. 12: 7-10), we should endure insults, persecution, rejection and a certain personal suffering as Paul's *thorn in the flesh.* We must also take positively and endure willingly the scars and bruises we would worn on our body and even in spirit because of our prophetic ministry. As a matter of fact, let us remember always: Those who reach out to others by witnessing always to the goodness and truth cannot travel through this life unscathed.

Fifteenth Sunday in Ordinary Time

With inner drive of our call let us win the world

> *Blessed be the God and Father of our Lord Jesus Christ, who has blessed us in Christ with every spiritual blessing in the heavens, as he chose us in him, before the foundation of the world, to be holy and without blemish before him. In love he destined us for adoption to himself through Jesus Christ, in accord with the favor of his will, for the praise of the glory of his grace that he granted us in the beloved... In him we were also chosen, destined in accord with the purpose of the One who accomplishes all things according to the intention of his will, so that we might exist for the praise of his glory... (Eph. 1: 3-14)*

Some among us consider life is unfair and so they dare to die soon; many others esteem there is nothing to gain after death and so they plan to live. This kind of confusion, distortion or negative view about life is a pest bugging all humans at one time on another. However God does not want us, his disciples, to live in that suffocating mindsetup. The Spirit instructs us today to go deeper into some Scriptural passages to help ourselves erasing these negative thoughts and to live our earthly life contently, smilingly and fruitfully.

One of the best advice the Scriptures offer us today for our life's survival and success is to clearly understand and uphold the glorious vocation of our life. Paul elegantly portrays our life's vocation in his writings: Our essence and existence are already predestined by God the Creator; he chose us even *before the foundation of the world.* The reason behind this startling deal of God to us is to *accomplish all his endeavors fully and realize all his intentions totally in his Son Jesus.* God's main intention for his calling us is every one of us *to be holy and without blemish before him like his Son*; and he chose us so that we might *exist for the praise of his glory*; and *to sum up all things in Christ in heaven and on earth.*

This is how all God's friends, prophets and disciples esteemed highly about their vulnerable lives. Let us take for example Prophet Amos. He was a humble shepherd but he was fully convinced that he had been called by God to prophesy. As he narrates challenging the king that he was in no way a 'professional' who is employed to prophesy, in order to earn his livelihood; rather he insisted the One in Upstairs urged him to do this hectic job and he obeyed him. (Am. 7: 12-15) When he was threatened by his king who ordered him to flee off from his territory, he challenged him with his audacious tenacity that *I am not a prophet, nor do I belong to a company of prophets. I am a herdsman and a dresser of sycamores, but the LORD took me from following the flock, and the LORD said to me, 'Go, and prophesy to my people Israel.'* (Am. 7: 14-15)

Above all, Jesus has been the best rolemodel to us in handling life's problems by our inner conviction. He showed it first in his own life and taught his disciples the same. He kept in his heart and mind that only God the Father called him for performing his Prophetic role as

People's Messiah; as Amos, he claimed it in public: Quoting Isaiah 61: 1-2, *The Spirit of the Lord is upon me, because he has anointed me to bring glad tidings to the poor. He has sent me to proclaim liberty to captives...,* he confirmed it was a prophecy about his identity: *Today this scripture passage is fulfilled in your hearing.* (Lk. 4: 16-21) Therefore being too zealous of God's will and his Kingdom-values, he esteemed God's will as his food and life. In the Gospels we read that all disciples were chosen by Jesus first to abide in him, meaning to become fully imbibed with his inner convictions of their Godly predestination and then to be sent out as the proxies of his Prophetic role, to bear witness to God's love by preaching and healing. *He summoned the Twelve and began to send them out two by two and gave them authority over unclean spirits.* (Mk. 6: 7-13)

He bestowed to his disciples authority and power to drive out unclean spirits, first from themselves and then from others; knowing how humans can easily be subdued by those unclean spirits, he commanded his disciples that they should be detach themselves from worldly things, instructing them *to take nothing for the journey but a walking stick—no food, no sack, no money in their belts;* but must totally cling on to God for their needs; he too advised them *to shake the dust off,* perhaps referring to the dust of feelings like resentment, anger, hatred and revenge in order to be free enough to let our faith in Jesus Christ shine not just in words but also in our actions. Then, he wanted them to drive out the demons from other people.

Even though we are proud to be born and bred in the post-modern Age we are living in a world which is still in desperate need of prophets and apostles sent by Jesus. Our human race continues to be enslaved by so many unclean spirits. Let us fully believe in the truth that we had been called and destined from all ages to come and to be born and reborn at this hectic period to continue the work of Jesus joining the team of messengers sent out by the Spirit to walk the walk of Jesus and certainly to work the work of Jesus.

THIRTY FOURTH WEEKEND

Sixteenth Sunday in Ordinary Time
*Jesus' Mission hangs in the balance
of both justice and peace*

*The apostles gathered together with Jesus
and reported all they had done and taught.
He said to them, "Come away by yourselves
to a deserted place and rest a while." People
were coming and going in great numbers,
and they had no opportunity even to eat.
So they went off in the boat by themselves
to a deserted place. People saw them
leaving and many came to know about
it. They hastened there on foot from all
the towns and arrived at the place before
them. When he disembarked and saw the
vast crowd, his heart was moved with pity
for them, for they were like sheep without
a shepherd; and he began to teach them
many things.* (Mk. 6: 30-34)

In the life on earth we feel as if living and moving
through a deserted place due to its inevitable risky
environment. In today's meditation time the Spirit asks us
to be enlightened by the Scriptures to see the right way to
survive and be successful in our earthly journey.

God is the supreme Shepherd to all of us. He cares his
flock; he cannot bear the sight of his sheep getting into
trouble, being scattered, suffering from hunger and thirst;
he is so compassionate to the flock that he cannot let them

remain in fear and trembling and lonely. It is this conviction, every day we join with the Psalmist in saying aloud: *The LORD is my shepherd; there is nothing I lack.* (Ps. 23: 1-4) People of the world, not understanding such faith may criticize it as some sort of weird and utopian claim. However we know we were confirmed on this belief by our Scriptures, especially by Jesus to whom, as Jeremiah prophesied, God has handed his leadership over. (Jer. 23: 1-6) Jesus never argued against it and he willingly accepted that role to shepherd us in God's name. He imitated the Supreme Shepherd and showed mercy and compassion to the needy and hungry people. As the Gospels spell out, *his heart was always moved with pity for the humans, for they were like sheep without a shepherd.* He discovered they were full of problems, issues and desolate experiences of life. He did within his limited and restricted power and situation all that he could. He was a round-the-clock missionary of preaching, teaching and performing healing deeds.

Very surprisingly, as his Father admonished him, he delegated his shepherding-leadership with other fellow human beings whom he called as his disciples. He had sent them to do the same missionary works in and around Palestine. They came back full of joy and enumerated to Jesus all the experiences with excitement. Jesus noticed they were tired and weary because of their tedious missionary journey. At this juncture, our Master taught them and through them to us, who are now engaged in his missionary endeavors, a very important lesson for our continued winning in leadership management. We can sum up that lesson in one single Biblical term: "Justice." God's prophecy about the identity of Jesus is *the Lord our Justice.*

The term justice also literally means "balance"; *'to stand in balance.'* All our mental, physical and spiritual problems come out of the imbalanced handling of our own lives and roles. We should know we are divided within ourselves; human life is a very risky business to deal with and especially when that business is full of responsibilities such as leading others as shepherds. While we place more attention or emphasis on one side of us the other side reaps its own toll. In this Jesus instructs us to be *in balance*.

When he observed his disciples were so tired and burnt out he said to them, *Come away by yourselves to a deserted place and rest a while.* This means he wanted them not just enjoying leisure time but being with him alone. This is for getting back more spiritual energy they lacked. Hence with Jesus they went off in the boat to a deserted place. However, as Mark narrates, people saw them leaving and many came to know about it. They hastened there on foot from all the towns and arrived at the place before them. Jesus saw the same crowd again from which he purposely wanted he and his disciples to be freed. Again he uses his justice, namely *balance*: His heart was moved with pity for them, for they were like sheep without a shepherd; and he began to teach them many things.

This is just to tell us how we should be balanced in our managing Jesus' Gospel-mission. The mission entrusted to us by Jesus is to establish in every human spirit the God's Kingdom consisting of both peace and justice as well. As Paul would write about the purpose of Jesus' mission, *he came and preached peace to you who were far off and peace to those who were near, for through him we both have access in one Spirit to the Father.* (Ref. Eph. 2: 13-18) This peacemaking work must first help us to cherish it within our life and spirit and then it should be intensely performed among the humans who are dissipated, hungering for rest and peace and better life.

Seventeenth Sunday in Ordinary Time

The magnanimous and restful way of helping the needy

...When Jesus raised his eyes and saw that a large crowd was coming to him, he said to Philip, 'Where can we buy enough food for them to eat?' He said this to test him, because he himself knew what he was going to do. Philip answered him, 'Two hundred days' wages worth of food would not be enough for each of them to have a little bit'. One of his disciples, Andrew, the brother of Simon Peter, said to him, 'There is a boy here who has five barley loaves and two fish; but what good are these for so many?' Jesus said, 'Have the people recline.' Now there was a great deal of grass in that place. So the men reclined, about five thousand in number. Then Jesus took the loaves, gave thanks, and distributed them to those who were reclining, and also as much of the fish as they wanted. When they had had their fill, he said to his disciples, 'Gather the fragments left over, so that nothing will be wasted.' So they collected them, and filled twelve wicker baskets with fragments from the five barley loaves that had been more than they could eat. When the people saw the sign he had done, they said, 'This *is truly the Prophet, the one who is to come into the world.' Since Jesus knew that they were going to come and carry him off to make him king, he withdrew again to the mountain alone.* (Jn. 6: 1-15)

We know how we, many times feel restless fretting over the impending problems of our life. Our littleness and frugal earnings, shrinking of our savings and our helplessness lead us to hopeless situation. Today the Spirit bids us through his Scriptural passages to come out of such gloomiest situation of life and try to rise up for bringing miracles to us as well as to the needy neighbors.

In the event of Jesus' miraculous multiplication of loaves, we hear Mark inserting the natural human reaction of the disciples when their Master asked them to feed thousands of hungry stomachs with the tiny little bread and fish available in their hands. They retorted: *There is a boy here who has five barley loaves and two fish; but what good are these for so many? Two hundred days' wages worth of food would not be enough for each of them to have a little.* However the miracle-worker performed his feeding job perfectly and even overflowingly. History tells us that at the time of perils and needs, while God's men behave calm and restful, ordinary human beings hassle and fuss over. We notice this, for example, in an OT narration about Prophet Elisha's miracle of feeding the hungry.

When the Prophet, receiving a devotee's offering of twenty barley loaves, ordered to give them to people to eat, his servant bothered about, and questioned the Prophet's unrealistic effort of feeding hundreds of people with few breads: *How can I set this before a hundred people?* Elisha tranquilly replied: *Give it to the people to eat, for thus says the LORD: You will eat and have some left over...* (2 Kgs. 4: 42-44)

This is the way Jesus expects his disciples manage any life's problems, retaining peace and calmness. His Spirit lists out some Scriptural tips for us to attain this remarkable ability. First he exhorts us to assure ourselves of the eternal truth: *'The LORD is near to all who call upon him, to all who call upon him in truth. He gives them their food in due season. He opens wide his hand and satisfy the desire of every living thing.'* (Ref. Ps. 145) Consequently the Spirit persuades us to totally surrender everything to the Lord and become his prisoner. That is what Paul and most of Jesus' followers did. Paul loved to call himself as *I am a prisoner for the Lord* and in that unthinkable calmness he could advise others from his dungeon that they should cherish Christian values such as humility, gentleness, patience forgiving, peace and unity. (Ref. Eph. 4: 1-6)

When this kind of mindsetup is established and maintained, the Spirit of Jesus, who has made our inner spirit as his abode, begins to urge us to share what we possess or procure with the needy, helpless and starving people as much as we can within our limit, as maximum as possible, and as much as it is needed. We become fully aware of the fact these unfortunate humans can find the compassionate God only through these sort of kind gestures. Plus when we handout and share our possessions and bread they first give thanks to God like Jesus did and then distribute the gifts. At the end of the day, we should never wait for the praise and appreciation from our beneficiaries, rather like Jesus with humility either fly away or shut ourselves in our private chamber and tell the Lord smilingly as any faithful servant would do: *We are unprofitable servants; we have done what we were obliged to do.* (Lk. 17: 10)

Eighteenth Sunday in Ordinary Time

The new Way of earthly living with the help of Eucharist

...Jesus answered them and said, 'Amen, amen, I say to you, you are looking for me not because you saw signs but because you ate the loaves and were filled. Do not work for food that perishes but for the food that endures for eternal life, which the Son of Man will give you. For on him the Father, God, has set his seal.' So they said to him, "What can we do to accomplish the works of God?" Jesus answered and said to them, "This is the work of God that you believe in the one he sent." So they said to him "What sign can you do, that we may see and believe in you? What can you do?... So Jesus said to them, "Amen, amen, I say to you, it was not Moses who gave the bread from heaven; my Father gives you the true bread from heaven. For the bread of God is that which comes down from heaven and gives life to the world." So they said to him, "Sir, give us this bread always." Jesus said to them, "I am the bread of life; whoever comes to me will never hunger, and whoever believes in me will never thirst. (Jn. 6: 24-35)

Christianity, in its first century, was not labeled as a religion or any sort of institution as we talk about it these days. Rather it was named as "the Way." Early Christians were called "followers of the Way." Today the Spirit invites us through the Scriptures to enter into the Way of Jesus especially in judging and using our earthly lifetime.

The first advice Jesus bestows us is to go beyond the present situation of our life. In our dealings with God, he says, we should not separate this present moment from the past. We read in the Gospels that the people, living in Jesus' time, ignored the power and identity of Jesus behind the miracles they saw, asking him some more miracles to do so that they could believe him. They said to him: *What sign can you do, that we may see and believe in you? What can you do? Our ancestors ate manna in the desert, as it is written: 'He gave them bread from heaven to eat.'* This is the mistake the old Israelites were doing in the desert. They were so much worried about today's bread that they did not trust that their God who had done wonderful things in their past would do the same. They grumbled against God. (Ref. Ex. 16: 2-15) Jesus cautions us therefore not to behave that way. We should not forget the great things that the Lord has done throughout our lives. Remembrance is a sign of gratitude. With renewed mind of Christ we should remind ourselves of the marvelous deeds of God in our past and connect this present situation to the past endeavors of God done in our lives out of his compassion and mercy.

Also, the Spirit inspires us through the Scriptures to see the Giver beyond the gifts. Everything that is happening is simply a sign for us to reach out the God who is the Provider. We should never ask in ignorance *"what is this?"* as the old Israelites asked in the desert. Moses indicated that it was a food beyond natural and artificial;

he explained to them, *"This is the bread that the LORD has given you to eat."* And the Lord God also pointed out to them: *"So that you may know that I, the LORD, am your God."* The Israelites were being called to accept the manna and the quail as gifts and to see beyond those gifts to the God who had brought them from Egypt and was guiding them to freedom and a new way of life. We notice the same ignorance and indifference of the people at Jesus' time, unable to see what was beyond his miracles. They ignored the power and identity of Jesus present behind the miracles and therefore asked him some more miracles to do so. Jesus answered and said to them, *"This is the work of God that you believe in the one he sent."* He adds: *"I am the bread of life; whoever comes to me will never hunger, and whoever believes in me will never thirst."*

Everything in this universe is the sign and symbol of the goodness, beauty and wisdom of the Creator. Any event that occurs, anything we handle, we see, we touch, we feel, we come in contact with and everyone whom we relate to are simply the outer signs of God, the Creator, the Provider, the Redeemer and the Judge. Therefore we have to go beyond these things and see what and who is beyond these. This is the "new Way" that we follow with our renewed mind and heart in Jesus. Referring to this 'new way' Paul writes: *"You should put away the old self of your former way of life and put on the new self, created in God's way as you were taught in Christ* (Ref. Eph. 4: 17-24)

Indisputably to follow such 'renewed way' is very hard. Therefore in order to get acquainted with this unique way of life, Christ entrusted to us the Sacrament of "the Eucharist." In this celebration we exercise our new-way spiritual ability by seeing and believing what is hidden beyond the bread and wine. If we are to accept the bread that God gives to us in Jesus for our new way of life, it is essential to look beyond and to see where the sign is pointing. Learning to look beyond in this way remains the challenge of Eucharist.

Nineteenth Sunday in Ordinary Time

*Rise up; eat Jesus' Food; continue
your Marathon on Hilltop*

The Jews murmured about him because he said, "I am the bread that came down from heaven"...Jesus answered and said to them, "Stop murmuring among yourselves. No one can come to me unless the Father who sent me draw him, and I will raise him on the last day. It is written in the prophets: 'They shall all be taught by God.' Everyone who listens to my Father and learns from him comes to me. Not that anyone has seen the Father except the one who is from God; he has seen the Father. Amen, amen, I say to you, whoever believes has eternal life. I am the bread of life. Your ancestors ate the manna in the desert, but they died; this is the bread that comes down from heaven so that one may eat it and not die. I am the living bread that came down from heaven; whoever eats this bread will live forever; and the bread that I will give is my flesh for the life of the world." (Jn. 6: 41-51)

Many seniors of this world consider the human life is a mystery; a bundle of problems and issues; though short-lived but with continued struggle; a challenge imposing on us many times heavy burdens of unfair treatments. This negative thoughts make them feel discouraged and depressed. But this weekend the Spirit inspires us through his Scriptures to rethink of our life very positively and to rise up and walk productively by using God's amazing resources.

We are exhorted by Scriptures to esteem our life in this world as a journey traveling from one end to the other. It is a journey of our inner spirit hidden but active in our body, and not just from the womb to the tomb. Rather, it is a journey from an eternal origin to an eternal destiny, namely from God to God. It is like a mountaineering to reach its peak as Hilary of Norway did for the first time ever to reach the Everest of Himalayas. It's not just a struggle but positively it is a sportive effort to reach our destiny. In this journey of climbing our goal is to reach the mountain of the Lord as Prophet Elijah tried to run to the mountain of God, Horeb, as we read in one of the Biblical episodes (1 Kgs. 19: 4-8)

This 'hilltop of our life', as I label it, is a destiny of pure love and justice, filled with peace and joy. Paul portrays it as a life, freed of all bitterness, fury, anger, shouting, reviling and malice; it is full of kindness, compassion, forgiveness and love. In other words, the 'hilltop life', which we are destined for, is simply a life of the children of God, imitating exactly God our Father in Jesus. (Ref. Eph. 4: 30 – 5: 2)

We know it is indeed a hard journey to pull through. Therefore we are told that our Creator has promised and continues to offer us a nutritious and medicinal food for our climbing. Jesus called it the 'Bread of life'. Whereas in OT times God directly bestowed this food through his Angels as he did to the Prophet, to lift him up from all his worries, today offers us this living bread from heaven through Jesus. To our surprise, John put words in Jesus' mouth to explain Jesus' mysterious personality and identity. Jesus claims himself as that *bread from heaven given by our Father to nourish us in our life-journey.* Generally the term 'bread' brings to our mind certain resource that offers life's nourishment, satisfying the hunger, and giving joy to community, family, memory and life.

This is what Jesus meant when he promised that he is the bread from heaven. In the Bible, in the church and in life Jesus Christ means all of these things. It is very ironic this Jesus who called himself the living bread was born in Bethlehem, which means 'house of bread.' Jesus himself is the source of the nourishment we need on our daily journey toward our destiny of Godly life.

As Mother Teresa made a remarkable observation about us who live and move in the developed nations, we, the people blessed by God with material and physical bread, are the ones who need very badly this 'Bread from heaven.' According to the assessment of this Saint, we have a long way to go on our journey to find our destiny and to reach God's hilltop peak. Like Elijah, we need God's true bread from heaven. Church guided by the Spirit understands the mystery enclosed in Jesus' promise of bestowing the heavenly Bread, and his explication of it as his own Body and Blood, which she calls the Eucharist, is the food from heaven to forgive, to soothe, to nourish, and to strengthen all who receive it in worthy manner.

Most of our maladies are generated from the soul. As we frequent to this Sacrament, like Prophet Elijah, receiving full energy we can start seeking the Lord forty days and forty nights; and certainly at the end we will reach the Realm of the Divine within us, where we will encounter God and continue to perform our daily duties of love in full commitment.

THIRTY EIGHTH WEEKEND

Twentieth Sunday in Ordinary Time

Let us long for the main dishes in God's Banquet

> *I am the living bread that came down from heaven; whoever eats this bread will live forever; and the bread that I will give is my flesh for the life of the world." The Jews quarreled among themselves, saying, "How can this man give us his flesh to eat?" Jesus said to them, "Amen, amen, I say to you, unless you eat the flesh of the Son of Man and drink his blood, you do not have life within you. Whoever eats my flesh and drinks my blood has eternal life, and I will raise him on the last day. For my flesh is true food, and my blood is true drink. Whoever eats my flesh and drinks my blood remains in me and I in him. Just as the living Father sent me and I have life because of the Father, so also the one who feeds on me will have life because of me. This is the bread that came down from heaven. Unlike your ancestors who ate and still died, whoever eats this bread will live forever."* (Jn. 6: 51-58)

Most of you, like me, enjoy any party that includes fun, drink and tasty food. In every country, in every race and tribe we notice people host sumptuous dinners on special occasions like weddings, wedding anniversaries, birth days and so on. Today the Spirit reminds us through his Biblical verses that such a lavish Banquet hosted eternally by God in his Son and invites us to meditate and pray to include us into this sumptuous Meal.

Bible tells us that our physical food, talents, IQ, natural resources are God's sharing with us in his banquet. Sometimes as it is labeled as a 'banquet of wisdom' (Ref. Wis. 9: 1-6). And in some other places the Scripture names it a banquet of life, banquet of joy, banquet of love and so on. *Taste and see the goodness of the Lord.* (Ps. 34) Jesus, summing up everything that was said in OT, refers to his own sharing of his Body and Blood as the 'Banquet of the Bread' declaring that *'whoever eats this bread will live forever; and the bread that I will give for the life of the world."* According to the description the Bible offers us about God's banquet, we can understand what sort of menu he serves us in his Banquet: Besides the side dishes of his physical, intellectual and social gifts, the main courses he places in our plate are: Eternal Life, Godly Wisdom, Sacrificial Love, Uncompromising Justice, and Never-ending Heavenly Bliss.

God's banquet is so remarkable that God expects some prerequisites from those who decide to participate and enjoy in it. First we asked to be fully aware of the greatest difference between the banquets humans host and that of God. Though both are lavish banquets, human banquets are limited only to certain guests. But God, to his Banquet, invites every human being with no discrimination whatsoever. Anyone who is hungry enough to hear and accept her invitation. They may be slave or servant or poor or dumb. *Let whoever is naive turn in here; to any who lack sense I say, 'Come, eat of my food, and drink of the wine I have mixed!'* (Wis. 9: 4-5)

Indubitably those dishes served in God's banquet are all nourishing our spiritual hunger. They are all covered dishes. We cannot easily open the covers and eat them as we like to. It is all in the hands of the Banquet host, God himself, who has to open them for us in his time. Hence the second condition we have to fulfill is to go on longing for such food, develop a deep hunger for the main dishes. Not all Scriptures of the world religions say that God offers himself as food. Only Jesus highlighted this truth which we call the incarnational aspect of Christian life. Being the Son of God Jesus boldly claims he is God's Banquet. Henri Nouwen described in his book *With Burning Hearts*: 'The Eucharist is the most ordinary and the most divine gesture imaginable. Jesus is God giving himself completely. He does not hold back or cling to his own possessions, not even to himself. He gives all there is to give'. Jesus desires that we should long for such eternal food. When he asks us to eat his flesh and drink his blood we should never take these Biblical words out of context; rather in Jewish terms both flesh and blood denote the entire life of Christ. Hence when we participate in the Eucharist, eating the bread, namely his flesh and drinking the wine, namely his blood, we show our faith and commitment there to possess the entire life of Jesus.

We firmly believe that in his banquet we receive all his attitudes and life's quests to be godly, to be wise, to be just, to be loving, to be blissful and thus to be a genuine Christian. As Paul advises us, *we will watch carefully how we live, not as foolish persons but as wise, making the most of the opportunity.* Adhering and assimilating Jesus' life, his attitudes, and his words will enjoy all the main courses in the Banquet he serves; consequently, *we will be filled with the Spirit, singing and playing to the Lord in our hearts, giving thanks always and for everything in the name of our Lord Jesus Christ to God the Father.* (Ref. Eph. 5: 15-20)

THIRTY NINETH WEEKEND

Twenty First Sunday in Ordinary Time

Do or Die...Choice is ours

Then many of his disciples who were listening said, "This saying is hard; who can accept it?" Since Jesus knew that his disciples were murmuring about this, he said to them, "Does this shock you? ...Jesus knew from the beginning the ones who would not believe and the one who would betray him. And he said, "For this reason I have told you that no one can come to me unless it is granted him by my Father." As a result of this, many of his disciples returned to their former way of life and no longer accompanied him. Jesus then said to the Twelve, "Do you also want to leave?" Simon Peter answered him, "Master, to whom shall we go? You have the words of eternal life. We have come to believe and are convinced that you are the Holy One of God." (Jn. 6: 60-69)

Life is made of millions of multiple choices. Great is the person who chooses the right choice at the right times and right situations. The Spirit moves us today by meditating on a few Scriptural passages to be sincere and faithful to our priority-choice of Christ as our only Way, Truth and Life.

God always emphasizes that at every decision-making occasion in our lives, especially when we arrive at a situation of making choice of adhering to a church or religion, not to distract ourselves at any time from him as our fundamental choice and to focus our attention on him and his Word. We observe this divine Will in many incidents narrated in OT. For a sample, we read that Joshua, assuring his and his family's faith, *'as for me and my household, we will serve the LORD,'* bid a challenge to his people: *'Choose today whom you will serve, the God who brought safely and bestowed you a land or the gods your ancestors'*. To him all people answered: *'Far be it from us to forsake the LORD to serve other gods'*. (Ref. Jos. 24: 1-18) This is the way all Biblical heroes got their final victory by deciding for God and taking sides with God.

This was the behavior of Jesus, God's Son, while he was living physically among humans. He wanted all his disciples take to heart all the challenges he proposed to them to inherit the eternal life. Those who heard him, have been able to understand and accept most of his words and works. Unfortunately when he proposed to eat his Body and to drink his Blood as the ultimate source of eternal life, they were shocked and many of them found Jesus' teaching on the Eucharist too hard to understand. Some were scandalized, others confused and unconvinced. The best option before them was to quit. Jesus watched them leaving. But he didn't dilute his teaching. Nor was he prepared to compromise in order to keep the flock with him. Rather, he went on repeating his extraordinary claim and unbelievable bid. He perfectly knew their weakness.

The only additional bid he made was to his disciples who were closely connected to him, mainly his Apostles. He asked them in a stringent but smiling style, *'do you also want to go away?"* More than anything else, this question was a bombshell them, creating horrible shockwaves in their spirit. But the Twelve remained, responding to him with Peter: *"Master, to whom shall we go? You have the words of eternal life.* They did not opt for a divorce from him. Though they didn't fully comprehend the mystery to which Jesus directed them, they didn't leave; they stayed with the one who could feed them unto eternal life.

Jesus continues today challenging us to have faith in him. This indomitable faith carries us to the point where we surrender all our rationality and will to his love and try to understand more on his challenges, especially that of the Heavenly Bread of Life. Very sadly, many of us may plan to leave him in ignorance and disbelief. His bidding regarding the Eucharist is considered by them as the heaviest Cross to bear. Seemingly they don't understand the indepth meaning of the Eucharistic participation as the source of integral unity with Christ and his Church, the community of believers.

Our relationship with Christ is very intrinsic and intimate. Exhorting married couples to hold such relationship with one another, Paul offers us a clue on this mysterious relationship: *He who loves his wife loves himself...even as Christ does the church; for this reason a man shall leave his father and his mother and be joined to his wife, and the two shall become one flesh. This is a great mystery, but I speak in reference to Christ and the church.* (Ref. Eph. 5: 21-32) Indeed, we cannot live with Christ without adhering to his Church because each one of us is only a member of Jesus' Body, the Church. So Jesus asks us with wounded heart: 'Do you also go away from the Church as many of your household members, community members did or do, because of my gift of the Eucharist?'

FORTIETH WEEKEND

Twenty Second Sunday in Ordinary Time

A true and fruitful religion is simple,
integrated and authentic

Now when the Pharisees with some scribes who had come from Jerusalem gathered around him, they observed that some of his disciples ate their meals with unclean, that is, unwashed, hands... So the Pharisees and scribes questioned him, "Why do your disciples not follow the tradition of the elders but instead eat a meal with unclean hands?" He responded, "Well did Isaiah prophesy about you hypocrites, as it is written: 'This people honors me with their lips, but their hearts are far from me; in vain do they worship me, teaching as doctrines human precepts.' You disregard God's commandment but cling to human tradition." He went on to say, "How well you have set aside the commandment of God in order to uphold your tradition!... You nullify the word of God in favor of your tradition that you have handed on. And you do many such things..." (Mk. 7: 1-23)

Among the people who claim they are affiliated to Christian religion, even from their cradle, many don't practice it as God demands from them and consequently never benefit from it as they should. Perhaps we may be included in that club by our carelessness or indifference to be fully aware of the right understanding of Christianity. In today's meditation the Spirit bids us to reflect over certain God's words that clarify the important characteristics of true Christianity.

First God offers us a simple religion that should not be filled with complicated views, ideas and practices; rather it should contain transparency and unfussiness. When the Lord bestowed his precepts he underlined saying: *In your observance of the commandments of the LORD, your God, which* I am commanding you, you shall not add to what I command you nor subtract from it. *Observe them carefully.* (Deut. 4: 2) God is simple and therefore he wants his children to be simple and expects them to observe simple religion, a simple way of relating to him. John Wesley calls it 'the simplicity of intention, and purity of affection'.

The laws, given by God through Moses, were initially rather simple in their governance of the relations between God and humankind as well as the relationships between human beings. Unfortunately those laws evolved eventually into a complex maze of legislation. By the time of Jesus, people were loaded with unbearable burden of thousands of laws and prescriptions both oral and written. The worst thing Jesus observed was that those people who were very meticulous in observing all tiny little prescriptions totally forgot the core of the demands from God. He addressed his grievances against this behavior pointing out that their dedication to so many minute details skewed their judgment and sensibilities. Also, he blamed how their observance devolved into external rituals that were very conscientiously performed but were becoming less and less informed by interior holiness. Jesus loved and proclaimed only a simple religion.

Secondly God demands from us an observance of a religion of integration. Integration is defined as 'a combining of parts or objects that work together well.' This is the real consequence of our observance of religion in simplicity with no distortion or distraction. Jesus' main instruction to his disciples was not to follow the disintegrated religion of the Pharisees who were giving only lipservice and not a heart-felt obedience. He emphasized that every religious performance we do outside must correspond to what we profess; what we say outside must be connected to our heart; our outward appearance should resemble our inner soul.

Thirdly God asks us to observe a religion of authenticity. Authenticity denotes the genuineness or truth of something; its legitimacy and validity. If we hold on to a religion which in our esteem is so great and a source of love, peace and justice, then we should prove it by our life. James the Apostle, following the footsteps of Christ instructs us to follow a true religion that is simply doing and living by exactly what we hear from God. He offers us a simplified version of a true religion: *Be doers of the word and not hearers only, deluding yourselves. Religion that is pure and undefiled before God and the Father is this: to care for orphans and widows in their affliction and to keep oneself unstained by the world.*" Do first what we try to speak and speak what we feel within us.

True piety is not a practiced and soulless routine but a holiness that arises from within a heart that is consciously in love with God. This is right way of practicing our religion in order to bring down peace and blessings upon us.

FORTY FIRST WEEKEND

Twenty Third Sunday in Ordinary Time

God's glory shines forth in human ailments

*And people brought to him a deaf man
who had a speech impediment and begged
him to lay his hand on him. He took him
off by himself away from the crowd. He
put his finger into the man's ears and,
spitting, touched his tongue; then he
looked up to heaven and groaned, and
said to him, "Ephphatha!" (that is, "Be
opened!") And immediately the man's
ears were opened, his speech impediment
was removed, and he spoke plainly. He
ordered them not to tell anyone. But the
more he ordered them not to, the more
they proclaimed it. They were exceedingly
astonished and they said, "He has done all
things well. He makes the deaf hear and
the mute speak." (Mk. 7: 31-37)*

Priests at our Baptism, making the sign of the cross both over our lips and ears, blessed our speaking and hearing senses saying Jesus' healing words: *"Ephphatha!"* '*Be opened.*' Regrettably many of us, being careless to what happened at that moment, abuse or misuse those gifts our Creator has offered us. Today the Spirit awakens us to understand more about these gifts and through the meditation of the relevant Biblical verses we are instructed on how to use them according to the Will of God.

The main intention of God to bestow special blessing to our mouth and ears is that our physical senses be opened widely and broadly to see and proclaim his lavishing openness: In creation he acts like a spendthrift; in forgiving he behaves like a crazy prodigal Father; in liberating he disguises himself as one-man liberation army; and above all in relating himself to the sick, the poor, and the broken disabled people he stands like their one and only champion. In OT we read God asking Isaiah the Prophet to encourage the poor, the weak, the sick, the fearful, the blind and the deaf and dumb saying to them: *Be strong, fear not! Here is your God; he comes with vindication; with divine recompense he comes to save you.* (Is. 35: 4-5) Through Apostle James he underlines his special concern for the poor and the needy: *Did not God choose those who are poor in the world to be rich in faith and heirs of the kingdom that he promised to those who love him?* (Jas. 2: 5) When his Son Jesus came to us, he made him execute such mindsetup of his benevolent Fatherhood and also proclaim it by many miracles of curing the disabled humans.

Secondly God wishes all our senses to see through the suffering Christ, a weeping God in those fragile people. We know our susceptibility to all physical, psychological and emotional ailments, sicknesses and shameful and incurable diseases. Indisputably our humanity has no complete escape from such maladies until we die. Though we cannot and should not attribute all these sufferings and evils to the sinfulness of humanity, they are closely and intrinsically connected to the disconnection of the body and the spirit. Besides all the words and deeds of God, we hear in the Bible, toward those who suffer such disorders, we are thrilled to observe Jesus' continuous and intense care and love shown to the disabled. His first thought that came into his mind at their sight was *it is so that the works of God might be made visible through him.* (Jn. 9: 3) He meant that every malady, every suffering, every sickness of human beings have a glorious and challenging story of humanity with and towards God.

Inevitably if we are fully conscious of the merciful interactions God in our life, we discover the mightiest glory of God actively demonstrated by so many miracles happening in the sufferers. Miracle one: These sick persons are consoled, nursed, strengthened by our Godly love-in-actions; second miracle is that we come to know more visibly that these desperate and socially-rejected people are the true friends of God. It is through them we gain God's favor and his blessings; as a third miracle these disabled persons become the right and effective source of our faith. Anyone who believes in God experiences this power and also shares this power with others. That is what occurring when we stand by these ailed humans.

The most amazing miracle, we encounter in our reaching out with no discrimination, to the poor, the disabled, the handicapped, the sick and physically, emotionally, mentally and spiritually impaired, is our inner spirit feels overwhelmingly that we truly imitate God. James very succinctly addresses about this amazing factor. He pinpoints to the human weakness of making hasty and faulty judgments of others based on preconceived notions and outward appearances; he too exhorts us to make our own the mind and heart of God, who does not show partiality. (Jas. 2: 1-5) Therefore God advises today to appreciate and glorify not the sickness but those who are sick because we encounter in them his miracles of compassion.

FORTY SECOND WEEKEND

Twenty Fourth Sunday in Ordinary Time
Partial Knowledge of the Master causes
half-hearted discipleship

Now Jesus and his disciples set out for the villages of Caesarea Philippi...he asked them, "who do you say that I am?" Peter said to him in reply, "You are the Messiah." Then he warned them not to tell anyone about him. He began to teach them that the Son of Man must suffer greatly and be rejected by the elders, the chief priests, and the scribes, and be killed, and rise after three days. He spoke this openly. Then Peter took him aside and began to rebuke him. At this he turned around and, looking at his disciples, rebuked Peter and said, "Get behind me, Satan. You are thinking not as God does, but as human beings do." He summoned the crowd with his disciples and said to them, "Whoever wishes to come after me must deny himself, take up his cross, and follow me. (Mk. 8: 27-35)

The whole dynamics of our Christian life is centered on our discipleship to Christ our Leader and Guru. The Spirit informs us today through God's words what kind of discipleship we should give to Jesus. The primary requirement to join his company Jesus demands from us a clear understanding of his identity. We notice him asking us today one of the hardest questions as he did to his Apostles: *Who do you say that I am?'* His disciples through Peter answered: *You are the Messiah.* It was a good answer but an incomplete one. This is why Jesus corrected them giving an additional note about him: *The Son of Man must suffer greatly and be rejected by the elders, the chief priests, and the scribes, and be killed, and rise after three days.* He explained that he was indeed a glorious Messiah but also a suffering Messiah as well. He was truthful to what Isaiah predicted of him in OT. We hear the Prophet, after exposing in his Book the future Messiah's glory, offers a clear portray of the same Messiah as a suffering Christ. (Is. 50: 5-9)

While his addition was a big surprise to us Jesus too instructed all his disciples to be both glorious and suffering as well. *Those who wish to come after me must deny themselves, take up their cross and follow me...* But how exactly do we pull this off? Do we actually arrange to have ourselves scourged, nails pounded in our wrists and feet, and raised up on a cross? Undoubtedly some of us, as Martyrs and Saints, are called to suffer in the same physical way in which Jesus died. But not all of us are called to be so. Jesus expects his disciples to suffer and die small deaths we encounter in daily life.

One series of deaths we encounter on daily basis is the troublesome situations in human relationship as Isaiah points out the Messiah's continued suffering. *If anyone wishes to oppose me, let us appear together. Who disputes my right? Let that man confront me. See, the Lord GOD is my help; who will prove me wrong?* It is nothing but a reference to how each one of us psychologically and emotionally is affected daily by the oppositions, misunderstandings, and disagreements occurring in our human relationships.

As a matter of fact we read in the Gospels such a relationship-situation of suffering between Jesus and Peter. While he rebuked Peter for his misunderstanding and wrong argument and little bit of opposition to the vision and mission based on God's Will, he told us: *Those who wish to come after me must deny themselves, take up their cross and follow me.* In other words, "don't cling to your silly self-centered attitude and conviction; when you stand for truth or against injustice for the sake of God's will there will be many deaths you have to undergo.

There is another kind of small deaths we should undergo. While the first kind is in our relationship with equals, the second kind is in our relationship with those who are considered below to us, the needy, downtrodden and neglected ones. Through James Jesus teaches that simply upholding our creed and faith is not enough to be called Jesus' disciples. We have to get out of our couches or comfortzones and say something about the God's values and do something about it among people so that our Father in heaven will be glorified. *What good is it, my brothers and sisters, if someone says he has faith but does not have works? Can that faith save him?* (Jas. 2: 14-18)

Due to our commitment to Jesus' command of charitable love to the needy as James tells us, we may lose our money, talent, and time which perhaps would have been used for our self-gratification and self-entertainment. It pinches truly our undisciplined self; it makes us many times feel we have lost a lot. This is our daily cross. When Jesus tells us today that we have to follow him in taking up the crosses that come our way, do we accept that as his today's disciples?

FORTY THIRD WEEKEND

Twenty Fifth Sunday in Ordinary Time

The only way to become number one is to be childlike

> *Jesus was teaching his disciples and telling them, "The Son of Man is to be handed over to men and they will kill him, and three days after his death he will rise." But they did not understand the saying, and they were afraid to question him. They came to Capernaum and, once inside the house, he began to ask them, "What were you arguing about on the way?" But they remained silent. They had been discussing among themselves on the way who was the greatest. Then he sat down, called the Twelve, and said to them, "If anyone wishes to be first, he shall be the last of all and the servant of all." Taking a child he placed it in their midst, and putting his arms around it he said to them, "Whoever receives one child such as this in my name, receives me; and whoever receives me, receives not me but the One who sent me." (Mk. 9: 30-37)*

Every human craves for coveting and holding power, primacy, supremacy, prestige, and number-one status in life. There is nothing wrong for us to desire to become first in this competitive world. Moreover Bible acknowledges that our Creator, by creating us in his likeness and image, shared with us his supremacy, honor, glory and power to control the creation. Unfortunately human history is filled with wars, infights, murders, killings and destruction of human lives mostly because of such human ambitions. The Spirit today wants us to reflect over this human failure and to meditate on how to get the most out of this desire in the light of Scriptures.

Gospels state how the first Disciples of Jesus held the same human power-seeking attitude. When Jesus noticed it, actually he does not condemn the desire to be first. Competition and development are part of human life's survival game. God in Jesus never denies this. The human ambition for growth, climbing up and progressing can very well come from God himself. Jesus did indeed have the desire to be the first, for God wanted it to be so. It was Father's will that Jesus become the firstborn of a multitude of brothers and the supreme Head of the Church. What Jesus condemned was our wrong ways of speaking and acting to win and covet the position by all means. The Word of God offers us some heavenly tips to realize validly and legitimately our ambitions of being the first.

Jesus would have spoken in details on these tips in many occasions of his public life. We read Mark summarizing them all in a tiny passage we have taken for our today's meditation. First Jesus foretells his disciples second time about his passion and death in order to make his disciples know how he was preoccupied with fulfilling his Father's will despite its perilous hardships. It was on this intense consciousness he built his life and its schedule. As Paul would verbalize his unrelented attitude, *being found in human form he humbled himself and became obedient unto death, even death on a cross.* It was by this fixation he was fully convinced he could realize his ambition of becoming number one. *Therefore God has highly exalted him and bestowed on him the name which is above every name.* (Phil. 2:8-9)

While Jesus was preoccupied with this remarkable program of life, we see the Apostles being worried with one worldly issue, namely if their Master died, who would then become the leader of their group? They were going on arguing which of them was the greatest in the eyes of Jesus. When he asked them what they had been talking about, they were highly embarrassed. Knowing their inner turbulence, but undisturbed by their pathetic attitude, began giving them a tip to be elected or to be promoted in his team. He offers a beautiful strategy with which they can win. *If anyone wishes to be first, he shall be the last of all and the servant of all.* He wants them to be humble, simple, and serviceable with no strings attached. He invites them to assert themselves as leaders who serve instead of seeking to be served.

In order to help them cultivate this attitude, Jesus placed a child in their midst, he indicated that they should be fully and totally depending on God as a child to the Father; and they too should receive his own childlikeness; *Learn from me, I am meek and humble of heart.* This is the only way for establishing peace, rest, hope, happiness in the war-stricken and rifted society is, as James indicates, *the wisdom from above is first of all pure, then peaceable, gentle, compliant, full of mercy and good fruits, without inconstancy or insincerity.* (Jas. 3: 16 – 4: 3)

We may be tormented and giggled by godless people seeing our childlike innocence and purity of intention in realizing our ambitions, as the Book of Wisdom indicates. (2: 12-20) As our Master and his faithful disciples, let us continue to be occupied with fulfilling our Father's Will, hoping one day he will make our ambitions realized of being number one in his Kingdom.

Twenty Sixth Sunday in Ordinary Time

Strengthened by God's blessings we become blessing to the weak, not a curse

> *John said to him, "Teacher, we saw someone driving out demons in your name, and we tried to prevent him because he does not follow us." Jesus replied, "Do not prevent him. There is no one who performs a mighty deed in my name who can at the same time speak ill of me. For whoever is not against us is for us. Anyone who gives you a cup of water to drink because you belong to Christ, amen, I say to you, will surely not lose his reward. "Whoever causes one of these little ones who believe in me to sin, it would be better for him if a great millstone were put around his neck and he were thrown into the sea. If your hand causes you to sin, cut it off. It is better for you to enter into life maimed than with two hands to go into Gehenna, into the unquenchable fire...* (Mk. 9: 38-48)

As disciples of Jesus, we have been called to take part in God's one and only work of universal salvation of the entire humanity. Among his people God is so concerned with the little ones. When some of us get strengthened by him, he expects us in turn to support the little ones. Today the Spirit of Jesus bids us to meditate on some Scriptural guidelines for how to handle this salvific work in the midst of our little ones.

First of all, Jesus expects us to possess a passionate concern for the salvation of all who claim they belong to his sheepfold. There are many sheep among us spiritually very poor, and so many of them physically and socially are weaklings unable to live a normal life. Jesus called them as 'the little ones' and promised a very big reward to those care for these vulnerable sheep. Besides he warns those who are scandalizing these little ones telling that they should be punished. It *would be better for him if a great millstone was put around his neck and he was thrown into the sea.*

The reason why Jesus expects us to hold such concern for the little ones is that we, as the People of God form one body, one organism. In this body, there can be members who are weak in their faith and small in their understanding of what spiritual life is. If the stronger members of the body mislead or put down the weaker ones, it affects the growth of the entire body. This is why he even wanted the valiant members of the Church to punish themselves by maiming their organs that are sources of scandal to the weak.

Secondly the Spirit also indicates to us when we do not possess such passionate concern and love for God's little ones we end up being a worst hindrance to God's salvific work. When we minister to the salvation of our little ones God expects us to use all that we are endowed with. Unfortunately, as James writes, there are too many of us who become selfish and very individual self-oriented people that we enrich ourselves and forget the little ones. Thus the elite and developed sheep not only scandalize the little ones and make them more vulnerable and subservient to evil spirit, but also do harm to their own salvation. (Ref. Jas. 5: 1-6)

When we do not have the passionate concern for the little ones we are prone to see our own good name, good position and self-glory. Pride begins to rule us. Thus even the good works we do in the name of Jesus, the Church or charity turn out to be a big source of scandal to the little ones. In our pride we begin to exclude others and criticize their good works. We give room for infights and jealousy. We notice this as a perennial problem in God's community. In OT we read God empowering 70 elders with the gift of the spirit and making them prophets, he too granted his spirit to many others outside 'holy campus'. This was protested by those inside that elite group. But Moses advised them not to be jealous because it was the will of God. (Num. 11: 25-29) The same way we hear from the Gospel some Apostles complaining to Jesus against someone driving out demons in his name. But Jesus replied, *"Do not prevent him."* This means, Jesus wants us to recognize and appreciate and include others in this ministry of salvation. In the body of Christ, everyone has the right and duty to be an instrument of God's healing and merciful love. There is no room for jealousy in this body. God has empowered everyone with his spirit for the benefit of the entire community.

Each member or soul is precious to God. It is true that each person is responsible for his own salvation. However, as mentioned earlier, there can be weak and small members who are vulnerable to be misled by the actions or words of others. Jesus tells us today that our duty as his disciples is to lead God's children to salvation and not to be obstacles in their way. Any sacrifice is worth making when it is a question of the salvation of a soul, even at the stake of sacrificing our life, as the Master did.

FORTY FIFTH WEEKEND

Twenty Seventh Sunday in Ordinary Time

*Being consecrated is the only solution
for any life's status-problems*

> *The Pharisees approached and asked,
> "Is it lawful for a husband to divorce his
> wife?" They were testing him. He said to
> them in reply, "What did Moses command
> you?" They replied, "Moses permitted
> him to write a bill of divorce and dismiss
> her." But Jesus told them, "Because of the
> hardness of your hearts he wrote you this
> commandment. But from the beginning
> of creation, 'God made them male and
> female. For this reason a man shall leave
> his father and mother and be joined to his
> wife, and the two shall become one flesh.'
> So they are no longer two but one flesh.
> Therefore what God has joined together,
> no human being must separate"* ... (Mk.
> 10: 2-16)

Being bored with the uses of private and social media's views and opinions, many of us seek a correct answer for our legitimate question: How can we successfully lead a blessed life? Through Scriptural passages the Spirit invites us this weekend to reflect on the exact answer of God who declares that it is nothing but leading a consecrated life. In Psalm 128 David and his people pray to the Lord: *May the Lord bless us all the days of our lives! And the entire Psalm* enlists all those blessings they want to be blessed with: That they would be favored by God; they would prosper with the prosperity of Jerusalem, meaning heavenly riches; they would enjoy everything they accomplish by their own hands; they would have long life; and they would possess peaceful life.

Now the question is how we, the humans, can be blessed with such remarkable life. The Psalmist writes: *Blessed are you who fear the LORD! Blessed are you who walk in his ways!* Enlightening us in this matter of blessed life, we read in NT: *He who consecrates and those who are being consecrated all have one origin. (Heb. 2: 11)* This Biblical verse underlines that all the disciples of Jesus are consecrated with our Master Jesus whom we hear praying for such gift for us at the Last Supper: *I do not ask that you take them out of the world but that you keep them from the evil one. They do not belong to the world any more than I belong to the world. Consecrate them in the truth. Your word is truth. As you sent me into the world, so I sent them into the world. And I consecrate myself for them, so that they also may be consecrated in truth.* (Jn. 17: 15-19)

In Biblical and Christian Traditional sense a consecrated life to the Lord means to become totally as God's possession. Look at the vessels and other clothes we use at the altar. All are consecrated and dedicated to God for the sole purpose of using for God and by God. This means they become God's properties. Everything should be used according to his will. It is simply like the consecrated life of Jesus, who did everything from his conception to his death with sacrificial love to fulfill God's purposes, namely to bring qualitylife to his God's children. Our Christian life becomes qualified as consecrated or holy, only by our lowering down our fake self, deep into the Sheol of sufferings, sacrifices and finally death in any kind as our Lord underwent.

This God's call to a consecrated life is not exclusively to some religious priests, sisters and brothers. It is a clarion call to every Christian. By lifesituation and need-base each one of us may choose different status in life: As our Lord pointed out, some are born to be singles; others chose to be singles for the sake of the community development; many others by natural causes, while most of humans choose married life and build up their own life-giving, life-producing and life-sustaining families. All, in every status, are called to be consecrated. In the Gospel passage, taken for today's meditation, upholds that those Christians who have chosen married life must lead also the same consecrated life as that of Christ, living with sacrificial love; selfless life, humble and stable relationship.

I personally know how hard it is for every one of us to fulfill God's demand of consecrated life from us. Certainly we are made of both light and darkness; however we can be strengthen ourselves in consecrated life more and more by our religious and spiritual endeavors, and by trying our best not to salute all the enticement of our own darkness. We may fail in conducting our lives in a consecrated way but when we fail, let us believe and hope our Christ is there always to empower us with his forgiveness, love and admonition and lead us to heaven. Once we are with God, we will finally live only a total life of light. We are certain that we will receive the glorious reward of blessed life as we *see Jesus "crowned with glory and honor" because he suffered death, he who "for a little while" was made "lower than the angels."*

FORTY SIXTH WEEKEND

Twenty Eighth Sunday in Ordinary Time

The eternal anomaly of the gift of wisdom

As he was setting out on a journey, a man ran up, knelt down before him, and asked him, "Good teacher, what must I do to inherit eternal life?" Jesus answered him, "Why do you call me good? No one is good but God alone. You know the commandments: 'You shall not kill; you shall not commit adultery; you shall not steal; you shall not bear false witness; you shall not defraud; honor your father and your mother.'" He replied and said to him, "Teacher, all of these I have observed from my youth." Jesus, looking at him, loved him and said to him, "You are lacking in one thing. Go, sell what you have, and give to the poor and you will have treasure in heaven; then come, follow me." At that statement his face fell, and he went away sad, for he had many possessions. Jesus looked around and said to his disciples, "How hard it is for those who have wealth to enter the kingdom of God!" The disciples were amazed at his words... (Mk. 10: 17-30)

'Fear of God is the beginning of wisdom.' This had been the Biblical verse, often used by our elders in their exhortations on discipline. We perhaps know the meaning of 'fear of God; but, most of us either don't know much about what wisdom means. In our weekend meditation the Spirit instructs us on the true meaning of 'wisdom' by sharing with us some related God's words.

All our sages and Saints who have been probing into this wisdom describe it as a breaking through the silence of nature and the loneliness of humanity; they too confirm wisdom demands an explosion of darkness of life and it is a painful journey to the other world beyond what we see before our eyes. From the light our forebears shed on our quest for wisdom we come to know wisdom is something beyond ordinary life; it is getting into the inner circle of our life and to understand what it tells us for our right living.

According to the Book of Wisdom, when we get this wisdom, *all good things together will come to us; and countless riches will follow it.*'(Wis. 7: 7-11) This is why King Solomon in his prayer could tell the Lord that he preferred the gift of wisdom to the material riches and power. (1 Kings 3: 1-15) Undoubtedly, wisdom is more valuable than any material good. However, we have to be cautious in demanding for appropriating this gift. In Biblical usage, wisdom is nothing but the 'word' that comes from God and specifically Jesus Christ, who is the Word incarnate. In this vein the author of the Letter to Hebrews writes: The Word of God, namely the Wisdom, is very *sharp, sharper than any two-edged sword. It penetrates and divides the soul and spirit, joints and marrow.* (Heb. 4: 12-13) This reminds us of the age-old saying: *'Truth always hurts'.* Let us remember here the saying of Jesus, who is the wisdom in personification: *'I did not bring peace but sword to the world'.*

However, it is worth paying the price of being the receiver of wisdom. Once we possess wisdom, we start working out our own plan of life; we know the knack of shopping around life's important seasons. Wisdom helps us in the choice of our carrier, job; and in the choice of our partner in life. Through wisdom, we learn how to live the life profitably; we get the power to work hard to earn enough money in just and right way according to God's norms; the money brings us properties and pleasurable entertainments; it leads us to earn popularity in and around our family and community; thus we get power over other people. At this juncture again the wisdom enters into our lives and really disturbs our peace of mind telling us the wise words of Jesus: *'How hard it is for the rich to enter into the kingdom of heaven'.* The same wisdom also orders us to *'go and sell what you have and give it to the poor.'* (Mk. 10: 17-23)

Doesn't it sound weird? The heavenly wisdom which encouraged us to choose the right status of life, a suitable job, a taste for hard work, a thrill to be sincere and duty-conscious, which in turn provided us enough riches and good positions, now names us 'foolish!' It curses us with no entrance to heaven and orders us to give away all that we have earned and secured, to the poor and the needy. It is indeed an anomaly. However we have to accept this norm of wisdom because it is the way to enjoy 'fuller life'.

The exhortation of our Master today may hurt our self-image and pride. Nevertheless positively speaking, it will have its reward from our Judge in heaven; negatively, it does not permit us to become oversize as a bubble. We know the characteristic of the bubbles. The bigger they become, the more vulnerable they turn to be victim of destruction. Therefore let us listen to the wisdom of God, and obey His practical advices in our day to day life.

Twenty Ninth Sunday in Ordinary Time

Anyone can be great because everyone suffers

Then James and John, the sons of Zebedee, came to him and said to him, "Teacher, we want you to do for us whatever we ask of you." He replied, "What do you wish me to do for you?" They answered him, "Grant that in your glory we may sit one at your right and the other at your left." Jesus said to them, "You do not know what you are asking. Can you drink the cup that I drink or be baptized with the baptism with which I am baptized?" They said to him, "We can." Jesus said to them, "The cup that I drink, you will drink, and with the baptism with which I am baptized, you will be baptized... "You know that those who are recognized as rulers over the Gentiles lord it over them, and their great ones make their authority over them felt. But it shall not be so among you. Rather, whoever wishes to be great among you will be your servant; whoever wishes to be first among you will be the slave of all. For the Son of Man did not come to be served but to serve and to give his life as a ransom for many." (Mk. 10: 35-45)

Some of our non-religious friends always make a cynical comment about Christian assertion that human sufferings play an important role in every person's life. They mistakenly criticize we worship a God who is bloodthirsty and seemingly a sadist who always enjoys in the sufferings of humans. Perhaps some of us may be tempted to join their club. The Spirit today bids us to open wide our inner eyes and ears in meditation of God's valuable teachings on human sufferings.

Undoubtedly our faith upholds that our God is in his essence 'all good'. He produced in his creation period every creature that is good and not evil. He therefore cannot be the source of any evil of which human sufferings are a part. Prophets and messengers of our God continuously declared this truth. At the same time they emphasized all evils entered into God's creation by the willful disobedience of human beings. This being said, it is crystal clear that every human being undergoes sufferings. And that also is interpreted by Biblical Writers that death and sufferings are the wages of sins or the inevitable results of each human's blunders. At this juncture a valid question arises: While sinful people are permitted to suffer as punishment, why do the just and righteous also suffer? There are many reasons for it; here let us meditate on a couple of reasons:

Our Master Jesus from the onset of his life recognized the importance of his sufferings and accepted willingly the title 'the Suffering Messiah' as prophesied in OT: *It was the LORD's will to crush him with pain.* He endured them victoriously with certain inner convictions. He dreamed of his followers to enjoy 'fuller life' in this world and the world to come. However to attain that eternal life, he preached a unique way. It is the Gospel of sufferings and death. As Paul claimed, the entire Church says aloud: W*e proclaim Christ crucified.*

Gospel of the Cross enumerates the glorious but costly results of Jesus' sufferings, as Isaiah writes: The sufferer will have a long life; the will of God, namely God's plan of fulfillment of his creation will be accomplished; he will see the light of fullness of days; through his sufferings many of his fellowmen will be surely saved. (Is. 53: 10-11)

Jesus was never tired of instructing his disciples follow his footsteps in carrying their own crosses. While being very human as they were, we notice them considering the way to attain fuller life is to covet earthly glory, appreciation, recognition, higher position, and an environment where all, except themselves, feel low and bow to them and serve them. Jesus never denied their eternal ambition for fuller life. But he pointed out that such dream can be realized only by sufferings and death. He asked them, *Can you drink the cup that I drink or be baptized with the baptism with which I am baptized?* Jesus expected his disciples to undergo daily death exactly like his. What he meant was that they should die of the self as the center of its own concern and should die to the world as the center of security and identity.

To put it realistically, deaths every disciple faces daily are: Totally surrendering to a God who always seems to be invisible staying in eternal absence, eternal distance and eternal silence; patiently living our human life which is unfair, unpredictable, vulnerable and slowly disintegrating; enduring the blunders our neighbors do out of their ignorance, arrogance and weakness; above all, in persevering in our charitable services to the needy, sacrificing our peace; our identity; our glory; our selfesteem; and even losing our grip of life. All these are ultimately for pleasing God by our sin-offerings for the world as our Master demands.

Thirtieth Sunday in Ordinary Time

The nuance-tips for becoming Christian adults

They came to Jericho. And as he was leaving Jericho with his disciples and a sizable crowd, Bartimaeus, a blind man, the son of Timaeus, sat by the roadside begging. On hearing that it was Jesus of Nazareth, he began to cry out and say, "Jesus, son of David, have pity on me." And many rebuked him, telling him to be silent. But he kept calling out all the more, "Son of David, have pity on me." Jesus stopped and said, "Call him." So they called the blind man, saying to him, "Take courage; get up, he is calling you." He threw aside his cloak, sprang up, and came to Jesus. Jesus said to him in reply, "What do you want me to do for you?" The blind man replied to him, "Master, I want to see." Jesus told him, "Go your way; your faith has saved you." Immediately he received his sight and followed him on the way. (Mk. 10: 46-52)

Adulthood in humans' life is not only the most precious period of life but also the most crucial and risky one. This weekend the Spirit takes us to some Scriptural passages to inspire us with the right meaning and properly cherishing of that special time in life.

First of all what does God think of Christian adulthood? We are given a thoughtprovoking words of God through Jeremiah (31: 7-9). According to the worthy adults in his kingdom are: those who are convinced of their origin and roots, namely they were once enslaved by various earthly things and persons but now they have been delivered by God as remnants of the human race; those who accept the reality of humanness, namely they have come together from different kinds of backgrounds, race, nationality, color, mind setup, IQ, disability, broken heartedness, different roles and needs, and hopelessly hoping for better life; and also those who put indomitable faith and trust and hope in the Creator, who never left them alone; they believe that their God is not like a child who kicking the ball away and stands there enjoying how it is rolling; rather he behaves like a Father to them.

Yes, if we want to be worthy adults tin God's kingdom we should be fully conscious of our being delivered by the Father and also set apart from other humans as his representatives, proxies, agents. However, to make us better adults in God's eyes, we cannot falsely glorify ourselves for such exclusiveness. We read in a passage from the Letter to the Hebrews that like Jesus, we should have a peculiar heart of praising and glorifying only our God who very early, even before we were conceived in mother's womb said to us: *You are my son, you are my daughter; this day I have begotten you.* (Heb. 5: 1-6)

All disciples of Jesus must try to get into the peculiar shoes of humans who have been already esteemed by God as his worthiest adults. In the Gospel event, taken for today's meditation, Jesus brings before us Bartimaeus as a rolemodel for attaining that outstanding position.

First Jesus wants us to stop begging only for material goods, but begin to cry out in prayer for becoming matured as the blind man was saying: *Jesus, Son of David, have pity on me.*" Even when the crowd restricted and rebuked him, he was louder enough with his prayer.

Secondly, when the blind man heard Jesus was calling through his Disciples, he immediately left everything and rushed to Jesus. We should, besides praying, get the support of our fellow-disciples in our families or parishes and rise up and do what Jesus tells us.

Thirdly, like Bartimeus, we should uninterruptedly demonstrate our faith to Jesus and during that process of faith-in-actions we will become matured Christians.

In the Kingdom of God the only sign for our reaching Christian adulthood is nothing but to share testimonies about all that went along the way. Therefore when we become adults, our 'becoming adults' would be proven through our abiding in Jesus, walking with Jesus and glorifying God with joy exclaiming the marvelous deeds he has done, not only in the past, in the Bible or among the saints but much more in our personal life how we have attained the Christian adulthood.

Thirty First Sunday in Ordinary Time

*we can simplify our religious rituals but
not our love for God and neighbors*

*One of the scribes...asked him, "Which
is the first of all the commandments?"
Jesus replied, "The first is this: 'Hear, O
Israel! The Lord our God is Lord alone!
You shall love the Lord your God with all
your heart, with all your soul, with all
your mind, and with all your strength.'
The second is this: 'You shall love your
neighbor as yourself.' There is no other
commandment greater than these." The
scribe said to him, "Well said, teacher. You
are right in saying, 'He is one and there is
no other than he.' And 'to love him with all
your heart, with all your understanding,
with all your strength, and to love your
neighbor as yourself' is worth more than
all burnt offerings and sacrifices"... (Mk.
12: 28b-34)*

Life is so much complicated. We are torn to pieces by
our own getups, setups, dreams, ambitions, opportunities,
ideas, philosophies, theologies, worldviews, cultures, and
so on. Many times in history some enthusiastic religious
teachers and leaders tried to add some more complications
to human life in the form of too many dos and donts,
commandments, rituals, rites, rubrics in religion. Today the

Spirit wants us not to be bugged down to such complexity of religious performances by meditating God's words on this matter and abide in peaceful religion.

Normally humans like to take a simplistic way of leading life. They want their teachers to help them to simplify our religious holding and requirements or they themselves would try to find ways and means to accomplish it. 'Let us simplify religion' is not just the cry of modern generation; but this has been the outcry of the Israelites at the time of the Lord. There were too many interpretations and subtle details on the Commandments of God. People were burdened with thousands of secondary laws and regulations to be observed as religious people. God in OT did offer to his people only the Ten Commandments through which he wanted them to realize their longer life of more prosperity, joy and peace. (Deut. 5 and 6) Regrettably religious teachers who came after Moses had a tendency to endlessly multiply the commandments and precepts of the law, creating norms and obligations for every minimal detail of life.

When Jesus noticed this awkward situation, he tried to simplify all the precepts of God into two, using verses from the OT Books: *The first is this: 'Hear, O Israel! The Lord our God is Lord alone! You shall love the Lord your God with all your heart, with all your soul, with all your mind, and with all your strength.'* (Deut. 6: 4-5) *The second is this: 'You shall love your neighbor as yourself.' There is no other commandment greater than these.'* (Lev. 19: 18) Jesus' simplistic form of his religion sounds so good and pleasing to our ears. However when we dig into it and live by it in our daily lives we go through nightmares.

Loving God is ok. Very simple and cozy to be out of the family, out of the street, pout of the town, out of the country and select a desert and live a monastic, isolated life and die.

All we perform there is solely for expressing our total love for God. But that is not the complete summary of Jesus' religion. He adds to it a second one like the first, *love our neighbors as ourselves.* This means we should in no way leave our neighbors and our relationships with them.

After living in the midst of our neighbors, namely, parents, spouses, children, friends and relatives and other strange neighbors we should by now are well aware of the hard truth about the neighbors. A French philosopher, Jean Paul Sartre, exclaimed: "Hell is nothing but our own neighbor". That is the reality. It is with them, through them, and in them we have to lead a life of love for God. Loving them as ourselves is a hard thing to do. What Jesus described about this command is that we should accept our neighbors with all their weaknesses, strengths, good and bad smells, sickness, health, inabilities, sinfulness, their wrong and good choices and their prejudices and hypocrisies as we condone our own.

This atleast is tolerable; but Jesus before he went back to heaven, demanded us further a step to go and love these unbearable neighbors as he had loved us. Namely, we have to love even our enemies, to forgive them as he forgave and be ready to share everything of ourselves, including our very lives for them.

I always divide these two commandments: First one is directed to the irreligious people who have developed a tendency to stop with their love for human beings; and the second one is focused on the religious people who already find God as their only Sovereign Lord and love him totally. The first group forgets God but concentrates on neighbors and the second group while focusing their attention on God totally forget their neighbors. We need to simplify our religion, but not our love for God and neighbors.

FIFTIETH WEEKEND

Thirty Second Sunday in Ordinary Time
Let us not act 'dumb' in handling 'dump' boxes

In the course of his teaching he said, "Beware of the scribes, who like to go around in long robes and accept greetings in the marketplaces, seats of honor in synagogues, and places of honor at banquets. They devour the houses of widows and, as a pretext, recite lengthy prayers. They will receive a very severe condemnation." He sat down opposite the treasury and observed how the crowd put money into the treasury. Many rich people put in large sums. A poor widow also came and put in two small coins worth a few cents. Calling his disciples to himself, he said to them, "Amen, I say to you, this poor widow put in more than all the other contributors to the treasury. For they have all contributed from their surplus wealth, but she, from her poverty, has contributed all she had, her whole livelihood." (Mk. 12: 38-44)

Practice of taking collections in religious circles has been a longtime ritual for pleasing their gods. Very disappointingly humans, who empty them or collecting the collections from those boxes or baskets, do not spend the money for which it has been filled; or the humans who fill those boxes do not hold a right intentions over their gifts. In Christianity it is the same situation. So today the Spirit calls us to ponder over through the Biblical verses how God considers our donations and their endresults.

Through Jesus, God expects us to have a Christ's consciousness in 'collection rituals'. Even though he sounded like totally being against them as he noticed horrible abuses were occurring in this kind of religious practice of offerings, he never replaced these practices. There are valid reasons for such practices of offering to the God. Jesus accepted these rituals as symbols and signs of outward expression of our love-response to God. God expects every one of his children to show in deed their love and gratitude toward him and his love. There is only one commandment to please the Lord; and that is, love thy God with your whole heart, whole mind and whole soul and with all your strength, and to express such love visibly and tangibly, love your neighbor as yourself. Jesus in his lifetime observed these practices very meticulously. He is quoted saying when he came down to this world: *"Sacrifice and offering you did not desire, but a body you prepared for me; holocausts and sin offerings you took no delight in. Then I said, 'As is written of me in the scroll, Behold, I come to do your will, O God.'"* (Heb. 10: 5-7)

Pointing out what the poor widows did, one in OT and another in the Gospel, the Spirit of God instructs us that, 'offerings' in the sight of God should be a sign of our total acceptance and recognition of God's providence. Never we should give only what is surplus in us; rather, as the widow in the Gospel, try to give really what we can with a sincere motivation and single-heartedness. Whatever we have belongs to him, he is the owner and we are only the stewards and instruments in his hands; therefore we are ready to offer everything to him even our own self if need be. Selfishness has no room inside heaven. Every bit of our selfishness must be broken to pieces and burnt in the fire of love. It is for this as one of the reasons why Jesus appreciated our offerings to God.

Besides, even though God does not need our offerings or money, he needs our efforts continuously to empty ourselves and make him to fill us; he offers too many of us ample and lucky chances and opportunities to gather his riches and become prosperous. It is for nothing but to be the cooperators in his job of providence, especially to those at the low level of their life. God through Jesus commands us in all religious practices we should include the love of neighbor. Every outward act we do as expression of our love to Him must be either through the love of others or together with the love of the same. We can have private conversation with God in prayer and in religious ceremonies, but if it is without any relation to our neighbor who is outside there, such a purely self-centered religious act cannot be a genuine expression of our love to God.

The widow's mite is mightier than all prayers and other religious practices. God, on his part, will surely reward us as he did in the case of the widow in the Old Testament, *'her jar did not go empty, nor her jug run dry; they were full all the days of her life as the Lord had foretold through Elijah'*. (1 Kgs. 17: 10-16) Let us also remind ourselves the golden promise of Jesus regarding his reciprocal gifts to us when we do these wonderful religious practice of paying our tithes to the Church with full understanding and without break, without murmuring: *Give and gifts will be given to you; a good measure, packed together, shaken down, and overflowing, will be poured into your lap. For the measure with which you measure will in return be measured out to you.*" (Lk. 6: 38)

FIFTY FIRST WEEKEND

Thirty Third Sunday in Ordinary Time
Tough times don't last; but tough people do

"But in those days after that tribulation the sun will be darkened, and the moon will not give its light, and the stars will be falling from the sky, and the powers in the heavens will be shaken. And then they will see 'the Son of Man coming in the clouds' with great power and glory, and then he will send out the angels and gather his elect from the four winds, from the end of the earth to the end of the sky. "Learn a lesson from the fig tree. When its branch becomes tender and sprouts leaves, you know that summer is near. In the same way, when you see these things happening, know that he is near, at the gates. Amen, I say to you, this generation will not pass away until all these things have taken place. Heaven and earth will pass away, but my words will not pass away. "But of that day or hour, no one knows, neither the angels in heaven, nor the Son, but only the Father. (Mk. 13: 24-32)

God through his Scriptures, Church teachings and our daily experiences desires that we should be fully aware of our end and the end of the universe as well so that we walk in line with him

and reach our glorious destiny. **Especially at the end of the Liturgical year we are asked by the Spirit to ponder about it more intensively.**

In the Synoptic Gospels and the Book of Revelation as well we hear so many frightening factors regarding the end of universe, including at the last breath of every human being. Such magnified speech rhetoric about the endtimes have been interpreted positively by Church Fathers in the light of Scriptures themselves. **While Jesus describes about the occurrences at endtimes, he actually quotes two OT prophecies uttered by Daniel** (12: 1-3) **and Joel** (Joel 3: 3-4). **We find in those prophecies two dimensions of the endtimes-happenings: One is negative prophecy:** *Those days will* be a time unsurpassed in distress since nations began until that time...In addition to these negative and horrible pronouncements there are some positive points too we hear from the Prophets. Jesus summed up: *And then they will see 'the Son of Man coming in the clouds' with great power and glory, and then he will send out the angels and gather his elect from the four winds, from the end of the earth to the end of the sky.*

Biblical scholars advise us not to take those negative prophecies literally. They are like stories and parables placed before us to straighten our lives and feel the urgency of getting back the image of Jesus Christ within us. In human history we observe similar to those calamities mentioned in the Scriptures have happened in the past, happening today and will continue in their own styles and forms. We may not know when and how those calamities will happen to us and to the entire universe. Jesus says: *"But of that day or hour, no one knows, neither the angels in heaven, nor the Son, but only the Father."*

Therefore God in Jesus expects us not to be panic or overanxious about these things. The main reason for this is he has drawn an indelible mark on our forehead through his grace at our Baptism and we confirmed it in our Confirmation. John writes about the identity of those remnants: *They will look upon his face, and his name will be on their foreheads.* (Rev. 22: 4) We should presume when we first try to transform ourselves into Jesus' image we feel we're putting on a mask. Down deep we know we're not the person we appear to be. Remembering such unique status Jesus wants us to wait for him with the unwavering hope. He has promised he is with us till the end of the world. With his presence we should live our faith even in the trials of life, not in fear but in the firm hope. For, we are people of hope in a loving and saving God.

The more we read these 'endtimes' stories, and the more we experience such calamities and disasters occurring in our lives and at our backyards, the greater our efforts should be in becoming like Jesus Christ. Every kind of end brings us to the conclusion that we will be judged according to our cooperation with God's grace. We may have tough times to go through—like death striking our family, accidents happening, terrorist attacks, losing our job and so on. But, because Christ has already won the victory for us, we will not let these tough times defeat us.

The one and only prophecy from the Spirit uninterruptedly ringing in our minds and hearts should be: *This is the covenant I will establish with them after those days, says the Lord: 'I will put my laws in their hearts, and I will write them upon their minds,' he also says: 'Their sins and their evildoings I will remember no more.'* (Heb. 10: 11-18)

FIFTY SECOND WEEKEND

Feast of Christ the King

*Jesus became universal King through
his ladder of sacrifices*

*So Pilate went back into the praetorium
and summoned Jesus and said to him,
"Are you the King of the Jews?" Jesus
answered, "Do you say this on your own
or have others told you about me?" Pilate
answered, "I am not a Jew, am I? Your
own nation and the chief priests handed
you over to me. What have you done?"
Jesus answered, "My kingdom does not
belong to this world. If my kingdom did
belong to this world, my attendants would
be fighting to keep me from being handed
over to the Jews. But as it is, my kingdom
is not here." So Pilate said to him, "Then
you are a king?" Jesus answered, "You say
I am a king. For this I was born and for
this I came into the world, to testify to the
truth. Everyone who belongs to the truth
listens to my voice." (Jn. 18: 33-37)*

Jesus Christ is King of the Universe. That is our belief
because the Scriptures and the Church say so. Today the
Spirit invites us, through our meditation, to get the clearer
portray of the kingship of Christ and to know more about
the genuine quality of our franchise in his kingdom.

In the Gospel we read Jesus accepting that He is King, even knowing that he was standing in front of Pilate, who was a great dignitary in that society as Roman Governor equally powerful as any king. And Pilate himself ascertained that he had power to release or to crucify Jesus. In the book of Revelation John saw in his vision Jesus as the ruler of the kings of the earth. *Jesus Christ, the faithful witness, the firstborn of the dead and ruler of the kings of the earth.* (Rev. 1: 5a) And the same belief was prophesied by Daniel. *When he reached the Ancient One and was presented before him, the one like a Son of man received dominion, glory, and kingship; all peoples, nations, and languages serve him. His dominion is an everlasting dominion that shall not be taken away his kingship shall not be destroyed.* (Dan. 7: 13-14)

It was a surprising historical story that Jesus, a man of Nazareth, son of a carpenter, became king, and that too not by political maneuvering, lobbying, shrewd diplomacy or purchasing people with unethical and undoable promises; rather, as Paul wrote in his Letter, God instituted Jesus so high above all principalities that at his name every knee should bend, of those in heaven and on earth and under the earth. The only ladder through which Jesus climbed up to this august position was made of humility, total surrender to God, and truthful and faithful behavior with integrity to God and to people. (Ref. Phi. 2: 6-10)

In this process of seizing his supreme status Jesus considered testifying to the truth was his primary job. *For this I was born and for this I came into the world, to testify to the truth.* His second purpose in life was to establish and run only a spiritual kingdom and not worldly or earthly one. *My kingdom does not belong to this world. If my kingdom did belong to this world, my attendants would be fighting to keep me from being handed over to the Jews. But as it is, my kingdom is not here.* And his third engagement was *to witness to this truth and die for it.* As an ultimate goal of life was to free us from our sins and make all of us naturalized as his citizens. *He has freed us from our sins by his blood, and he has made us into a kingdom, priests for his God and Father.* (Rev. 1: 5b)

All that Jesus did willingly in his life as he was pursuing his life's remarkable goals, were not wasted. All were resourceful and very productive: He gave his very life, but we got his life back; he gave out his breath, but we were filled with his spirit; and he was buried, but we with him rise up; he was a slave before God for our sake, but then we with him became kings and queens in his kingdom.

Humans traditionally greet their kings or queens exclaiming, whenever they appear in front of the public: 'Long live the King/Queen!' We too certainly can greet Jesus today 'Long live the King of kings!' It is not because he left behind him kingship through his posterity as humans do; rather, with John we firmly believe the words of Jesus: *I am the Alpha and Omega, the one who is and who was and who is to come, the almighty.* (Rev. 1: 8)

Other books by Rev. Benjamin A. Vima

SONDAY SONRISE: Sunday Homilies for three
Liturgical Years

DAILY DOSE for Christian Survival: Daily Scriptural
Meditations and Spiritual Medication

PRAYERFULLY YOURS: Qualityprayer for Qualitylife

**CATHOLIC CHRISTIAN
SPIRITUALITY** for New Age
Dummies

MY RELIGION: REEL OR REAL? A Postmodern
Catholic's Assessment of his religion

MINISTRY IN TEARS: International
Priests' missionary
Life & Ministry (Co-authored by his brother Rev. Dasan
Vima, SJ)

"Blessed theMerciful"
The CHESED-Oriented Christian Life

HILLTOP MEDITATIONS for Year C weekend Spiritual
Nourishment

Printed in the United States
By Bookmasters